GOVIND BALLABH PANT
The True Gandhian

Indian Freedom Fighters Series—17

Govind Ballabh Pant

The True Gandhian

S.R. BAKSHI

Anmol Publications

ANMOL PUBLICATIONS
4378/4B, Ansari Road,
Darya Ganj, New Delhi-110002.

Govind Ballabh Pant : The True Gandhian

ISBN 81-7041-430-X

PRINTED IN INDIA

Published by J.L. Kumar for Anmol Publications and Printed at Sangita Printers, Maujpur Delhi-53.

Preface

In the long-drawn political struggle of our country Govind Ballabh Pant's role is unique and most significant. He began to take interest in the socio-economic conditions of the people of his district and soon after his sphere of influence extended to the whole province as well as the other regions of India. He was a disciplined worker of the Congress and did remarkable work as a prominent member of this organisation. He was much respected and admired by Mahatma Gandhi, Motilal Nehru, Jawaharlal Nehru and other leaders of our Country. Indeed his contribution to the several spheres of administration is unique and praise-worthy.

The chapters deal with Govind Ballabh Pant's early life, his political ideology, Congress leadership, participation in the freedom struggle and his role in the administration have also given a glossary and a brief bibliography.

I have consulted the research material from the Sapru House Library, Indian Council of Historical Research Library and the Nehru Memorial Museum and Library. I feel grateful to the authorities of these institutions for giving me their academic support during my researches.

S.R. Bakshi

Contents

1

Early Career

Govind Ballabh Pant who played a most significant role in the freedom movement of our country was born on 30 August 1887 at village Khoont in the Almora district of Utter Pradesh. His father Pandit Manorath Pant was a revenue official of the provincial government. The family originally belonged to Maharashtra from where it migrated to the Himalayan district in the tenth century.

Pant was an intelligent student and showed the signs of his greatness by hardwork and sincerity in studies. He was educated at Almora and Allahabad. After his B.A., he joined the Law College and came out successful with the Lumsden Gold Medal. Besides he used to participate in several extra-curricular activities of the College. At this point of time, he began to attend political meetings addressed by S.N. Banerjea, Gokhale and other leaders who happened to visit Allahabad. Thus he fully acquained with the socio-economic and political developments in all the regions of India.

Initially, Pant started started his legal practice at Almora, but he changed over first to Ranikhet and then to Kashipur. Soon he established himself well as a lawyer in the region. Besides he began to participate in the public activities and soon he became an acknowledged leader of the Kumaon region. He establishad to the Kumaon Parished in 1916 to study the problems of Kumaon and these were *coolie-begar*, the old practice of forcing villagers to work for government officials without payment, and other social problems. This movement had the blessings of Mahatma Gandhi and Pant achieved success in many way. In 1916 he was elected the member of the All India Congress Committee.

At the call of Mahatma Gandhi, Pandit Pant gave up his legal practice and devoted his time for the constructive work, i.e., spinning, weaving, communal amity, prohibition, eradication of untouchability and development of education. In 1924 he was elected to the U.P. Legislative Council on the Swaraj Party ticket.

During his tenure in the Council Pantji either himself raised or vigorously participated in several important discussions. Some of them related to development of the rural areas, forest fires, report of the Reforms Inquiry Committee, and the newly appointed all-white Simon Commission. Pantji speech on the Simon Commission which had raised controversies and had aroused political passions was couched in sober, simple language but it was at the same time most eloquent. It was punctuated with frequent applause. Exhorting the people for boycott of the Commission he said in echoing words:

> "If you are dissatisfied with the all-white Commission, it is your duty, the duty you owe to your country, the duty that you owe to your conscience the duty that you owe to your future generations to assert yourself unambiguously before it becomes too late. And if you fail to do so, mind, you are taking a great and irksome and very terrific responsibility on yourself and it will be for you to answer the generations to come for having stood in the way of the progress of this great country at a critical hour. It is your duty in your own interest to support the movement of boycott so that there may be more places available for you there. So far as we are concerned, we are soldiers in this battle of Swaraj and we do not ask for anything until and unless we have reached that glorious goal which can be attained only through the

path of righteousness, rectitude and self-abnegation. So in your own interest, I ask you, to think twice before given your vote against this resolution."

The resolution was ultimately carried.

However, Simon Commission came to India in October 1928 and visited Lahore where it was confronted by a huge "Go Back Simon Commission" procession led by Lala Lajpat Rai. He was assaulted and beaten in a lathi charge by the police. The injuries caused to him proved fatal and he died eighteen days later. Paying his tributes in the Council Pantji said: "He devoted every particle of his energy, every minute of his time, and every pie of his income to the service of his community"...He was not a man of words only, he was above all a hero of action. His words however were equally applicable to his own case.

The Simon Commission visited Lucknow on 30 November after its visit to Agra. The boycott procession led by Pandit Nehru and Pantji was lathi-charged and both received body injuries. Nehru in his autobiography described the scene thus:

> "Almost every part of me seemed to ache, and I was covered with contused wounds and marks of blows. But fortunately I was not injured in any vital spot. Many of our companions were less fortunate and were badly injured Govind Ballabh Part, who stood by me, offered a much bigger target being six feet odd in height, and the injuries received then have resulted in a painful and persistent malacy which prevented him for a long time from straightening his back or leading an active life."

Speaking on an adjournment motion moved by Chintamani in the Council Panti however said:

> "If I have ever stood before this House with a genuine feeling of embarrassment it is today. My name has been

prominently mentioned with me spleadid activities that are associated with this city of Lucknow in connection with the visit of the Simon Commission I can say this much that I am not swayed by any feeling of anger or resentment. If a personal explanation or a confession of faith can be permitted I am prepared to say with all humility that I am proud of the part I took on November 29 and 30, and it is my payer, my sincere and earnest, humble prayer to the Almighty that He may give me the strength to face the brute force of which we are the victims not only when it is displayed by means of batons, but when we have to face more severe ordeals, for it is only thus that one can put an end to a Raj which is based entirely and exclusively on brutal, physical force, on might and on nothing else."

As Pandit Jawahaılal Nehru said:

"Govind Ballabh Pant is a big man, tall and heavy of body and slow of movement. He is a son of mountains and carries something of their imperturbability about him. I had sometimes seen him irritated and angry, but I have never seen him lose his temper. He and I had shared together lathi blows of the police in 1928 and we had also had adjoining cells in prison. A man of outstanding ability, he was the obivious leader of the Congress Party in our province. It was an aggressive party, more so than in any other province, and not easy to manage. But by his unfailing good humour and tact and his amazing patience, he surmounted every obstacle and was liked even by this critics and opponents. He is not a revolutionary type and his whole bent is towards constitutional activity. But, like so many other in India, circumstances have compelled him to other causes. The chief criticism made of him has been that he is too good, too soft. He is indeed the perfect gentleman."

Yes, Nehruji was unquestionably right. It was these qualities of leadership and tremendous human dimension of Pantji's personality which gave a distinctiveness to his government and to politics in U.P. during his Chief Ministership and to the office of Home Minister he held at the Centre till his death.

Pandit Pant was very clear in his mind about the aims and objects of education which are right ideals of living. While moving a resolution in the Uttar Pradesh Legislature Council on 28 February, 1925 Pantji said:

Unless and until nationalism is given a proper place, an adequate place, prominent place, an all-absorbing place in the system of education, the purpose of education, which is service of the community through the individual the attainment of self fulfilment for country through the actions of the individual, will not be attained, and if that object is not attained then all effort is vain. You may make men better animals, but that is not the object for which humanity exists. If education does not in any way inspire in us a longing for a higher life, a desire to live for our country, a desire to die for our country, it is education that has lost is main object. I submit it is in that sense I am using word nationalism.

He further said:

Then, Sir, education has another aspect about it, and that is the fire, the flame to be free. A self-centred secular system of education makes the people so very cowardly and so very timid. Where self-reliance is lacking in everything, there can be no enterprise and no manly co-operation; these things come out of men who are born with a sense of national dignity with a sense of national self-respect, with a faith in their national glory and in their future and with reverence for the past when none of these exists how can you expect that spirit of enterprise, how can you expect that backbone on which alone national life grows? If education has any use it is to create those ideals for which humanity, for which man, should exist, and one of the noblest of those ideals is freedom for the country, the desire to live in a free country. If education in a way leads us to conceal our little life under the shell, to acquire the habit of concealing the truth and not telling that which we feel, how can you expect that education to solve the larger problem which humanity expects from every individual? Education has its object and that objects is the promulgation of right ideals of living. With that object is needed the real genuine ideal of freedom for the country, the emancipation of the land. Those who have read the history of France must have noticed the nationalism as it existed in that country after the year 1870, that nationalism which does not acquiesce in foreign rule, which burns out of education. I do not say it should lead to a conflagration, but it should lead to a constructive, and selfless effort to be in one's land what others are in theirs: it should lead to the desire to attain one's full stature in one's own country; it should resent every obstacle, everything that is done to put down man from attaining the highest position in the land; it is that which can inflame an Indian to be a Napoleon Bonaparte; it is which can inflame an Indian to be in his own country what the greatest statesmen have been in theirs; it is that which can make an Indian feel that there is a day when he can be Gladstone, when he can be a Wellington, when he can be a Lord Reading in his own country. Until and unless you can put education in such a form as to lead man to think that the highest is attainable by him you are stfling the essential object of education. It is that what I mean by "nationalism". It is the substratum, it is the basis on which all that is good all that is desirable grows, has its being and is bred.

2

Political Ideology

Govind Ballabh Pant's political ideology revolved round the burning issues which had deep linkage with the freedom struggle of our country. During the early years of his participation in the freedom movement, he took up local issues touching upon the political happenings in his district and, later on, in the United Provinces. But this was not the end of his long political career. His ideology soon shifted towards the national issues and his participation in this regard was of much value.

In the U.P. Council and elsewhere he gave vent to his feelings regarding the report of the Lee Commission, on additional representation to Zamindars in the Council, on the need for occupancy tenure for tenants, resolution regarding the Simon Commission, issues having linkage with the Civil Disobedience Prisoners, nationalisation of key industries, press and its liberty, Indianisation of the Indian economy and several other problems.

ON THE REPORT OF THE LEE COMMISSION[1]

First of all I must congratulate the honourable mover of this resolution on the good luck he had in getting the permission of His Excellency for discussing this resolution. There were other motions proposed by other members, but they were ruled out, and I bow to that decision. I however beg to submit that on the present occasion one question is of greater importance to these provinces than that of the constitution of the services and the constitution of the Government. The two are closely connected together and it is very difficult to deal with one without touching on the other. As it is, it may be within the recollection of honourable members of this House that this Commission was appointed after there had been a discussion in the Leglislative Assembly in respect of the Indianization of the services and the famous document known after the name of the Hon'ble the Finance Member—the O'Donnell Circular —had been issued by the Government of India. During that time there was another resolution before the Legislative Assembly, and that related to the question of constitutional reforms. In respect of both of them, although, according to the temper of the assembly as it existed at that time, very conciliatory speeches were delivered by Sir William Vincent, who was then in-charge of the department, later on some sort of change came in, and the result was that while this Commission was appointed to inquire into the question of the services, the more important question of constitutional reforms was relegated to the background. The question of the constitution of the services was also referred to the Commission. That, I believe, was a very late afterthought of the authority which appointed that Commission in response to the agitation that had been organized in this country for the increase of the emoluments of the services. Later on the other part was tagged on to the terms of reference in order to make it less unpalatable to the people of this country. However, the Commission was there—it was appointed—and it entered into its field of work. It must be known to the honourable members of this House that the Legislative Assembly as representing the people of India was opposed to the constitution of this Commission. It twice recorded its considered opinion against the appointment of this Commission, and while in one of the resolutions that it passed it expressed its opinion, in the other it denied the demand for the money that was required for the Commission. All the same, as I understand, in spite of the opposition of the

Government of India, and overriding the wishes of the representatives of this country, this Commission was appointed, demonstrating once again the irresponsibility of the Secretary of State who is responsible to the Parliament for India, but who in fact carries on the administration of this country, as was stated by the Right Hon'ble Mr. Shastri, with the assistance of the grandmammas of the India Council. However, the Commission was there and there were members of it, but the fact remains that not one of them was an elected member of the Assembly. The Commission took its task with more than usual earnestness, and it so hastily recorded its recommendations that it took less than 4 months in disposing of the very complicated questions that were referred to it. I submit that it is very difficult for any person to form any opinion on the merits of the recommendations, and that for more reasons than one. No part of the evidence has been published, and not even one-third of the witnesses were examined by the Commission in public. Apart from that the Commissioners relying on their own wisdom did not care even to give any reason for their recommendations. Under the circumstances it is difficult for anybody, apart from the knowledge that he possesses outside and apart from what has been written by the Commissioners, to form an independent opinion on the merits of the bold recommendations that have been made by the Commission. I submit that they have made serious omissions in considering the question of emoluments of the services. They have not paid any regard to—they have not even taken into consideration—one of the most important factors which alone can determine the salaries that should be paid to the members of the public services. They have not made even a pretence of referring to the financial conditions, to the economic resources of the country with whose services they were dealing. They have not even cared to suggest that the country which is provided with these services and which is served by them has or has not the capacity to pay them at the rate which they recommend. The Commission makes all their recommendations in support of the increment in emoluments mainly on the ground that there has been a rise in prices I would very respectfully submit that, as mentioned by the honourable mover so late as the 20th of May, 1922—rather it was perhaps 30th—the Hon'ble the Finance Member, who was then incharge of the department concerned in the Government of India, held that there were enough attractions and that the pay and allowances that were given wered adequate enough, but the way in which he is looking at me suggests that I am not correctly reporting him; but we do think that the suggestion was there, that there could be no difficulty in getting recruits on the terms that were then in vogue. Anyway, that was the idea of the responsible officer-in-charge of the department on the 30th of May, 1922. Now this House will have to consider the changes that have taken place in the market from that time, and particularly to compare the rates that have then prevailed with those that are now prevailing. I would like to say that there has been probably a fail in prices of about 25 per cent all round, and the index price has altered too. I submit that under these circumstances if you take that position into consideration it would be difficult to say that the increase that has been recommended on the ground of rise in prices is justified. Then it must be known to the honourable members of the House that between the years 1917-1919 a number of allowances and privileges were given in pursuance of the recommendations of the Islington Commission combined with the paramount desire Mr. Montague had for placating the services who were going into revolt against his constitutional proposals. He took all this into consideration and tried as much as he could to raise the rates that were then in foree. Subsequently there was also the option to retire on proportionate pensions, and it would have been an indication of the inadequacy of the emoluments that were then obtainable if it had been seen that many of the members did not consider it worthwhile to continue in the service; but that was not the case. I am inclined to think that even those who left the country did so, not because the pay they received was not adequate, but because of their aversion and of their hostility to the new order of things to which they could not reconcile themselves. So I submit that there is no reason for holding that there has been such a change in the circumstances as would entitle the All-India Services to an increase in their emoluments on account of the rise in prices. But whatever be the case, we have to cut our coat according to the cloth that we have, i.e., according to the financial condition of our provinces. We are here concerned only with the Provincial Services. I am not speaking anything about the Central Services as they are designated in the report and as all the members must be knowing the Military Services are not touched by it at all. I was just putting a question about the financial condition of these provinces. There have been consecutive deficits for about three sessions. During that time additional taxes have been imposed; during that time executive orders have been passed raising the fees under various heads, and even loans have been raised and money that would ordinarily have been found out of the current revenue for certain works has been diverted out of the capital account to keep the Government going. You must be remembering the speeches that were made by the Hon'ble the Finance Member at the time he was introducing the taxation bills soon after the budget session, and from them you must have all arrived at the conclusion that our treasury is depleted and that we are on the verge of bankruptcy. That is one side of the question.

On the other, all the members must have seen the recommendations of the Economy Committee. According to those recommendations even scholarships had to be discontinued and the grants that had been made for purposes of education had to be cut down. I know the zeal that the members of that committee had for all beneficent activities and for objects that lead to further development, but even they were constrained by the financial limitations which cannot be overridden by anybody to make the recommendations which were not at all after their taste or after their choice. We also know that while Madras and Bengal have almost the same population as we have in these parts, and while the population not only of these Presidencies but also of India as a whole has risen during the last two decennial censuses, having gone up in 1911 by about 6 per cent and in 1921 by more than one per cent, in these provinces in both of these censuses a shortage was noted: in the last census it was as low as 3 per cent. We also know that the standard of living of the people in general—of those residing in the villages, of the masses in particular is of such a poor order, of such an unthinkable destitution, that it is difficult for anybody outside India to realize it. We also know that the mortality in our provinces is higher than in any other province. The speech that was delivered by Sir John Hewett in 1907 at the Sanitary Conference holds good to this day, when he said that the mortality in jails was much lower than that in the general population. The mortality, as we all know, in the case of children in these provinces is the highest. We also know that on the scale of literacy we hold almost the lowest rung of the ladder. Further, we know that the progress that has been made during the last thirty or forty years in this connection is almost negligible. Still further we know that the institutions that we have in these provinces for the education of children and of the youth are not even half as many as they are in Bengal and almost a third of what they are in Madras. The number of scholars is also in the same proportion. With all this record before us one can very well understand where we stand and what an amount of money we require for purposes which cannot be postponed even for a day. Of all the provinces we have the largest number of officers of the Imperial Services, including the Indian Civil Service or Indian Police Service. With all that before you, and in the present state of our financial resources, where are these ten lakhs to be found that have been calculated by the Finance department as the cost if the recommendations of the Lee Commission are carried out? If we were a rich country perhaps we would not have minded. Situated as we are and knowing as we do that the Imperial Services are the best paid services on the face of the earth, knowing as we do that while we are paying the highest salaries to the members of these services, without casting any reflection on their capacity, we also know that the state of our finances is such that we are the poorest people on the face of the earth. How are the two ends to be met if extravagance of this sort is to be encouraged? You may be remembering, and quotations have been made from Mr. Ramsay Macdonald where he says that this is the most extravagant system that is in force. This is what he wrote in his book in 1910, and since then it has grown much more costly. He also said that so far as possible every European should be replaced by an Indian. Under these circumstances, I submit, Sir, that considering our financial condition, considering the demands of an urgent character which cannot be deferred for a day, which have to be met, it is not possible for us to make any provision of the sort that is being sought. If we look ahead we can see that there are no chances of the resources being expanded further, of further money being raised. Of that I could not give a better proof than this, that when driven to find money the Finance department had to resort to a measure which was expected to bring in about Rs. 50,000 or at most a lakh. When the financial position of a country is of such a character that when money is needed for very urgent purposes, as the Government even in this country I hope does not report to taxation unless constrained to do so, then no better source could be found than one which was expected to yield between half a lakh and one lakh. The position is also clear if you look at the sources of revenue. They are mostly land revenue, excise and stamps. So far as land revenue is concerned we are paying a quarter of the whole that is raised in the country. And even if you were to raise land revenue by 50 per cent at every settlement, the increment, would per year not be more than 1.5 per cent. If you look at excise it is a tainted source of revenue, and so far as lies in our power we are determined to bring about its death as soon as we can. So far as stamps are concerned, when there are no trades, no industries, their room for expansion is very narrow indeed. From this one can easily see, and it is quite obvious that there are very little chances of our revenues expanding. Under these circumstances there is no ground, there is no possibility of finding money for any increase. I do not consider it necessary to go into the question further, as any person who looks into it with an unbiassed mind will see that so far as this province is concerned we have no money. Whether the Government of India or the Imperial Government at home is prepared to give any doles or any allowance for this purpose, I that have to them and they can settle it between themselves and the Imperial Services.

The next question relates to the organization and structure of the services. The recommendations of the Commission come mainly under there heads—the one relating to financial measures, which I have referred to already, the other relating to the provincialization and Indianization, and the third to the appointment of Service Commissions and other safeguards. As to the second, the proposals of the Commission are bifurcated under two categories, those relating to service operating in transferred fields and those operating in reserved fields. These are obviously based on a misapprehension. They are inadmissible because they are severed from the more important question of constitutional reform; but apart from that they are not admissible because the question of services in this country is not a political issue. It is a moral issue and an economical issue. The laws of economics, the laws of finance are inexorable, and no Government however mighty can successfully defy them. The laws of ethics are superior even to that. We claim to be in our country what others are in theirs. We are thankful to the services for all that they have done for us. I do not want to enter into the question in a spirit of carping criticism at this stage. I am prepared to extend my gratitude to them, but what I do want to put forward with all the earnestness and humility at my command is that India situated as it is can no longer afford to engage for its public services men from abroad, firstly, because there is the constitutional question as I submitted, secondly, because the economic condition does not in any way permit it, and thirdly, because with the goal of responsible government before us it is out of the question to man our services through foreign recruits or for the Secretary of State to regulate and control them from a place 4,000 miles away from the shores of India. So long as the services were there to govern, to rule, to control, there was a motive for them, there was a stimulus for them, and we being prepared to be governed and ruled, were there to obey their dictates. As Mill says, there cannot be any sort of compromise between that stage of things in which one is to command and the other to obey, but I believe that stage is gone and gone for ever, as our manhood does not submit to it, our sense of self-respect does not permit it. So under these circumstances it is necessary that the question should be looked into from that aspect. This is a moral question: it affects our national pride and stature. This view is not of a recent date. Men like Mr. Gokhale have so long ago as the time of the Welby Commission expressed opinions of this character. Those who have read the books of Dadabhai Nowrojee must have seen how keenly he felt this question of the services. I submit the question of the services is very important from the aspect of our national self-respect. We are not asking for too much. It has been admitted even by administrators that were not very friendly to India that in the matter of recruitment to these services there have been promises made to the ear that have been broken to the heart. It was stated by one of them that all sorts of subterfuges had been put into practice in order to get over the difficulties created by the Act of 1833. That Act was never given any sort of respect, to say nothing of operation. After that, when in 1853 the Act was revised, at that time Mr. Bright and others referred to this question, but it was again shelved. In 1853 the competitive system was introduced. In 1858 we got the gracious proclamation, and this was followed in 1860 by the report of the Sir Erskine Perry's Committee, who again recommended simultaneous examinations, but to no effect. In the early eighties it was prescribed that one sixth of the services should be manned by Indians. Even that was not done. Then there was the Commission of 1886, and its recommendations were of a retrograde character, but even what it recommended was not given effect to. My learned friend the mover has referred to the notes of Mr. Coupland and Sir Reginald Craddock even in this very report, so I need not cite them again.

So when we ask for the stoppage of recruitment today, we are not asking for anything drastic. We see that so far an effort has been made to stifle even the orders of the authorities—even the status and the resolution passed by the House of Commons at the instance of Mr. Paul in 1893. If necessary action had been taken on these, by this time all the services would have been Indianized, but this was not done and now we cannot wait any further. What do we see in the Philippines? It came under the Americans only in 1899. Today, except the Governor and the Deputy Governor, all the services are manned by the Philippinos, every post is held by them. Look at the progress Japan has made during the last fifty years when they introduced the western system. They can now manage their own affairs all right. With all this before us now to think that we can submit to any further humiliation is to count too much upon our sense of inferiority and self-distrust. Apart from that there is a very important consideration of a fundamental character which I would like to bring to the notice of the honourable members of this House. It is a matter which savours a little unpalatable and I regret I have to say it. After all the goal of British policy has been declared to be the attainment of responsible government. Is it in any way expected that the Imperial Services, if recruited from England, will be able to carry out this goal as expeditiously as it was intended to be at the time it was announced or as it ought to be? I think that there would be very great difficulty. They are perhaps not to be blamed, looking at the traditions in which they have been brought up. They believe, at least most of them, that India can never be fit for self-government. They believe that Mr. Montague and those who shared his opinion have been playing with a new experiment which will never be successful. Under these circumstances, how they can possibly work towards the attainment of the goal of responsible government? They can think of material improvement of the condition of the masses. The can think of better organization, but it is not possible for the majority of them to think of the acquisition of the powers of self-rule by Indians. It is not necessary for us to go very far to elucidate this position. What was after all the reason of their opposition to Lord Ripon, or of the White Mutiny at the time?

Why was there the organized though suppressed revolt against Mr. Montague which was only averted because of the sudden removal of Mr. Montague from office? Even today if one were to probe into the depths of their hearts he will find that they are more in sympathy with Sir Michael O' Dwyer or Mr. Justice Mc Cardie than with Mr. Montague or Lord Olivier I would be very glad if I was disabused of these notions. Then, I repeat, as the goal is responsible self-government, we want as agents of that policy those people who have an undisputed and an invincible faith in every rung of the ladder. For if they do not believe in them, you can certainly not make them work for it as heartily and as earnestly as you would wish. Looking at this the services have to be radically altered. Indians have to be introduced in the services, so that they may be conducted in the right spirit. The notion of overlordship has to be abandoned; the interest of the masses should be looked to, and for that an Indian alone is suited. He alone can go to the masses clad in simple clothes, talking to them in a homely manner, realizing their difficulties, trying to remove them, and all the time feeling that he is doing this for his country, that it is his duty not because he is paid, but because he has the opportunity of doing it. It is because we desire and believe that this is the only process that can lead to the realization of self-government, we think that further recruitment from abroad cannot possibly be tolerated under these circumstances. The whole question is before the Legislative Assembly, and my only object in moving this amendment is not to tie down their hands but to bring to their notice the opinion of this House. I hope the honourable members of this House will in that spirit accept the amendment which I have ventured to move and pass the amended resolution unanimously.[2]

ON ADDITIONAL REPRESENTATION TO ZAMINDARS IN THE COUNCIL[3]

I really regret that this resolution should have been brought before this House at this time. It would have been much better if this too had been ruled out like Thakur Manjit Singh's resolution which was I believe of much less far-reaching character, but any way it has been admitted and it has been discussed so long. I only hope that it will not prove another apple of discord as it may be designed to be or it may accidentally happen to be. I find myself in a peculiarly difficult position. So far as our regard to the zamindars is concerned it is unstinted and unreserved. Their names has always been associated with benevolent educational and other activities and they have done much for the good of the province. On the other hand we do not want the zamindars to remain away from us; we want them to be part and parcel of ourselves; we want to remove any line of distinction that may have existed so far. They are advanced enough; their nationalistic ideas are as good as those of many others, though, owing to the situation which they occupy the attitude which they have to adopt towards those with whom they have to deal more closely perhaps than many of us may impose certain restraints upon them, but so far as the good of the country is concerned, I should think that they have as large a heart as any of us. So if we are unable to support this proposal that is before the House at present, it is not because of our distrust of them, it is not because of our lack of recognition of the good they have done to the country, but because a vicious principle if perpetuated leads to the growth of vice and consequently it must be eliminated as soon as circumstances permit. Anyway nobody should be allowed to feed fat on vice in order to propagate it further. The points of difference between various groups in India have been emphasized and much stress has been laid so far upon them. Are there is reality any points of difference? Is there any necessity for providing any safeguards for protecting the interests of the zamindars? Where is it that their interests differ and from whom? So far as the rates of seats allotted to the taluqdars of Oudh to those allotted to the zamindars of Agra is concerned, I need not apply myself to that at all, as I am concerned with a question and a principle of a more comprehensive character. What and from whom do the interests of the zamindars differ? Is it from the tenants or is it from the urban class? If they differ from those of the urban class then the representatives of the latter class on the Council are much less in number than those of the rural parts. If it asserted that there is a conflict of interests between zamindars and tenants, then you are setting up a principle which will bring nemesis in its wake and that of a disastrous character. Why should you encourage a sentiment in the tenants that zamindars are so situated that they want to be safeguarded against them? Why should not the tenants feel that zamindars are one with them and that their interests are identical with them? I have just heard that the progress of the country depends on agriculture. I have just heard that the agricultural interests deserve the greatest consideration. I hope the honourable members on the other side will pardon me for saying that we realize the importance of that statement. We realize the vitality of that subject. We feel that it is the agricultural interests, it is the agricultural classes, it is the peasantry and the zamindars on whom the future of this province depends. It is because of the realization of that fact that we do not want to widen the gulf or broaden the differences, if any have been introduced, between the zamindars and tenants by means of special electorates. After all who are here in larger numbers? Is it the tenants or is it the zamindars or the urban classes? Whom are you going to protect by adding to the numbers? If I had asked for protection for tenants because of the present state of things, it would have been right, because so far as I know there are very few here who can claim to belong to that honourable class. Perhaps there might have been some plausibility about my argument taking the present alone into consideration. But when I see the zamindars of the province arrayed before us here, and that in such fine order, it does not look very generous on their part to come forward with further claims. Well, times may change, they say. Let us assume for the moment that times will change. What will it come to then? If the interests of the zamindars and tenants are identical, the times can change only in bringing a larger number of tenants. So far as the agricultural interests are concerned, they will be as strongly and as soundly looked after then as they are today. On the other hand the zamindars profess that their interests do not differ from those of the tenants. Such being the case I submit that their plea for more representation on the Council becomes much weaker. For whom do you seek the protection? For those who are in large numbers here or for those who are practically not represented at all? I accordingly submit that it is because I hold that the tenants and the zamindars should form one body, because I hold that every one who has a vote must be entitled to use it not for any particular individual but for the good of the country, for the promotion of progress, order, liberty and emancipation of the land that I think it is not proper to encourage any sort of differences which may have accidentally crept into the system. It is only on account of the fact, Sir, that we feel that we will not be serving the best interests of the zamindars or of the province or of the country by further emphasizing the imaginary line of difference which has length but no breadth that I have come forward to oppose this proposition. I assure the honourable members of the aristocratic class that we do not in the least mean to cast any reflection on their importance and on the position which they deservedly hold, but after all we have to look to the higher interests. If for the time being I am unable to appreciate the needs of the country and the necessities of the times or if the lights within me lead me to a further and different line from that of others, it becomes necessary for the latter to warn me not on the right track. Now what will it lead to? Suppose the zamindars have four representatives or six representatives that I am? if the general electorate has interests opposed to those of the zamindars, what will these six seats matter? What position will you have? Not much better than ours. I tell you, we are more than six here, but still it is very seldom that we can make ourselves felt and the Hon'ble the Finance Member as the leader of the House has very seldom to bother about it. So I submit and tell you that the number of two or four will not make a very vast difference. If the interests are identical, then please for the sake of the country, for the sake of progress, for the sake of liberty which is the vision of all of us, wipe off that imaginary line as soon as may be; at least do not lay any further stress on it and do not built any further walls of prejudice which only shut us from one another and thereby create needless misunderstandings which have absolutely no reason to be there.

I do not consider it necessary to go into the question of history. The matter has been discussed again and again outside and it hat also been discussed on the floor of this House previously. But the Southborough Committee held their inquiry and I had an opportunity of seeing the original notes that were prepared by the Government in that connection as I had the honour of appearing before both the committees. I believe that this distinction came in because there had been a recognition of that principle in the past. Now it is rather a very queer way of doing things that because something has been there, though it be on principle unsound, still in order to bring that injustice in line with the injustice that is already existing in the other scale of the balance, we should raise it up. That is not the right way of doing justice at least. I feel it.

Nawab Muhammad Yusuf

What about the representation of the universities?

Pandit Govind Ballabh Pant

Well, I have no objection if you take it away. Only I will then manage, so far as it will lie in my power to get Dr. Ganesh Prasad through some other constituency.

Dr. Ganesh Prasad

I would not like to stand from other constituency.

Raja Jagannath Bakhsh Singh

What about the Chambers of Commerce?

Pandit Govind Ballabh Pant

Well, I am asked about Commerce. I would submit that so far as Commerce is concerned, there is a certain amount of suspicion of racial interest in the matter. So long as we cannot bring the Europeans and Indians closer, which should be the aim of each of us who are in the national field, I will not grudge it. But on the question of principle, I submit that the constituencies of the University as well as of Commerce stand on a different footing from that of the zamindars. For, if the zamindars seek special protection, I venture to submit it is only against the tenants, and that principle I would not like to be introduced in the polity of our province.

Raja Jagannath Bakhsh Singh

Not against tenants.

Pandit Govind Ballabh Pant

That is my humble submission. You may rule it out. Because most of the voters are tenants in rural constituencies, and if their interests are identical with those of the zamindars, why should the zamindars seek special protection? The tenants will send only those people who will protect their interests. I remember—if I am wrong I am open to correction—that in the Montague-Chelmsford Report it is stated that the subject of land revenue is not being transferred as the authors apprehended that the tenants would not be adequately represented in the Council. If that impression of mine is correct, then what I feel is that from the outset the apprehension of the Government and the authors of the scheme has rather been that it is the tenants whose interests will not be fully looked after in these Councils. It is sometimes said that there is a sympathy between vested interests, but I consider that we all have vested interests and we all have common sympathy, because well have one common interest and that it is the good of our country. But if you take a false view of vested interests and say that it is the interest of those who are holding the lion's share in the administration on the one side and in land and business on the other, then perhaps such a false combination may lead one party to support the other for the time being, but that cannot be based on grounds of justice. I feel that it is the weakest and the poorest who, if any, should be protected; but I would not like even to encourage such special protection for them.

It is no use referring to the House of Lords or to other places. There the development has been on different lines: their oligarchy has gradually enlarged itself into democracy. Here we are beginning with a certain advantage, so false analogies taken from other institutions do not suit our circumstances as we are moving in different times. I never meant to argue, but unfortunately I have happened to introduce some arguments. I would beg of the zamindars not to misunderstand me, and I assure them that our inability to support this resolution does not in any way indicate any lack of regard on our part for their position or for their interests. It is only the good of the country which we think requires that there should be no divisions, and that at least divisions should not be accentuated.[4]

THE NEED FOR OCCUPANCY TENURE FOR TENANTS[5]

Well, Sir, a sort of flutter has followed from my amendment. I knew that it would cost me some effort to convince the honourable members of the reasonableness, the necessity and the wholesome character of this amendment, and I hope that by the time I sit down at least I will have dispelled the misgivings of those who are still doubtful about it. Whether I will do so or not will depend on the reasonable attitude of the members of this House and on their listening to me with an open mind. I hope they possess both. Well, Sir, as to the merits of the amendment I may inform the honourable members of this House that about five or six paragraphs of our minute of dissent dealt with it and from that the honourable members can very well understand the strong feeling that we have on the subject.

I have absolutely no doubt that the Bill as it is entirely lacking in vitality and vigour because of the absence of a provision of this character. The Bill was the outcome of the labours of a committee that was formed by the Government with a view to find out a lasting solution of the agrarian problem. Not only was it to be lasting, but it was also to be satisfactory. I put it to the honourable members of this House whether they are satisfied that the present Bill does furnish a lasting and satisfactory solution of the agrarian problem. Are they satisfied that it is anything but a makeshift arrangement, which is being provided to meet only the exigencies of the present situation, and that in framing it, its framers have been inspired only by the requirements which thrust themselves upon those who are actuated by nothing but the principle of expediency? I have no noubt that the Bill as it is, though it may for the time being serve as a palliative to meet what has been said in the original resolution issued on the subject by the Government to be the keener realization of grievances and a growing determination to press for their redressal by the cultivators in the province of Agra, cannot but lead to further legislation after a short time. I do not see any reason why the time of the public should be wasted again on a question which raises bitter controversy or why such a measure should be dealt with in a tampering spirit to be brought forward again and again to embitter controversy and create splits between us. Again, I think it is in the interest of Government too that they deal with the question in a generous manner with a view to find out an ultimate and final solution of it. It is because I feel that it is absolutely necessary that this Bill should provide some solution for a reasonable time to come that I am proposing this amendment. Sir, this is a very great defect in this Bill that it gives the go-by to the policy which has been in force in this province for at least 125 years. This Bill is making an abrupt break from the policy which has been recognized, approved, confirmed and developed by means of legislation during the last 70 years in this province. From time to time efforts have been made to give further strength to the principle of occupancy tenure in these provinces. By this Bill an end is being put to that for ever. We have to see whether we can satisfy the tenant by means of any provision which will give him only the privilege of continuing in possession of the holding for his lifetime, provided he goes on paying rent at a very high rate; whether a provision like that can solve the agrarian problem. The arguments that were advanced by Hafiz Hidayat Husain Sahib and Rao Abdul Hameed Khan Sahib in the course of their discourses on a prior clause of this Bill can very well be brought to mind by honourable members of this House in this connection. They were very right when they said that among us a tenant cannot appreciate anything that does not continue the advantage of that thing beyond his lifetime to his children. We know that in Indian homes one's own wife, if she fails to bring forth a child, is codemned by her own husband. So in the places where we live, where sanctity is attached to the principle of heredity, a principle that will put an end to the heritable character of the land tenure in this province altogether and will terminate it after the lifetime of the tenant concerned is nothing if not altogether vicious. I hold that it is absolutely necessary that this amendment should be made. As must be known to honourable members of this House, there is no provision for the acquisition of occupancy rights in this Bill. I am not taking into account the provision with which we have just dealt with, which enables a landlord to confer occupancy rights. I am concerned with the acquisition of occupancy rights, not with the conferment of such rights. So far as the conferment of rights is concerned, it is open to any person to confer any rights on any person so long as there is no law prohibiting such conferment. But the acquisition of rights is an entirely different thing. Sir, I do not know if our honourable friend, Mr. Gavin Jones, is here. I want to ask him if there can be any agricultural development in the province, if he can think of people putting their money, putting their labour and investing what they possess in their holding when they know full well that whatever they invest will come to an end after their death. And after all what does a man live for? Does he live for himself or for those whom he procreates? If it is for those who are to follow him that a man lives, works and labours—that is after all the weakness of us Indians even in this materialistic age—then I say that this provision cannot serve a beneficial purpose, it will be detrimental to agricultural development and will be detrimental to the growth of genuine interest in the land on the part of the tenants and it will lead to such a precarious tenure as will be harmful in more ways than one. I do admit that the principle of statutory life-tenancy is useful to the extent that it secures the tenant in the enjoyment of his holding for his lifetime—to that extent it is to his benefit. I request you to look at the thing from the larger standpoint. I am asking if it can solve the problem. I know that the scheme of this Bill has been framed on the basis of the Oudh Rent Act of 1921 and that is exaclly the reason why I think that this clause should be added to the present clause 16. In Oudh we had practically no occupancy tenure prior to that year. The number of occupancy tenants did not exceed a few thousands. The proportion did not go beyond two per cent. In Agra that the state of things is entirely different. Here we have a large number of occupancy tenants. The growth from year to year of about half a per cent of occupancy area shown that great importance has been attached to it by those who have acquired the privileges. Then we also know that in province of Agra these rights have not been prohibited by anything in the form of Oudh Compromise. I say and claim that it is the inherent right of the tenant in the province of Agra that he should acquire occupancy rights in these provinces by virtue of prescriptive usage. It is his inherent right by virtue of the Statutes which have been in force for the last seventy years and it is in conformity with the sacred principles which have been observed for such a considerably long time. By limiting the tenant's rights to his lifetime you are doing an injustice to the vast class of tenantry concerned. You are doing an injury to the larger interests of the landlords concerned, because I do believe that it is in the interests of landlords that the tenants should feel that their holdings are their own. It is in the interests of landlords that the tenants should feel that their children and their children's children will ever be associated with the children and children's children of the landlords. But when their tenure is to come to an end with their lifetime they must feel the weakness of their position. They will feel that their landlords have only an ephemeral and temporary connection with them. It is because I desire that their should be harmony between the landlords and the tenants that I advocate this course. What I am proposing is not after all an unknown innovation. As may be known to honourable members of this House, in the Central Provinces occupancy rights were conferred on all non-occupancy tenants. There was nothing in the form of statutory tenure. I wish to invite the attention of the House to another point. Here under this Bill the zamindars are deriving many more advantages than the zamindars in Oudh got from the Bill of 1921. So if the provisions of this Bill are supplemented in any way it is not unfair or unjust to the zamindars. If this Bill had taken this shape from the outset, there would not have been any serious objection on the part of anybody. Sir, the principle of occupancy tenure is desirable also because we want that the tenant should go on adding to the productivity of the soil. We want that the tenant should work for his field knowing full well that his son has to be a tenant. He should not be driven from his holding. If he has to do it, he has only to lay up every shell for something else. If his son has to cast about for his living after his death, how can he feel inclined to improve his holding? So, Sir, from whichever aspect the question may be looked at, it is necessary that a provision of this character should find a place in this Bill. It has been said by some of our friends here that they have been returned by the votes of one class or another. Who have also been told that we should remember that we have been returned by the votes of the zamindars and the tenants. To us the occasion is much more solemn than that. We think that this is hardly an occasion for tactics or manoeuvring, when such large issues are at stake. Millions of people are looking up to this Council today as to what we do. They may not be as wide awake and vocal as others who are more familiar with the activities of parliaments are. But we know what we do today will reflect upon their well-being, will bear upon their welfare for at least some time to come. All of us may be wiped out from the floor of this Council. That is after all an altogether inconsequential consequence. What does it matter to us? The principle before us should be whether in the interests of the country, whether in the larger interests of the people whom we happen to be representing here today is it or is it not necessary that an amendment of this sort should be made in this Bill? If the majority of the people tell us that it is reasonable that such an amendment should not be made, it may be thrown out. But I appeal to the honourable members of this House, on whichever side of this chamber they may be sitting, not to be influenced by any other considerations in disposing of the amendment which I have just moved.[6]

RESOLUTION REG. THE SIMON COMMISSION[7]

At the outset I should like to congratulate the Hon'ble the Finance Member on his lucid speech; about its merits I will say a few words later.

As the Hon'ble Home Member just remarked the question before the House is of momentous and vital importance. It is not possible for me to do justice to it within the few minutes that are at my disposal. Nor is it necessary for me to deal with it at any length. The entire attention of the country has been focussed on it for the last four months and every shade of opinion has been fully expressed. Besides, nobody is in a mood to listen as all are anxious to move the lobbies. Nothing that may now be urged can demonstrate the strength of the cause that we sitting on this side represent as the passage of this resolution in this Council, specially when one bears in mind the frantic efforts that have been made by the Government in every possible way and through every possible means to secure support for their forlorn cause.

I wish I could survey the strip of ground between the two good men, namely, the Hon'ble Finance Member and the Hon'ble Home Member. The latter does not call for any special treatment as he was no more than an echo of the Finance

Member, I have however noted with interest that though the Hon'ble Finance Member is a novice in the art and has just entered the arena he has found an apt disciple in the Hon'ble Home Member who has been in the Government for some years.

Sir, as I just observed, the resolution has been discussed threadbare. The objections raised by the speakers on the other side have been fully answered by those whose ability, patriotism or public spirit cannot be disputed by any sane Indian. One cannot convince him who will not be convinced. So I will not waste the time of the House by stale and insipid repetition.

The monstrous plot brought forth by the Baldwin Birkenhead cabinet has been torn to pieces by almost every one from even among those Indian politicians who have received solemn testimonials about their sobriety and moderation from the accredited representatives of the burceaucracy. So far as the Indian National Congress is concerned, its differences are fundamental and go to the very root of this scheme. We stand for self-determination and at least for round table conference and as it has not received sufficient notice here so far I will confine my remarks to this important aspect of the constitutional problem before the House. I am certain that every one who is in right earnest will be driven by the logic of incontrovertible historial facts to the conclusion that there is no alternative to a round table conference. The suggestion has not been made by doctrinaire politicians but by serious people who have grappled with hard realities of the situation, explored every avenue and found that nothing short of a round table conference can serve any useful purpose. The history of the growth of self-groverning institutions within the British Empire has demonstrated that there is only one way for the solution of constitutional difficulties, and that can be found only in the country for which the constitution has to be devised and only by those people who are to be affected by that constitution. This principle had been discovered by actual experience before the sacred doctrine of self-determination was formally proclaimed from the housetops by self-seeking egoists, at an hour of crisis, to save their own skins. That is a principle which history has vindicated as being the only sound principle on which a lasting constitution can be based. Do you not know what happened in the various dominions that are comprised in what is grandiloquently called the British Commonwealth? Sir, in South Africa, certain constitutions were imposed by British Parliament in 1876 and 1877, but they came to naught, because they had not been framed by the citizens of countries affected. They were thrust on an unwilling people; and what was the sequel? There was a lot of strife and bloodshed and Parliament had to give way. After the Boer War, in 1906, a constitution was embodied in a statute by Parliament which to the very latter gave effect to the wishes of the people of South Africa. What happened in Canada? There too, the British Parliament imposed certain consitutions at a certain stage which proved equally disastrous. In the end Parliament was forced to adopt the same expedient which it later followed in the case of South Africa, and a constitution framed by the people of Canada had to be accepted. Only home-made constitutions put an end to the fierce bitterness, hostility, and misery in these countries and secured peace and progress. Exactly the same thing happened in Ireland. The British people had a scheme of Irish Home Rule before them in 1884. The Parliament framed a certain Act in 1914. They followed it up by another in 1920, but still there was no peace in sight, and it was only when in 1921 the Parliament accepted the constitution that had been framed by the representatives of Ireland itself that chaos and suffering ceased in Ireland. So, Sir, history has established two or three principles indubitably and they are indisputable. It has been repeatedly proved that unless and until a constitution framed and formulated by the representatives of the people of the countay for which the constitution is intended is introduced, makeshift contrivances cannot put an end to the struggle for liberty nor can they secure satisfaction or stability. It is equally clear that whenever efforts have been made to superimpose something from without, it has only added to complications and bitterness and has made things worse. I cannat do better than quote to you a speech of Sir John Simon himself, which gives a conclusive and direct reply to the authors of the present scheme. It is a wonder to me that Sir John Simon with his reputation, statesmanship and integrity should have agreed to be a party to the working of a scheme which goes fundamentally against the principles which he enunciated in 1921. Sir, speaking on the Irish Constitution Bill on November 27,1921, Sir John Simon in the course of his speech, made the following remarks; considering the significance of the speech and to avoid the least possibility of any misapprehension, I will quote it at some length—"I rise to express on behalf of myself and my friends with whom I am associated, our complete concurrence with what the Prime Minister said at the opening of the Debate. He pointed out, and I think it is one of the encouraging features of the situation, that this constitution is a constitution which has been drafted in Ireland by Irishmen for Ireland. In that respect it differs from the two Gladstonian schemes, from the Act of 1914, and from the Act of 1920. The procedure that has been followed is, however, by no means a novel or a revolutionary procedure. As the Prime Minister pointed out, the constitutions under which different parts of our Empire are now working are in a very large measure constitutions which have been settled on the soil where they were to operate by the people who were to live under them. The Dominion of Canada, which, in Art. 2 of the Treaty, is specially referred to, lives, it is true, under a constitution which is contained in an Imperial Act; but that Imperial Act did nothing more than embody in legislative form the great collection of resolutions which had been arrived at, in Quebec as a result of long debate and ultimate agreement between the Canadians themselves. The Constitution of Australia is not to be found in any enacting section of any British Act of Parliament at all. The Constitution of Australia is scheduled to a Statute of 1900, in exactly the same way in, which it is proposed that this Irish Constitution should be scheduled to this present Bill. Perhaps the most remarkable case of all is the most recent, for the Constitution of the Union of South Africa was at length arrived at as the result of discussion in South

Africa itself, and it was carried through this House within the recollection of a good many honourable members, in the year 1909, without the alteration of a single sentence. It may be suggested that these instances are not exactly in point, because they are all instances of a union which is being effected between areas that hitherto have not been so closely federated; but but the principle that constitutions in our Empire have usually been found to have a permanent basis in the cases where they have been arrived at and settled on the soil affected by them, is by no means limited to the different federal unions under the British Crown. I believe it would be true to say that constitutions which promote prosperity and loyalty and which have been found to be lasting constitutions for subordinate States in our Empire, have almost, without exception, eitheir actually or virtually, been framed by those who were to live under them themselves. I think that that circumstance may well be set against some of the gloomy records and forebadings of the honourable and gallant Gentlemen for at any rate, there is a real element of hope and confidence here, in that this Constitution which the British Parliament formulates and offers to confer upon Ireland; it is a Constitution which Irishmen themselves have drawn up, and which they now apply to the Imperial Parliament to ratify.

Sir, in all these cases the British Parliament was the supreme authority and absolute power of enacting the law under which those various Governments in these countries were to function was vested exclusively, so far as the legal aspect of the matter wont, in the British Parliament and nobody else. Their position then did not in the least differ from the position of India today, I ask my honourable friend from Cawnpore-cum-Fatehgarh and others who have raised the constitutional question to digest what that eminent jurist, Sir John Simon, has pointedly observed in this connection. That is the last word on the subject. I will not comment on this speech, every word of which should give food for reflection to Sir John and his colleagues and to those who are opposed to the proposal of a round table conference. It is not a strange irony that with his belief "that constitutions which promote prosperity and loyalty and which have been found to be lasting constitutions for subordinate States in the Empire have been framed by those who were to live under them themselves" Sir John Simon should be the friend, philosopher, and guide of the outrageous Commission, the outstanding feature of which is the rigid exclusion of Indians. I am reminded of a sentence from the speech of the Hon'ble the Finance Member that in politics the unexpected often happens. But, will those in power always wait for surprises and never agree to do anything in good grace out of goodwill to satisfy those who stand for the vindication of their invulnerable birth-right? Sir, in the year 1920 when the Home Rule Act was passed Mr. Asquith and others urged that Dominion status should be conferred on Ireland. The Government in power then did not agree. What wast the result? The reign of law was over. There was repression and there was oppression, there were assassinations and there were murders, and within a year of the passage of that Act, in 1921, the British Parliament had to confer on Ireland a constitution going far beyond the Dominion status. The unexpected happened and it happened within a year. I am not using the language of intimidation. I ask the Government in power here who are in close touch with the state of things in this country, to tell those who are their masters and who have appointed them our masters, that the unexpected happens so often and the unexpected may also happen in India. The British people and Parliament accepted to a letter the Home-made schemes in the case of Canada, in the case of South Africa, and in the case of Ireland. Why do they fight shy even of a round table conference in our case? Is it because they think that old India is lying prostrate today? Will the lessons of history be of no avail to them? They were deluded by appearances in Ireland but within a year Ireland proved its might and British Government had to brind. "Too late" is inscribed in dark letters in so many chapters of British history. Will they realize their blunder in the case of India only when the opportunity of befriending her is past and gone? They refused to accommodate the United States and this recoiled on them. Do they want the horrors and tragedy of a rebellion as in Canada, of an open fight in South Africa, or of Sinn Fennism as in Ireland before accepting the credentials of Indians to effectively determine the future constitution of their country? Is it only after people have taken to stern and gruesome ways that they are considered fit to be treate as men? That is a grave and serious question. We have entered the fight for freedom. We will attain it, attain it, it today, attain it tomorrow, attain it in ten years or in twenty years. We are not going to give it up. So I ask the British people to beware and not to spurn at our proposals. They similarly rejected the suggestions that were made by others who were similarly circumstanced but had ultimately to pay back the principal with interest.

Let Parliament make its choice while there is yet time and settle a scheme for this country now and unite the East and the West in bonds of fellowship and friendship. But if you persist in your own ways just consider who will suffer in the end. Our ultimate triumph is assured but what will be the position or prestige of the British Empire without India or with India, hostile and independent? At the most you can only put off the evil hour by obstructing us in our onward march: but pray imagine the volume of human suffering, loss, and misery that such resistance has always entailed. We beseech you as friends of humanity and peaceful progress to stay your hands and to save the world and this country from a catastrophe which you can easily avert.

It is not given to those who throughout their lives have been pompous, arrogant, and vain, to solve great problems. Only those who are possessed of a spirit of humanity, humility, and saintliness and undertanding can handle large issues. So I appeal to you in that spirit. There is yet time and the catastrophe may yet be averted. But if you do not; rest assured history will blame you.

May I request you, my honourable countrymen there who are not seeing the tragic consequences which their complacent attitude, and narrow-minded vision—which does not go beyond their nose—can entail, to take account of the disastrous consequences that they will bring upon their people if they lose sight of the goal which they and we could share equally? Sir, I will now ask them to make their choice, Parliament can make its own, but what have the honourable members sitting there with their wavering and feeble hearts to settle for us and for themselves? Do they know that the scheme which we are considering, today has the blessing of Sydenham, of O'Dwyer, of the London Times, of the Allahabad Pioneer, o.' the Lahore Civil and Military Gazette, of Col. Crawford of every individual under the sun who has been an implacable and unbending opponent of Indian aspiration? Whom are they going to stand by, Lord Birkenhead or Mahatma Gandhi? Do they owe allegiance to the principles of liberty, progress, and freedom, or are they so self-centered that even in this grave and solemn moment they cannot rise above their own petty interests and surroundings? I ask them to take account of the opinion in the country and of the welcome change that is noticeable in quarters that were supposed to be reactionary or stagnant. I ask my honourable friends to bear in mind the parting will and testament of that great and good man Hakim Ajmal Khan, who died with the words on his tongue "boycott this Commission" what response will they make to this great man who in that solemn and sacred hour when one is in touch with the world beyond made this appeal? I appeal to them in his name to cast their vote for this resolution.

One thing more and I have done. I do not see how any one can oppose this resolution after hearing the speech of the Hon'ble the Finance Member. Leaving aside all questions of principle, the resolution must be supported by everyone on the ground of expediency. One may or may not agree with me in my view about the undeniable right of the country to determine a constitution for itself, but almost every speaker has condemned the present scheme of the Commission and has deplored that there is no Indian on this Commission. Even the Hon'ble the Finance Member does not justify or defend it.

He practically admits that it is defective but asks the Council to wait for further developments in the hope that suitable changes might be made. I say that it is exactly what you should not do. Those who are not satisfied with the present scheme—and even the Hon'ble the Finance Member did not express his approval of it and the resolution is restricted to the present scheme only—and who are anxious to see it modified can further their object by passing this resolution and not by defeating it. The Hon'ble the Finance Member says that the resolution is premature. Perhaps you are already late but if you decline to record your opinion even now it will be a blunder.

When the time for appointing the Committees is reached the scheme will have been finally cast and if you let it solidify and crystallize while it is said to be in fluid state and let judgement go against you by default any objections which you may then care to raise will be ruled out on the ground of their being too late. This is just the time when even those who are practically minded should bring maximum pressure on those with whom according to them their destiny rests. Their masters are at a distance of hundreds of miles from the shores of this country and it will take their feeble voice some time to go beyond the roaring seas in case it is not drowned in the way.

If you are dissatisfied with the all-White Commission, it is your duty, the duty that you owe to your country, the duty that you owe to your conscience, the duty that you owe to your future generations, to assert yourself unambiguously before it becomes too late. And if you fail to do so, mind, you are taking a great and irksome and very terrific responsibility on yourself and it will be for you to answer the generations to come for having stood in the way of the progress of this country at a critical hour. The Hon'ble the Home Member said that we should owe allegiance to the country and to no party. That is exactly the point that I want to lay stress upon. Owe allegiance to the country not to the tin gods who may be installed in the House of Mammon today and toppled down tomorrow.

Owe allegiance to the country; and where is the embodiment of that allegiance? Is it not in Mahatma Gandhi? Is it not in Dr. Ansari? Is it not in Pandit Madan Mohan Malaviya? Is it not in Pandit Motilal Nehru? Or is it there in the Hon'ble the Minister, Local Self-Government's keeping? Let everyone of you answer the plain question. Take a country-wide view of the thing and do not be misled by those who are centered in and cannot look beyond themselves.

Look at the matter from a correct standpoint, take a true perspective of it, do not forget your country; be true and honest and remember that if today the Nawab Sahib of Chattari and the Nawab Sahib of Jaunpur are two of the members of the Government, it is because of the sacrifices of those who are asking you to boycott this Commission.

It is your duty in your own interest to support the movement of boycott, so that there may be more places available for you there. So far as we are concerned, we are soldiers in this battle of swaraj and we do not ask for anything until and unless we have reached that glorious goal which can be attained only through the path of righteousness, rectitude, and self-abnegation. So in your own interest I ask you to think twice before giving your vote against this resolution.[8]

THE INDIAN STATUTORY COMMISSION[9]

With your permission, I wish to make a few remarks before the Finance Member moves the motion standing in his name. Having given careful consideration to the matter I and those with whom I have the privilege of acting here arrived at the conclusion that it would be in the best interests of all concerned if we dissociated ourselves from the motion which is to be made by him. I may at once state that I personally feel that having regard to my own sense of personal decency, national dignity, and the honour of this House no alternative course is open to me. For what to these legislatures exist, if their verdicts, recorded after careful, elaborate full-dress debates are going to be re-opened every day, if the executives takes it into its head to bring forward the question again? On February 25, as the House knows full well, a clear, emphatic and definite verdict was recorded by the members of this House. That verdict was not the outcome of any precipitate hurry. The Finance member had sounded his note of caution in a very persuasive tone then before the votes were cast. The members had the benefit of hearing all that he had to say, and after careful consideration of all he had to say, after carefully weighing all the pros and cons of the proposition before them, they definitely determined that this House would never have anything to do with this Statoryut Commission at any stage and in any form. Now we are being asked to trample upon that resolution, to treat it as thrown into the waste-paper basket, and to proceed with the formation of a committee. However euphemistically the resolution may be couched, the point is clear enough that Government wants the House to co-operate with the Commission. There can be no doubt in the mind of any sane person that the country is against the Commission. Those who have been following the trend of thought and opinion in this country, those who have any regard for the enlightened opinion of this country must be convinced that every man who cares for the good of this country is against this Commission. Even now I stand here to say with full confidence that the majority of the members of this House are against this Commission (Voices of "no"). I have absolutely no doubt that if a referendum were made the country as a whole would record its opinion against this Commission. There are those who have the audacity to question my remark on this matter in spite of our experience to the last few months. Who does now know the result of the two bye-elections that were held? Was not this distinct issue placed before the people and were not these votes cast on it? Did not the Hon'ble Minister for Local Self-Government use every resource, resort to every tactics, adopt every device which he could have found on the face of the earth in order to get votes cast in favour of the candidate he sponsored, as he was himself the sponsor of Sir John Simon's Commission? And were not those votes cast against him, and was not his candidate defeated by an overwhelming majority in each case? Does that not indicate the direction in which the wind is blowing outside this House? And I again emphatically declare that I am convinced that the majority of the members of this House are against this Commission. If I do not want to take part in the deliberations that will take place over this motion today it is because I consider it a waste of time. Not only that, I consider it a very improper course to reopen a question over which the verdict of the House is in accord with the sentiment and enlightened opinion of the country and over which this House has recorded an unambiguous, emphatic and positive opinion. Besides, I see that even if we continue the process, even if we throw out this motion again, if the Government is determined to go on definitely, it can go on interminably with similar motions again and again until they have either coerced or cajoled or bribed or intimidated or otherwise forced or seduced the members of this House to submit and succumb to those influences of which they are past masters. It is because I want to save my country from the stigma which is sometimes brought on everyone of us, because of the ignoble, because of the intolerably objectionable, I may not say mean, methods that are adopted by the Government that I feel it is better that they, the Government, are given a long rope and allowed to do what they like than that their wishes should be resisted and India should be made the further victim of their machinations, especially in demoralizing our character. It is because I value the moral factor highly that I would rather that the Government did what it chose. Besides, do you not know what the Government is after? The Assembly threw out the resolution, or rather the Assembly adopted a resolution similar in form to the resolution that we passed. The Assembly is now being coerced to send some of its representatives to this Commission. They stoutly declined to do so, but the Government comes to their aid and says they will nominate members if the Assembly does not elect them. If the wishes of the highest house in this country representing the most enlightened of our leaders are going to be flouted like that, what is the use in carrying on a sham controversy inside the four walls of this House when we know full well that ultimately our verdict is to be disregarded most unceremoniously? If the Government is determined to nominate people even if we throw out the resolution, why should we waste our time over this discussion? So we leave it to them to do what they like. Besides, I feel that there can be a duel only when we stand on common ground. Our valuation of vital matters and eternal verieties of life, our opinions about moral factors, differ fundamentally. What the Government are after is entirely different from what we can conceive to be the normal rule of life for a normally moral course and under these circumstances we cannot even meet to part. We decline even to stand face to face so far as this particular proceeding goes, for in their activities, regarding this matter in particular, they have demonstrated it in an unmistakable way that they are after purchasing every one among us, they are after compromising our honour, and after reducing us to impotent figure heads and then to press all these matters into service against us in order to demonstrate the weakness of Indian character and Indian courage and Indian intrepidity. The Government's attitude has never been anything if not hypocritcal. They bemoan the differences between us and they foment those differences day in and day out. They think that we not being fit for the defence of our country cannot have self-government, and they take every step for the emasculation of our people. They on the one hand, make a false pretence of respecting public opinion; and, on the other hand, they throw over board those people who show any deference for the recorded wishes of this House and instal in most responsible offices those who have shamelessly swallowed their solemn declarations. In these circumstances it is not worthwhile to waste the time of this House. I may also state here, and I will be pardoned for saying so that it has been fully disclosed by the proceedings of this House as well as outside that there is a fundamental difference of outlook and of ideals between those who want to co-operate with the Commission and those who do not want to have anything to do with it. There are those in whose scheme of things the central figure is the starving skeleton in the field, and there are those in whose scheme of things there is the pampered fat man on the pedestal to whom everything and everybody must bend and submit. Between these two classes there is little chance of agreement. There are those who want the people to rise; there are those who want the economic uplift of the masses; there are those on the other hand, who would only desire to have more of the loaves and fishes, who would care more for high posts and for high salaries than for the service of those for whom these services are meant. If there are people who want to whine before the Commission let them have unrestricted scope. If there are people who want to make a demonstration of their petty wranglings before the Commission let them do so. We need not stand in their way. Let those who desire dance to the tune of their masters and have the joy of it. But we, on the other hand, Sir, have only one goal before us, that is, the goal of liberty, of freedom for the country. We feel that in the present circumstances, when all constitutional methods, when everything that savours of constitutional has been thrown to the winds, has been trampled upon, there can be only one goal, that noble goal, that glorious goal of Independence for this great country. We cannot think of anything else. We have to live and to die for that, and for us these little juggleries in the form of commissions and committees, these little devices in one name or another have little meaning. We must steer clear of them all. We refuse to be deluded, to be misguided, to be misled by these things. We see the vision of the glorious mother installed above all these bickerings, above all these little handicaps, high up in the clouds, and we want to seek that road which will lead to that, that road which is not to be found inside the nets of this House, that road which is not to be found inside the machinations of the bureaucratic nets, but which is to be found apart and away from that; that road, which, however long it may be, is sure to lead us to our goal. We depend on ourselves to crave over future. We know that nations by themselves are made. We care not for your commissions, we care not for your manipulated, manoeuvred factious intrigues. We are after something better. We know that it is only through self-sacrifice, through self-abnegation that that object can be a tained. For the present we make to you a present of your commission. Make use of it as you like. For us there is room elsewhere, and enough of it. Our sincerity has been put to test not once, not twice, but on numberless occasions. I will only refer to their latest performance. They had been talking glibly and incessantly of the unfitness of Indians to frame any constitution. The moment the Nehru Committee's report was out, the moment it received the seal of approval of the All-Parties Conference, a campaign of calumny and ridicule was set up against it. Every device is being adopted in order to pooh-pooh it, in order to show that Indians are not fit to do anything, and when they produce anything it is altogether unfit to be considered seriously. We know our aims very well. They must know now that there is no occasion for any confusion, for any misunderstanding, or for any sort of misrepresentation. Everything is so clear. We know them well. We know also the history of Ireland, of Canada, of the United States of America, and of South Africa. We know that they have nowhere yielded. We know that they will not yield here of their own free accord. We know that they will have ultimately to yield to those forces to which they had to yield in other places. They are demonstrating to us every minute by their utter disregard of organized public opinion in this country that they are determined not to part with anything real and substantial in this country, and we must chalk out our own course. We must let the lessons of history burn deeply into our hearts. We must act up to them. The Government is welcome to enter into alliance with friends like Raja Jagannath Bakhsh Singh. There may be others who may take similar sommersaults hereafter. So far as we are concerned we take note of their boundless capacity to act in an ignoble manner. So far as we are concerned we will follow only the trying path of rectitude, of honour and of righteousness, and that path will lead us on to the glorious goal before us. We will not be misled by the false talk of this unnatural

Commission. You may arrive to your decision and elect your representatives. So far as we are concerned we challenge you again to go to the country, to dissolve this Council, and see whether you can get a single representative from the whole of these provinces from one end to the other. If you have not that courage, then accept that you want the committee whether the House agrees to it or not. You want the artificial committee to prop up your own unrighteous system. But we are determined to bring it down. Its collapse is near. We will work for it and work for it by those ways and means which have succeeded in other places and which will succeed in this country in vindicating the honour of our motherland and restoring our nation to its sublime eminence.

The members of the Nationalist and Congress parties then withdrew from the Chamber.[10]

CIVIL DISOBEDIENCE PRISONERS STILL IN PRISON

Pandit Govind Ballabh Pant

(a) Will government be pleased to state how many civil disobedience prisoners are still in prison in the various provinces?

(b) What are their names, and what is the remaining period of imprisonment in each case?

The Honourable Sir Henry Craik

(a) and (b). I lay a statement on the table. It is not in the public interest to give the names of these prisoners.

Statement showing the number of Civil Disobedience Prisoners undergoing imprisonment with periods of Sentence in each case.

Province	Number sentenced	Date of sentence	Period of imprisonment
Madras	One	1.2.32	6 months' rigorous imprisonment plus further sentence on 22nd February, 1932, of 3 1/2 years' rigorous imprisonment.
Bombay	Do	4.2.32	4 years' R.I. and Rs. 150 fine or 8 months in default.
Do	Do	19.2.32	4 years' R.I. and fine of Rs. 250 or 18 months in default.
Do	One on two charges	16.4.32 26.7.32	3 years' R.I. and fine of Rs. 500 or 9 months, 28 days in default.
Do	One on three charges	28.1.32 11.2.33 12.2.32	Two and half years' R.I. of Rs. 200 or 13 and half months in default.
Do	Do	26.1.32 28.1.32 30.1.32	5 years.
Do	One on two charges	16.4.32 16.7.32	Three and half years' R.I. and fine of Rs. 500 or 10 months in default.
Do	Do	26.9.33 10.4.34	2 years' R.I. and fine of Rs. 165 or 5 months in default.

Province	Number sentenced	Date of sentence	Period of imprisonment
Do	Do	15.11.32 23.12.32	(1) 6 months' R.I. and fine of Rs. 50 or 6 weeks in default. (2) 2 years' R.I.
Do	Do	14.2.34 1.6.34	(1) 6 months' R.I. and Rs. 50 fine or 6 weeks in default. (2) 2 years' R I. and Rs. 50 fine or 3 months in default.
Do	Two	26.10.33	18 months' R.I. and fine of Rs. 200 or 6 months in default each.
Do	One on two charges	31.7.33	18 months' R.I. and Rs. 500 fine or 6 months in default.
		13.9.33	6 months' R.I. and Rs. 50 fine or one and half months in default.
Do	Two	31.7.33	18 months' R.I. and Rs. 500 fine or in default 6 months each.
Do	One	20.3.33	2 years' R.I. and fine of Rs. 300 or 6 months in default.
Do	Do	27.3.33	Ditto ditto
Do	Do	7.4.33	Ditto ditto
Do	Do	24.4.33	2 years' and 3 months R.I. and fine of Rs. 350 or 7 and half months in default.

Province	Number sentenced	Date of sentence	Period of imprisonment
Do	Do	13.4.33	2 years' R.I. and Rs. 300 fine or 6 months in default.
Do	One on two charges	25.4.33	(1) 6 months' R.I. (2) 2 years R.I. and fine of Rs. 150 or 3 months in default.
Do	One	6.11.33	2 years' R.I.
Do	Do	17.7.33	Ditto.
Do	One on two charges	7.7.33 15.8.33	(1) 2 years. (2) 6 months.
Bombay	One on two charges	28.6.33 1.8.33	2 years' R.I. and Rs. 50 fine or 6 months in default.
Do	One on three charges	26.7.33 28.7.33 1.8.33	2 years' R.I.
Do	One on two charges	5.9.33 16.9.33	(1) 2 years' R.I. (2) 1 years' R.I.
Do	Do	22.8.33 8.9.33	(1) One and half years' R.I. (2) 6 months' R.I. and fine of Rs. 100.
Do	Do	9.9.33 11.9.33	(1) 6 months' R.I. (2) 1 years' R.I.

Province	Number sentenced	Date of sentence	Period of imprisonment
Do	Do	31.8.33	(1) 1 years' R.I. 4 months' R.I. (Concurrent).
		19.9.33	(2) 1 years' R.I. and Rs. 200 fine or 6 months in default.
Do	Do	17.3.33	6 months. 2 years (concurrent).
Bengal	Two	14.2.34	1 year, 9 months' R.I. each (including 3 months' R.I. in each case in default fine of Rs. 50).
Do	One	5.3.34	1 years' R.I.
Do	Two	21.4.34	1 year, 6 months' R.I. each.
Do	One	1.5.33	2 years and 42 days' R.I. (including 42 days' R.I. in default of fine of Rs. 50).
Do	One on three charges	17.8.33	3 years' R.I. and Rs. 100 and Rs. 50 fine or in default 3 months' R.I. and 2 months' S.I., respectively.
Do	One on two charges	17.8.33	1 years's R.I. and fine Rs. 50 or 2 months in default. 1 year's R.I. and fine Rs. 50 or 2 months in default.
Do	Do	3.8.33	1 years' R.I. and fine Rs. 100 or 3 months' R.I. in default.
		28.8.33	1 year's R.I.

Province	Number sentenced	Date of sentence	Period of imprisonment	
Do	Do	7.2.34	1 years' R.I. and Rs. 100 fine or 84 days' R.I. in default.	
Do	One	25.9.30	20 years' R.I. under Sections 302/34, I.P. Code and sections 145, 120-B/353, I.P.C.	
Do	Two	25.9.30	7 years' R.I. each under Sections 302/34 and 145, 120-B/353, I.P. Code and Section 325/147, I.P. Code, respectively.	
Do	Two on two charges	25.9.30	20 years' R.I.	each under Sections 302/34 and 143, I.P. Code.
		27.10.30	6 months' R.I.	
Do	One on two charges	25.9.30	20 years' R.I.	under Sections 302/34 and 143, I.P. Code and 120-B/353, I.P. Code.
		27.10.30	2 years' R.I.	
Do	One	26.4.34	1 year's R.I.	
United Provinces	Three	3.2.34	2 years' R.I. and Rs. 200 fine or in default 6 months' R.I. each.	

Province	Number sentenced	Date of sentence	Period of imprisonment
United Provinces	One on two charges	10.8.33	2 years and 6 months' R.I.
Do	One	21.3.33	2 years' R.I. and fine of Rs. 100.
Punjab	Do	20.9.33	2 years R.I.
Do	One on three charges	6.6.32	6 months' R.I. and Rs. 100 fine or, and half months' R.I. in default.
		23.6.32	2 years' R.I. and Rs. 200 fine or 6 months' further R.I. in default.
		19.11.32	3 months' R.I.
Bihar and Orissa	One	28.4.34	1 year's R.I.
North-West Frontier Province	Four	4.9.31	5 years' R.I. each
Do	One	31.1.34	5 years' R.I. and fine of Rs. 200 or 6 months' R.I.
Do	Two	21.9.33	3 years' R.I. each.
Do	One	20.6.33	3 years' R.I. and fine of Rs. 200 or 9 months' R.I.
Do	Do	13.1.32	6 years' R.I.
Do	Do	13.1.34	3 years' R.I.

Province	Number sentenced	Date of sentence	Period of imprisonment
Do	Do	9.7.34	2 years' R.I.
Do	Do	5.10.33	3 years' R.I. and fine of Rs. 100 or 6 months' R.I.
Do	Do	20.12.34	2 years' R.I. and fine of Rs. 200 or 6 months' R.I.
Do	Do	6.6.32	4 years' R.I.
Do	Do	27.11.34	6 months' R.I.
Total	71		

Pandit Govind Ballabh Pant

Why have these prisoners not been released yet?

The Honourable Sir Henry Craik

That is a question which should be addressed to the Local Governments concerned.

Pandit Govind Ballabh Pant

Did not the Honourable Member, in the course of one or two of his speeches in this House, say that if the Civil Disobedience Movement were withdrawn, Government would expedite the release of civil disobedience prisoners?

The Honourable Sir Henry Craik

I think the Honourable Member is referring to speeches

made by my predecessor.

Pandit Govind Ballabh Pant

I am referring to speeches made by the Honourable the Home Member of the Government of India, whosoever he might have been.

The Honourable Sir Henry Craik

Yes, Sir, those speeches were made and the process of release has been expedited.

Pandit Govind Ballabh Pant

Will the Honourable Member be pleased to state how many prisoners convicted for offences, connected with the Civil Disobedience Movement have been released before their time during the last two months?

The Honourable Sir Henry Craik

I cannot say that.

Pandit Govind Ballabh Pant

Is it not a fact that persons convicted of offences connected with that movement are not being released now?

The Honourable Sir Henry Craik

No, Sir; the process of release is still going on. The Honourable Member will see from the statement that there are at present only 69 prisoners left in the whole of India. A few months ago, there were several thousands.

Pandit Govind Ballabh Pant

It is because no more persons are now courting imprisonment or is it because persons are being let off before their time?

The Honourable Sir Henry Craik

I cannot say definitely, but I think both reasons contribute to it.[12]

DETENUS IN THE DEOLI DETENTION CAMP AND IN THE ANDAMANS[13]

Pandit Govind Ballabh Pant

(a) Will Government be pleased to state the names of "detenus", and state how many and which of them are at present located in the Deoli camp?

(b) Are there any detenus in the Andamans? If so, who?

The Honourable Sir Henry Craik

I invite attention to my reply to Mr. Mohan Lal Saksena's question No. 86 on the 6th February, 1935.

Mr. D.K. Lahiri Chaudhry

Is there any detenu in a solitary cell in the Deoli jail?

The Honourable Sir Henry Craik

Not as far as I know.

Pandit Govind Ballabh Pant

Have any prisoners been released from the Deoli jail during the last two months?

The Honourable Sir Henry Craik

Yes, Sir.

Pandit Govind Ballabh Pant

How many?

The Honourable Sir Henry Craik

I must correct myself. Certain prisoners have been transferred back to Bengal.[14]

NATIONALISATION OF KEY INDUSTRIES[15]

It was my intention that I should restrict myself strictly to the budget. It is unfortunate that certain remarks made by the Honourable the Law Member, and not only the observations made by him, but the attitude and the temper displayed by him, cannot be overlooked by me. When an Honourable Member of his position, holding the most responsible office in this House, exhibits temper. I think we little men here cannot but make a request to him to show a little more indulgence and restraint. Sir, the Honourable the Law Member reminds me of Lord Carson who once occupied a place in British Parliament exactly similar to what he is occupying here. He is in every way qualified and competent, but perhaps lacking in the saving grace of humour. Sir, the Honourable the Law Member has all my sympathy. I know he has not had to rub his shoulders with other men as a manly public man. I know, on the other hand, he had not to resist the blandishments to which public servants, as such—I would not call them "effeminate"—are exposed. (Laughter.) He does not belong to either of the two normal groups. I would not use any biological simile, but the fact remains that he often exhibits impotent rage, which, Sir, does not befit him. (Hear, hear,) Sir, after all does the Honourable the Law Member or his colleagues, sitting opposite, claim and assert that the ranks of the services are absolutely free from corruption? That is not what even the Honourable the Law Member dare say.

The Honourable Sir Nripendra Sircar

Yes, I don't say that.

Pandit Govind Ballabh Pant

He does not. Then, does he think that corruption can be only of the gross type? Are not there insidious ways of corruption? Sir, I was reading the life of Lord Carson recently and was struck by the fact recorded in the book that thirty Irish Members in the British House of Commons, who, as a rule, voted with the British Government, were appointed to eminent offices within a short period of a year or so. Well, is not that corruption in a subtle form? So the Honourable the Law Member need not be dogmatic in these matters. Let him look at them with a proper sense of proportion and without losing the balance. And, then, Sir, who set the ball rolling? Does not the Honourable the Law Member remember that the other day he indiscriminately charged everyone in the Congress with corruption of the worst type? He went out of his way, on an occasion when his remarks were absolutely out of point, and he said that the Congress people had embezzled one crore of rupees out of the Tilak Swaraj Fund.

The Honourable Sir Nirpendra Sircar

On a point of personal explanation, Sir, if my Honourable friend wants to attack me, I do not mind in the least, but I do hope he will quote me correctly, and I deny that I said that it was all Congressmen who had been corrupt and who had been concerned in all these things. I said nothing of the kind.

Pandit Govind Ballabh Pant

I do not mean to misquote anybody, much less the Honourable the Law Member, who, as I said, has my sympathy, if not my respect. Sir, the Honourable the Law Member does not deny that he said that Congressmen had been corrupt. I think I remember what he said: that Congressmen had embezzled one crore of rupees, that no accounts had been published, that Congressmen had been practically exploiting others, wearing fine clothes and using motor cars and the like! My complaint against him is definite. His statement was thoroughly incorrect, inasmuch as no less a person than Seth Jamnalal Bajaj was the Treasurer of the Fund and the accounts were properly kept, audited and duly published.

The Honourable Sir Nripendra Sircar

I rise again, Sir, to correct my Honourable friend. I deny that I said that no accounts were published of the Tilak Swaraj Fund or of the proceedings.

Pandit Govind Ballabh Pant

Well, if the Honourable the Law Member is vehement in his denial, conclude he realizes the blunders that he made. (Laughter.) Sir, let me humbly tell him that that was a momentous occasion, the debate on the Joint Parliamentary Committee Report was sure to engage attention in England, the character of Indians was on its trial, and on that vital occasion, when such delicate and large issues at stake, he was certainly guilty of a rash and unwary—and if he will permit my saying so—an absolutely incorrect and baseless remark. (Hear, hear.)

The Honourable Sir Nripendra Sircar

Which was never made!

Pandit Govind Ballabh Pant

There I settle my accounts with him. I have now to settle my accounts with the Honourable Member sitting opposite to me with whom I have come in close contact in another place more than once.

Sir, the budget that has been presented was received by me with a genuine feeling of disappointment, but I am here not to give expression to sentiments, but to deal with it in the cool light of reason. The Honourable the Finance Member, Sir, opened his speech with the observation that in this country the budget estimates were complicated, as they referred to three years: the actuals for the last year, the revised estimates for the current year and the estimates for the next year. I agree with him in that view. I feel, Sir, that if our figures were restricted to two years, —namely. the actuals for the preceding year and the estimates for the coming year then that course would provide correct data for our budget, would remove the element of uncertainly and speculation, and might, in certain circumstances, save us against unnecessary burdens of taxation. I may just give an instance. In the year 1933-34, the actuals show a real surplus of 2,72 lakhs, while the revised estimates indicated only 1,29 lakhs. Had the Honourable the Finance Member before him the actuals of the year 1933-34 when he framed the budget for 1934-35, perhaps he would have refrained from imposing some of the taxes that he then proposed. From several other points of view, too, it would be a better and financially a sounder method. Sir, in the circumstances of our country, a financial year from the 1st of October or November would be more appropriate. We are mainly an agricultural people, our indigenous bankers renew their annual accounts from either the Diwali or the Dusserah, and the monsoon is an important factor. It has been repeatedly said that in our country the budget is a gamble in rains. So if our budget year started on the 1st October or November, after the rains, that would suit this country better, and such a suggestion had, in fact, I think, been made by the Welby Commission. I do not know if the Honourable the Finance Member will give any thought to this matter. As we are situated, we are tied down to the fetters of the English practice connecting the advent of the New Year with the fool's day. I wish that the brithday may be changed to the wise man's day according to the Indian calendar from that of the fool's. Sir, the Honourable the Finance Member has, in my view, over-estimated expenditure and certainly under-estimated revenue. There are signs of recovery. The experts testify to this welcome change. The volume of exports and imports has gone up. The goods traffic in trains is improving. All these things point to a greater surplus in the coming year than we have actually realised in the last or in this year. In fact, our surplus has been steadily going up. It was 2,72 lakhs last year, while it is bordering on 3,50 lakhs this year. I think the Honourable the Finance Member would have been well-advised in calculating a larger amount of surplus. I know that financiers have the weakness of under-estimating revenue where the claims of exemption from taxation confront them, as they have the weakness of over-estimating expenditure where the claims of retrenchment are likely to be pressed upon them. So I am not surprised at the attitude taken up by the Honourable the Finance Member. Sir, I similarly think that the surplus has not been properly disposed of. I am entirely opposed to the diversion of the surplus to such purposes as civil aviation or the removal of the Pusa Institute. (Hear, hear.) I hold that the entire surplus of the current year should have been transferred to the rural reorganization fund. (Hear, hear.) This is one of the subjects which constantly engaged my attention at another place where I repeatedly pressed for the establishment of a rural reorganization fund. I am glad that the beginning is being made here. I hope the Honourable the Finance Member will make it a rule to automatically transfer all surpluses to the rural reconstruction fund. I make this suggestion on more grounds than one. Sir, as I said, financiers have the habit of under-estimating revenue and generally of over-estimating expenditure. But if they know that all surpluses are likely to be transferred to a consolidated permanent fund, then that serves as a check and a restraint on them. A surplus ordinarily covers many sins like charity, and I do not want any loophole or temptation for the Honourable the Finance Member to so manipulate his budget as to conceal the surplus only to be sprung upon us in the revised budget to be appropriated for doubtful sundry objects at the close of the year.

Sir, I will not refer to many other points which have been covered by other speakers, especially as we will have on occasion to discuss them later. But I should like to point out that the Honourable the Finance Member's statement as to the actual increase in the military budget is certainly misleading. He told us that there was an increase of only two lakhs after providing for the increase in salaries. I find, in reality, as compared with the actuals of the current year, the increase borders on about 1,60 lakhs. He has not taken into account the amount that is to be transferred to the army defence reserve fund this year as well as that to be drawn from it in the budget year. Those sums we have obviously to take into account, and, if we do so, we find that the actual increase, as compared with the current year, is not 58 or 60 lakhs as he tried to make out, but in reality it is about 1,60 lakhs. I hope he will accept my statement. I am really sorry that the actual state of affairs should not have been correctly represented in the budget. Sir, I am not going to refer to other items in the budget at this stage, as I want to address myself to questions of fundamental policy, as to what is the real financial policy of the Government of India? What does it stand for? After all, the matter of budgeting is in a way a mere matter of arithmetic, and any Finance Member can, in a country that is under subjection and under a Government resting on bayonets and rifles and with a people under disarmament, always balance any budget and establish equilibrium in figures for he can impose any amount of burdens on the people. But that is not what budgeting really means in the modern sense of finances and in the sense advanced financiers use the expression. I fact, if there is one dominant characteristic of our budget, it is one of Imperialism. The budget in all its salient features, reminds us of the Imperialist regime, to which we are subject and under which we breathe and exist today. The top-heavy administration, the fabulous salaries and emoluments of the higher ranks with similarly miserable pittances of the lower ranks, the restoration of salary cut, the drain of gold, home charges and the continuous, perpetual drain in so many other ways point to this stranglehold of Imperialism. Along with these I might mention the pegging of the rupee to the paper sterling detached from gold standard and retention of gold reserve in London.

We are told that the Honourable the Finance Member has balanced his budget, but what does that mean? How has he done it? I remember a couplet that I had read in one of the Sanskrit books in my younger days. It means that the sovereign like the rain god absorbs superfluous and surplus moisture in order to irrigate the arid lands for the production of rich, fresh and plentiful crops. But what has been done here? We all know what has happened during the last five years. Prices have gone down by about 50 per cent. I have the index figures with me. We find that the revenue budgeted this year is more than the revenue of every year since 1921-22, when present system of accounting started, except 1933. We find that the expenses of collection are about 25 per cent more than in 1921-22 and 50 per cent more than in 1923-24: please note, in spite of the colossal fall of an unprecedented character in prices. We find, further, that during the last five years, the Government of India proposed fresh taxation measures with a view to raising 48 crores of rupees per year from time to time. That is the tragic tale. While we asked for bread, we got stones. While people were starving, Government were adding to their burdens. That shows the state of their mind, the outlook and the angle from which they look at the affairs of this country. They initiated measures aggregating in additional taxation burdens to the tune of 48 crores in the course of five years at a time when the country was passing through the severest stress and unprecedented economic slump. I am reminded of the way some people manage their dairies. I will not speak of a Chicago stock house or of a slaughter-house, as that has a bad odour about it. So I will take the illustration of a dairy. Suppose a man keeps a dairy and he earns thereby a certain amount of profit each year and pays a certain amount by way of wages and emoluments to the staff in charge of the dairy, and the rate at which milk sells is four seers to a rupee. Assume that the price of milk goes down from four seers to eight seers per rupee. Still, the keeper of the dairy, or, in case it is held by a company, let us say the company, decides that the servants and the staff would continue to receive the salary that they had been receiving, but that the cattle will be provided with only half of the fodder that they had been getting and the calves will be weaned and will not be allowed any drop of milk. You can run a dairy like that; you can earn all the profits that you had been doing, but how will it react on the cattle? Sir, I repeat here what I observed last week regarding railway finance, that the general financial policy of the Government is equally perverse, equally anti-national and equally detrimental to the larger interests of this country.

A word more as to what we want and what we think can be done. I am convinced, Sir, that this is not the time when petty patchwork can cure the body-politic. Today the world stands for new ideals. It has devised new measures and new standards. It is not a time for a sordid outlook or matter of fact methods. My Honourable friend, the Finance Member, though young, happens to possess a great dread of jails. I have been there more than once, and I am not afraid of them. I would advice him to shed off that fear and to plunge into the right path and to march forward with a determination to raise the wealth and productivity of this country and to introduce at higher standard of living among the masses along with easier rates of taxation than he found when he reached here. Sir, first of all, the imperialistic outlook has to be abandoned. Modern science and modern economics have proved that those shibboleths, which obsessed the generations before us, have really no substance and no reality whatsoever. The twin spectres of the growth of population in a geometrical progression and of diminishing returns of exhaustible resources have been exercised completely by modern economics. There might have been some sort of biological pretext for an Imperialist policy when men were under the dread of a growing population and diminishing returns. But today we find the problem in England is not how to stem the tide of the growing population, but how to maintain it. The problem in the world is not how to produce more, but how to restrict production. Today our impoverishment is of our own choice. Today science has added to the bounty of providence and there is happiness ensured to everybody if men cease to be stupid and petty-minded and do not isolate themselves from the realms of light and bliss that lie before humanity through sheer conceit, prejudice or panic. In all earnestness, I ask the Honourable the Finance Member to look at things from a chastened outlook and to plan out a big scheme for mechanisation, for industrialisation and for rural reorganisation of this wonderful country. It can be done only on national lines now. At present our taxes are mostly indirect, and 75 per cent of them are being raised by indirect means. They react on our productive capacity. They hamper the growth of trade, and retard the progress of industries. And wherein lies the remedy? It lies only in the nationalisation of the key industries, it lies only in the State taking an active part in the reconstruction of the economic life of the country. If there was a Swaraj Government, I would have most humbly suggested to that Government to float a loan of a hundred crores forthwith in order to rebuild the economic life of this country. (Applause). Unfortunately, it is not so, we live under a foreign rule. So, it is but a dream, and, howevermuch our friends may blame us for our negative attitude, unless we remove this stupendous impediment and this tremendous obstacle, no progress is possible.[16]

PRESS AND ITS LIBERTY[17]

(Part—I)

Sir, it is needless to say that I rise to oppose the motion for the consideration of the Bill. So far as the Government and some of the Honourable Members who have supported them are concerned, they may treat this Bill as a mere administrative device for the maintenance of order under coercion. Some of them may look upon it only in a light spirit of frolicsome frivolity. But so far as I and those of my way of thinking are concerned, it gives rise to momentous issues. It is nothing short of an outrage on the cherished acquisitions, the cherished possessions, and the cherished institutions of modern age and civilization. Take away the right of freedom of thought, take away the right of freedom of expression, take away the right of freedom of association: just ignore the achievements of science, its discoveries and inventions; and what is left of modern civilization? What is, above all, the greatest achievement of the modern age and how has it been attained? Is it not only through the clash of ideas and through the impact of mind upon mind that humanity has been progressing and steadily advancing forward? I oppose this measure, because, in its effect to maintain artificial calm, it is creating, at all events even if it succeeds, the peace of the desert as Lord Irwin once said, or a fettered and muzzled India as Lord Morley had said on a previous occasion. Sir, is it not a tragedy and an irony that in this year of Grace 1935 such a Bill should be placed before this House? I am reminded, Sir, that it is just 100 years almost to a day that Sir Charles Metcalfe, known as the liberator of the press in India, issued orders withdrawing all restraints on the press. I would like just to read out a few sentences from the reply he gave to the deputation which waited on him in the year 1835 for the withdrawal of restraints on the press. This is what he said:

> "It rests with them" (meaning the critics and opponents), "to show that the communication of knowledge is a curse and not a benefit, and that the essence of good Government is to cover the land with darkness; for otherwise it must be admitted to be one of the most imperative duties of a Government to confer the incalculable blessing of knowledge on the people, and by what means can this be done more effectively than by the unrestrained liberty of publication and by the stimulus which it gives to the powers of the mind."

I would appeal to Honourable Members opposite to give a little thought to those words of wisdom. By what other means can you carry the torch of light in this country? Sir, we deplore illiteracy, we deplore superstitions, we want to find out remedies for them, we want to carry on a propaganda that may turn even the man who lives in the most remote hamlet in the village into a literate man, we want even the humble dweller of the thatched hut to be an intelligent citizen. We want him to be capable of taking an active interest in the affairs of our country. How can it be done otherwise than by the extension of the activities of the press?

Sir, before proceeding further, I should like to tell the House that whenever any restraints were imposed on the press, they retarded the growth and extension of printing presses as well as of newspapers and other periodical publications and even of books. As Honourable Members are aware, between the years 1910 and 1920, the press in India was subject to the octopus of the Press Act. In 1921, the Press Act was repealed, and, between 1921 and 1930, the press was free from fetters. The reaction was striking. Sir, between the years 1911 and 1920, when the press was under the Press Act, the rise in the number of presses was from 2,780 to 3,371 an increase of about 600 in 10 years,—or, on an average of 60 per year. When these fetters were withdrawn in 1921, what was the result? Between the years 1921 and 1931, the number of presses went up from 3,371 to 6,520, which shows an increase of about 3,200. The number was almost doubled. The growth in the number of presses in two years was more than in the whole of the ten preceding years. Similar was the case with newspapers. The number of newspapers and publications was 2,924 in 1911 as against 3,093 in 1920. Thus, the total increase during this decade was only 169. But, thereafter, between 1920-21 and 1930-31, the number went up to 4,500, with the result that the increase during this decade came to 1,500 in place of 169. Thus, in one single year, after the withdrawal of the fetters, there was a larger addition to the number of newspapers and publications in this country than during the whole of the preceding ten years when the press was under the repressive Press Act. (Cheers from Congress Party Benches). Let us now look at the number of books published. The number of books published in 1911-12 came to 11,584. And what was the number in 1919-20? It was in reality only 11,100. There was thus an actual reduction, a shrinkage to the extent of 500 in the number of books during the period the Press Act was in force. But what was the result when the Press Act was withdrawn? Between 1919-20 and 1930-31 the unmber went up from 11,100 to 17,427,—an increase of more than 6,000. Sir, can you have any doubt in your mind in the face of these figures and statistics that restraints on the press are a grave menace and a great hindrance to the diffusion of knowledge and culture, and stand in the way of all the well-wishers of the country and of all those people who are interested in promoting truth, light and learning?

Let us look back again on the history of the last few years. Sir, as I have just said, but for two short interludes, there were no restraints on the press between 1835 and 1910, when the Press Act was introduced which remained on the Statute-book up to the year 1921. Sir, I should like to remind Honourable Members of the Report that was issued by the Press Laws Committee. I will not repeat what they said. Important extracts from their report have been brought to the notice of the House by some of the speakers who have preceded me. What I want to tell Honourable Members is this: that in July, 1921, when the Press Laws Committee issued its Report, and shortly after when the Press Act was repealed, the commotion in the country was much more grave, much more alive and much more kicking than it is today. At that time, Sir, the Civil Disobedience Movement was almost at its zenith, there were no local laws, and there was no law at all in Bengal for the control of terrorism. Besides, all the political prisoners, whether convicted for violence or for non-violence offences, who had been released in pursuance of the proclamation issued in December, 1919, on the passage of the Montford Act were at large then. Sir, the state of terrorism at that time was much worse than what is said to be today. I think the Home Member, the Government of India and Secretary of State, all claim jointly and severally that the state of the country, so far as terrorism is concerned, is better, and has considerably improved since. May I know what is the reason for proceeding with a Bill like this at this time of the day when there is undisturbed tranquillity, when, so far as terrorism is concerned, you admit and declare that the position is much better, and when, so far as Civil Disobedience is concerned, it is at least suspended and quiescent. I ask, in all humility, what is the justification for proceeding with a measure of this sort today when it was considered proper, appropriate and safe to repeal the Press Act of 1910 in 1921-22. So far as terrorism is concerned, there are provisions in the Bengal Act which are most stringent and rigid. There it is open to the magistrates to issue orders to the printers and editors not to publish anything they do not like, irrespective of its being lawful or unlawful, wholesome or unwholesome. The Bengal Criminal Law Amendment Act contains provisions which do not leave any room for any free activity to any person or journalist in Bengal. Whether those laws are tolerable or not, I am not concerned with. What I am concerned with is only this, that, so far as terrorism is concerned, the remedies that you are providing in this Bill are altogether insignificant, negligible, useless and superfluous in the face of the Bengal Criminal Law Amendment Act, and there is no reason why, in the circumstances, you should plead terrorism as an excuse for putting this Bill permanently on the Statute-book. Then, Sir, may I know what, after all, has been the efficacy, the benefit, the advantage of the last three years' administration of the Criminal Law Amendment Act which is and was intended to expire in December next and will then die an unlamented death? I should like to know what has been the advantage, what has been the consequence, what has been the fruitful sequel to the passing of that measure and its administration for the last three years. It was admittedly an emergency measure. It was devised with a view to treating a passing phase, temporary malady, and what has been its reaction, and what has been its effect? A malady that was then no more than local, transitory and incidental, has now become chronic, and a permanent, inseparable and unsavoury feature of the body-politic is not that by itself sufficient for condemning that measure and for throwing it out? There is a proverb among us as to a disease coming on worsening with the treatment. Where the treatment has, after regular trial of three years, proved to be altogether inefficacious, and even harmful, and detrimental to the patient, is it in any way wise to persist in that wrong and erratic course? So, I submit, the Bill shoudl be thrown out, because the parent of the Bill, the existing Act, out of which it has sprung, has proved a monster which may kill, but cannot possibly cure or heal. There is one more reason why I think there is absolutely no justification for this measure. Here I have before me the report of the speech that the late Home Member delivered, while introducing the Criminal Law Amendment Bill in 1932. I have also before me a copy of the Bill which was then introduced with its Statement of Objects and Reasons. It was repeatedly said by the Home Member then that the Government had introduced that Bill only because of the Civil Disobedience Movement. He said:

> "The origin of the Bill is very plain. It can be said in two or three words, the civil disobedience movement. It is unnecessary to give a history of that movement."

Further, he went on to say:

> "Those Ordinances expired after six months and as the period for their expiry approached, it became, evident that we were in no position to discard the weapons with which the civil disobedience movement was being fought. Accordingly, at the end of June the Governor General issued a new consolidated Ordinance. This in its turn will expire at the end of the year. Now, Sir, the problem is, what action are the Government to take. The civil disobedience movement, though its manifestations have been much curtailed and though I think I can claim that its supporters have lost a good deal of the impetus with which the movement was started, is still in existence and no one can prophesy when it will come to an end. It certainly will not end so long as the leaders still feel that there is any prospect of gaining their objects. Now, Sir, what stands between them and success is mainly the power conferred by the Ordinance and therefore it is the view of Government that the best method of ensuring a speedy end of this movement is to make it clear that the powers with which the movement is being fought will be continued."

As I observed a minute ago, a similar explanation is given in the Statement of Objects and Reasons. Now, the Honourable The Home Member has admitted in his Statement of Objects and Reasons here that the Civil Disobedience Movement is at present in abeyance. He has also withdrawn certain clauses which formed part of the old measure. So far as he is concerned, this Bill has not been introduced in order to provide a ready weapon to meet the menace of Civil Disobedience if it is ever revived and resumed. That is admitted by the Honourable the Home Member himself in the Statement of Objects and Reasons. Sir, in these circumstances, I submit that there is absolutely no justification for this Bill and it is but the outcome of the morbid tendency of the executive which is ever avaricious to retain such arbitrary and autocratic powers as it manages to acquire in moments of crisis. That alone is the reason for this measure. It is easy for them to invent reasons for preserving their autocratic powers, even when those powers are not needed for combating any critical situation. I submit that the reasons that have been mentioned herc are merely fictions born of a fertile imagination, as in fact and in reality, these reasons did not affect the Criminal Law Amendment Bill of 1932. There was no reference to anything of this sort in the Statement appended to the Bill or the opening speech of the then Home Member.

The Honourable Sir Henry Craik

No, no. That is not correct.

Pandit Govind Ballabh Pant

I am definite. I challenge the Honourable the Home Member to show me the contrary. I have before me the Statement of Objects and Reasons, and I have before me the speeches. I know the Honourable Member will have a right of reply. I have absolutely no doubt that, so far as published literature on the subject goes, the Government had nothing in mind except the Civil Disobedience Movement when this measure was placed on the anvil in the year 1932. Obviously, the question is this, whether, in the present circumstances, it is proper and it is reasonable that a Bill of this sort should be placed before the House. I do not care if a slip here or a word there is pounced upon by the Honourable Members opposite who seem to be helpless and confused, but the exponents of official view then made it abundantly clear that they were not actuated by any other motive except that of meeting and combating the Civil Disobedience Movement when they introduced their Bill in 1932. But, Sir, that is not all that I have to submit. I should like to know what are the reasons then for this measure. Government want it to be permanently lodged in the Statute-book. I want Honourable Members to remember that it is not an emergency measure to tide over a crisis. It is, so far as the present Government is concerned, to form, if their object can be carried out, an integral part of the Statute-book of this country for all time to come. Among the fantastic reasons advanced in support of this measure, there is one which seems to surpass all others in its amazing nature. I have not heard anything more astounding, and had it not been a hard fact, I would be loath to accept, even as regards the Government of India, that they were capable of such stupid audacity. They say that it is to prepare the country for responsible Government that they want to impose fetters on the press. I have not heard anything more ridiculous, more ludicrous, more perverse and more untrue in any argument in my life. Sir, what does responsible Government mean? The press provides the lungs and arteries to the body-politic. Responsible Government sways and swings in the enlivening breeze which only a free press can produce and generate. Take that live force away, and what is left except blank dullness, foolish obstinacy and a nauseating sense of complaisant self-sufficiency for those who are commissioned to carry on the administration of the country. Has anybody ever heard of responsible Government with dictatorial powers in the hands of the Government, and can there be absolute powers of a more comprehensive and farreaching type than those provided in this Bill? Assume for a moment that you form a responsible ministry in a province and arm them with this Bill. I say, if they have a little-grain of sense in them, they can perpetuate their existence. I have no desire to get into those officers. They may be beyond my reach or outside the scope of my will or ambition, but I have no doubt, that a politician cannot conceive of a better weapon, and a better instrument for the perpetuation of his hold and grip than the powers which this Bill provides. What is the scope of this Bill? Government can declare any association unlawful. It may be even the European Association and, if I am in power tomorrow, perhaps Mr. James will think twice before equipping me with this power. Or it may be the Indian Civil Service Association, and I may declare it unlawful, for there is no control, no restraint, and no appeal. There is no other authority to which you can appeal against my decision. What I say is absolute: what I do is final. I can suppress any press. I can call for security. I can forfeit the security of any press on the pretext on any one of the innumerable grounds mentioned in section 4. I do not care to read out that section at this stage. I may have to do it later, but one of the things provided there is incitement to disaffection, and disaffection was defined by one of the High Court judges, Sir, John Strachey, as want of affection. If I am a Minister, and if any Member on the other side says anything that, instead of promoting affection on the part of other people towards me, tends even indirectly to drain their ardour for me, it will be within my competence to crush that press and to call for security from that paper. Well, Sir, could I desire for more if I wanted to be a Hitler or a Mussolini? I think you are doing the gravest injustice to the intelligence of this country and also the cause which you seem to espouse by placing this Bill on the table of this House. Then, Sir, I do not know how you will interpret and enforce these things. Charlie Chaplin was hauled up in the divorce Court by his wife on the ground that he had been guilty of hatred towards her. Plain Charlie protested in naive earnestness that his affection for his wife was unbounded and he had never been guilty of any lapses. But it was of no avail to him and the divorce was decreed. I do not know how publicists and public men will manage to protect themselves against such charges of disaffection against them, whether by the existing Government which has never made any secret of its animosity for them or by their successors that may follow hereafter.

There is yet another aspect which seemed to me to be still more strange. Example is better than precept. The Honourable the Home Member and his fraternity want us to trust the Ministers and the Governments of the future implicitly and to surrender to them the most valued rights and privileges in advance: but how have they themselves behaved? I do not know if Mr. Griffiths is here. The safeguards, even as they appear in the Government of India Act in their final form, do not satisfy some of the members of the Indian Civil Service, at least in Bengal, who held out a veritable threat which, when the Bill was in the last stage in the House of Commons, caused a little flutter at the time, even in the ranks of the bureaucracy in this country. Sir, may I put a question to the Honourable the Home Member as well as to others in his fold. So far as the Imperial Services are concerned, they cannot trust the Ministers. The Ministers should not even touch them. The Secretary of State alone will have exclusive control of the Imperial Services. Even the Governor General cannot be trusted, leave aside the Ministers. Even the Secretary of State cannot be trusted. Unless his advisers representing the Services support a change by a majority, even the Parliament will not sanction any amendment of service rules or conditions. Sir, even in the matter of postings, the Minister has got to go to the Governor and to appeal to him. He has to pray to him to get Mr. Griffiths appointed to Midnapore or some other place, and, so far as the medical services are concerned, no Indian can be appointed to certain reserved posts even by the Governor. Well, Sir, does that indicate the confidence of the bureaucracy in the Governments of the future? Is it just on their part to ask us to trust these Governments and to place the most valued rights which alone constitute life worth living at the sweet mercy and disposal of these discredited suspects? Is it sincere? Can hypocrisy go further? Can dishonesty go further? I ask the bureaucracy now and here—what justification have they to force us to surrender to the mysterious, to the obscure, to the unknown and the 'unknowable Ministers of the future the most valued heritage, the most cherished fundamental rights which form the very basis of civilised existence? How dare they impose these fetters on this country, while keeping themselves strictly and meticulously and completely out of the orbit and influences of these Ministers? (Loud Applause).

Sir, I am reminded of a story I once read. There were two fine cousins, Eve and Mary. Eve was younger, but had two divorces to her credit. They had a common friend, John, with a here-lip and squint eyes. John wanted to marry, and Eve very seriously, very earnestly, very persuasively suggested it to Mary that she should marry John. Mary gently said: "you have greater experience of married life, you have already had two husbands. John has queer looks. Why don't you marry him?" Well, for some time, Eve beat about the bush, but ultimately she gave out the truth. "My dear Mary, your parents were married only once. Your grand-parents were married only once. You are, by nature, by heredity, faithful. So far as I am concerned, my mother was the third wife to my father, and my father was the third husband to my mother. (Laughter.) So it won't be safe for me to marry such a husband. Besides, Mary, I know you want a husband, so that you may serve him, and I want a husband so that he may serve me. So, so far as you are concerned, John will be safe and you will be happy. But if I were to enter into this alliance, both of us will be unhappy. But I will be prepared to help you both, and I will make full use of either or both of you on every occasion for any purpose I like and choose." (Laughter.) That, Sir, is the state of affairs that obtains in this country. It is very well to suggest to us, to the innocent Marys in this country, to marry hare-lipped and squint-eyed Johns, so that the shrewd and the astute Eve may always be able to command the services of both to her heart's content. (Laughter.) Are we really such credulous, stupid fools? And, then, Sir, what is happening today? How are the high and mighty behaving?

Do you know how the constituencies are being delimited? Do you know how the Delimitation Conferences and Committees are being formed? Do you know in how many diverse ways efforts are being made to manage and manipulate things, so that the Bureaucracy may ever continue to rule, and, while the mask and figure may be of an Indian, the power may always rest and vest in the hands of the European?

Mr. President. (The Honourable Sir Abdur Rahim)

Would the Honourable Member like to stop here and resume his speech tomorrow?

Pandit Govind Ballabh Pant

All right, Sir.[18]

(Part—II)

Mr. President (The Honourable Sir Abdur Rahim)

The House will now resume consideration of the following motion moved by the Honourable the Home Member on the 5th September, 1935.

"That the Bill to amend the Criminal Law be taken into consideration."

Pandit Govind Ballabh Pant

Sir, the case for this Bill rests mainly, if not exclusively, on the two pamphlets that have been supplied by the Home Department, one containing extracts from newspapers and other publications and the other containing the statements that were furnished by the Honourable the Home Member in reply to the Short Notice Questions put by Seth Govind Das. I submit that if anybody had ever a fantastic of raising a sky scrapper on an arch of straw, he could not have hit upon anything better. Sir, look at the extracts that have been placed in this pamphlet which is headed. "A few selections from press articles made in connection with Press legislation". Sir, I reminded Honourable Members yesterday that there was no Press Act in force in this country between the years 1921 and 1931, I assume that the Government with their infinite resources, after making a microscopic examination of all the publications that have issued during this interval of ten years, have been able to cull together all that appears in this pamphlet.

The Honourable Sir Henry Craik (Home Member)

There are thousands.

Pandit Govind Ballabh Pant

Well, I do not know if they have anything up their sleeves. If there is anything secret, in the dark which they dare not expose lest it should burn and evaporate in the light we cannot take notice of it. If they have anything else in their possession we do not know. What they have considered deserving and worthy of being placed before us is contained in this pamphlet. Sir, this pamphlet does not contain anything for the years 1922, 1923, 1924, 1925, 1927 and 1929. It does not contain anything for the Presidencies of Bombay and Madras or for the Provinces of the United Provinces, Bihar and Orissa, Assam, Central Provinces and the North-West, Frontier Province. The extracts that have been given here are confined to the Provinces of Bengal and the Punjab and to the years 1926, 1929 and 1930 only. Sir, this general survey can lead only to one conclusion, namely, that the state of the press was never really as lamentable scandalous and dangerous, ominous and disastrous as is now sought to be made out. Sir, what do these extracts contain, even as they are? Before I do so I may tell the Honourable Members that so far as the United Provinces are concerned, I have read the Administration Reports issued by the Local Government and it is definitely, positively and unambiguously mentioned in those Reports in the year 1923 and again in the year 1924 that the tone as well as the language of public press in the province improved considerably after the withdrawal and repeal of the Press Act. Sir, these stray extracts containing only a part of the article and being for the most part indifferent translations cannot be a safe guide, but even if we take them at their face value, what do they indicate, and what do they prove? The first nine extracts relate to the single district of Pabna in Bengal and were all published in the month of July, 1926. When we proceed further, we find a number of descriptive articles. I have examined every article and I am satisfied that if this pamphlet is placed before any judicial tribunal, at least half of them will be declared to be perfectly innocent; and that demonstrates unmistakably the mentality of those who have put them before us as the examplars in support of this repressive piece of legislation. This pamphlet contains not only extracts from newspapers articles but also reprints from pamphlets, books, and cyclostyled and other posters. Well, Sir, I do not know how this Bill is intended or expected to reach cyclostyled posters, unless the Government have the intention of introducing an amendment at a later stage. Otherwise, so far as the present Bill goes, I do not see their relevancy. We find no jot or title smacking of Communism anywhere in it except in the cyclostyled poster or pamphlet. There is nothing in it, that could amount to a direct incitement to violence, except one or two sentences from two articles from certain obscure papers which have revealed their existence for the first time in this pamphlet: and so far as communal dissensions are concerned, Sir, as I observed as many as nine concerning Pabna District were shot off within a week. We do not know what happened there at the time. Perhaps there was an immense excitement in those districts in Bengal then. I would like to know, Sir, whether, on the basis of these extracts, any responsible Government would dare to approach the Legislature for such a piece of legislation as they have placed before us after a lapse of nearly ten years. We were told the other day, Sir, that there were 4,600 newspapers and publications in this country. We are here making a survey of everything that emanated from the press, whether in the form of newspapers, or pamphlets, or posters or books or otherwise during the period of ten years. Remembering that some of these papers might be dailies, some weeklies, some bi-weeklies, some monthlies and so on, the number of publications must have amounted to millions if not to billions. Of these, the selections come to about thirty, and on those thirty, we are asked to penalize the press of this country for ever!

The Honourable Sir Henry Craik

There were hundreds more.

Pandit Govind Ballabh Pant

I do not know whether the "hundreds more" are merely in the brain or imagination of the Honourable the Home Member.

The Honourable Sir Henry Craik

No.

Pandit Govind Ballabh Pant

So far as the published papers go, he has placed before us only these. I presume that these are the worst samples that he could lay his hands upon, and I would ask Honourable Members to read them and to see what they are like. I have a definite impression, Sir, of the articles that I used to read in newspapers in 1908, 1909 and 1910 and I dare say from the recollections I retain very distinctly to this day that some of the papers then published had more objectionable stuff in one issue than what is contained in the whole of this pumphlet today. Well, Sir, this is the comparative state of affairs. I could like to know from the Honourable the Home Member the true state of affairs. He has told us that communalism has never been so acute in this country as it is today. Well what measures has he taken to put an end to that? And if this is the result of three years' administration of the Criminal Law Amendment Act—namely, that communalism today is in its worst phase—then, I ask, why should he prolong and prepetuate the tortuous course which has resulted in this calamity? Then I would ask the Honourable the Home Member if he ever took action under section 153A in respect of these papers mentioned here, and whether he took any action under section 108 against the printer or the publisher of any of these?

The Honourable Sir Henry Craik

If the Honourable Member refers to my speech in introducing the Bill, he would have found that repeated action was taken.

Pandit Govind Ballabh Pant

So far as I am aware, none of these persons were prosecuted for any of these writings.

The Honourable Sir Henry Craik

We cannot get at them.

Pandit Govind Ballabh Pant

That is an untenable proposition which I cannot accept. Sir, if the police are really so inefficient that you cannot get at the culprits, then you have no business to continue to employ them (Loud Applause), then you should disband your staff. Why do you engage this police force and impose taxation on us in order to keep them going, if you and they cannot get at the culprits? (Hear, hear.) Sir, if your police force is designed only to get at innocent people, and if that is the purpose for which you are here, if your object merely is to frame these weapons and engines of oppression for innocent people, so that you may have some sort of fun and your police a ready handle and something by way of bait to book the innocent. The cat is out of the bag and I concede that, this Bill will eminently and fully fulfil that object. Sir, I was just telling you that this bogey of communalism is a curious figment of the imagination: it has been sprung upon us with a view to frightening us. Sir, when I hear Members of the Government talking of a communal crash I feel as though the chauffeur is losing hold of the brake and the crash is imminent. Perhaps, in some cases—I do not attribute any malice or malignancy—the wish may be the mother to the thought. (Hear, hear.) But, whatever it be, I say, Sir that if the Government feel that communalism is in its worst form, then we must be prepared for the crop which must ensue out of such open declarations from the most responsible quarters. (Hear, hear.) They may not want their prophecies to turn true, yet we must be on our guard. Sir, we had once a good, old sturdy gentleman as Commissioner in the place where I live. In 1924-25, as Honourable Members are aware, there was a recrudescence of communal trouble. Once he was having a talk with me and he told me: "Well, Pandit, there is too much of communalism these days. Why is it so?" I said there are many reasons. He said: "No, no. It is very easy to put an end to it." I said how? He asserted: "Well, put me in charge of the worst district and I will see that communalism will come to an end". I asked him how he would manage it? He gave me a story. He said that in his younger days while he was the District Magistrate at a certain place, a Tahsildar approached him and told him that his Tahsil was on fire and that a communal outburst was inevitable. He told the Tahsildar that that was the first time when he had ever heard such a report and while directing him to see him the next day with the latest information, warned him in the following words: "If you repeat tomorrow that your Tahsil is still in a combustible state, then I will make an entry in your service book and report you for transfer from this Tahsil." He told me that the Tahsildar approached him the next day and told him: "Give me time: things are improving." He replied: "Very well, you can have some more time." The man went back to him the next day and said: "Everything is all right 'Sub Khairiyat'." That is how communalism can be put an end to. I say if you are determined to put a stop to it, you can do it. I do not want to make remarks of an unpalatable and unpleasant type. But I would ask the Honourable Members opposite to read of some of the letters published by Lady Minto that passed between Lord Minto and Lord Morley.

I ask them to ponder over what Lord Olivier wrote in the article that appeared in the Times soon after he retired from the office of the Secretary of State for India. I ask them to read what Wedgwood Benn observed some time ago and I ask them to read what the Earl of Salisbury has said only recently. I would not say more. But Sir, I would remind them that communalism is not the monopoly of this land. Wherever you have foreign domination, there is a natural tendency to foster all those forces which contribute towards the perpetuation of that domination. It is but natural. That does not, however, absolve us from the responsibility that we owe to our country. I am one of those who feel that if our enemies can outwit us, we are fools. If our enemies can beat us, they must be abler. But I do not want to be beaten by them in any way and on any score whatsoever. I am not putting this forward as an apology or defence for any failure or lukewarmness on our part, but I am stating only a fact because it is a fact. In this connection, I would remind the Honourable Members that only recently there was an outburst in Belfast. Belfast is not Dublin which is the capital of the Sinn Fein or Irish Free State; but it is Belfast, the capital of the favourite province of the superb Lord Carson. I will just read out to you what happened in Belfast from an extract that appeared in the New Statesman and Nation recently. It says:

> "More than the usual political significance underlies the rioting which has developed in Belfast from the annual celebrations on July 12th of the Battle of the......better known in Northern Ireland as the glorious twelfth. The newspaper reports which have reached England tell us only of this great fighting, the rioting, the looting, the burning out of a dozen Government homes, the deaths of five persons and the wounding of well over a hundred, the use of rifles, revolvers and machine guns by the police and finally the calling out of the military who were patrolling the streets with fixed bayonets and steel helmets returning the desultory fire of the snipers who lie hidden in the network of poverty-stricken slum streets of the York Street area."

This is what happened in Belfast last month. Belfast is the place where the catholics are in very small number and where the protestants dominate. So, let not our people be entrapped by any insinuations about communalism being worse today than it has ever been before. I, for one, honestly believe—and I claim to possess some knowledge of the people and some experience of the affairs of this country and it is certainly more intimate and reliable than what any Honourable Member opposite can acquire as none of them has a direct approach to the hearts, to the sentiments and to the convictions of people,—than the worst phase of communalism has passed. There is more of harmony today than there was at any time before, at least during the last ten years. But for a few self-seekers and those who can always be incited to promote hatred between communities, the heart of the country is sounder today than it has ever been before, and I am convinced that if artificial restraints are not devised which must tend to cause greater distrust and mistrust in the future, the present rate of progress will continue until we have reached the millennium and the haven which we all desire.

Sir, I would like to refer to some of the extracts which have appeared in other places. I do not know if the Honourable the Home Member is aware of the sort of literature that is published in England. Has he ever seen the extracts that appear in the pamphlets or articles there? I do not know if he has been reading the Workers' Daily or whether he has been reading the Labour Leader or whether he has been reading such like other papers. I see that there is more of Communism in a single issue of these papers than in all that you can collect here during the last ten years and yet they are not proscribed here and I am occasionally reading them. I will read out to you a few extracts from some of the pamphlets that have been published in England. These pamphlets have been published almost continuously and regularly by people who have taken pretty good care to keep themselves in the background just as the imaginary dummy editors are supposed to be doing here. Well, Sir, now I propose to read from the Hansard and it is part of the speech delivered by the Attorney General of England in the last autumn session. He says:

> "There is a corresponding leaflet with reference to the Navy, entitled 'The Red Signal', which claims to be the organ of Communist sailors. I will trouble the House with a few illustrations, in order that honourable Members may have in their minds the sort of incitements which are offered to members of His Majesty's Forces in this secret, underground fashion. The Soldier's Voice of October, 1931, invited its readers who were soldiers to understand that: 'The way to victory lies, not through voting, but through mass struggle. What is needed is a repetition of the general strike.' The issue of May, 1932, contained this passage: 'Let us use the knowledge of arms which they give us, when the opportunity presents itself, to overthrow their rule, and, in unity with our fellow-workers, to establish a free Socialist Britain.' In November, 1932, the same production said: 'We suggest that you, comrade reader, should make a beginning now in your unit. Get in touch with that other fellow in your lot who thinks like you. And then start in to convert the rest of your mates to your ideas. If you don't quite know how to begin, what about writing for advice to that Communist or member of the Unemployed Movement you used to know at home?' These are incitements addressed to and intended for members of His Majesty's Forces. The Red Signal, the organ of Communist Sailors, in October, 1932, said:
>
> 'They will put a gun in your hands. Take it and study the art of war. This knowledge is essential for workers in order to fight against the capitalists of their own countries, in order to put an end to capitalism.'
>
> In May, 1933, it said:
>
> 'If war does come, then it must be turned into a civil war against the capitalist warmongers and their bankrupt system. We urge our comrades of the lower deck to get into touch

with this great movement wherever possible.' "

Sir, I ask the Honourable the Home Member whether he has seen anything approaching this even within a hundred miles in this country. Has he seen such pamphlets being distributed in the Army anywhere in this country? Has he seen people taking any interest of this wicked and malicious sort? The Attorney General says in another place:

"The effect of the two or three prosecutions which have taken place in the last year or so has been to drive the chief offenders underground. A somewhat sly and almost skulking breed of inciter has come into existence. They are too shy or too cowardly to put their names and addresses to the literature which they are in the habit of producing."

The Attorney General again quotes from another paper:

"They say in the Soldier's Voice of May, 1932:

'Leaflets were printed in English, French and Japanese and careful plans were laid for their distributions. They were strewn on parade grounds, stuck on walls and fences, put in the dance halls and cabarets frequented by men of the Forces, and many soldiers and sailors alike were surprised to find leaflets in their pockets or thurst into their hands.'

As I say, they are published anonymously by people who prefer to employ comparatively harmless and ill-paid persons to distribute them. The persons responsible for them have taken very good care to keep well in the background since the prosecutions of two or three years ago, when some of the offenders were properly dealt with under the existing law."

He says further:

"Some one may ask: How much of it is there? During the year 1932, there were 17 different subversive pamphlets.

I do not mean 17 issues, but 17 different pamphlets of different titles—The Soldier's Voice is the one and the Red Signal another—containing such incitements as I have mentioned; and in that year there were 20 places of distribution. In 1933 there were 11 different subversive pamphlets and 14 places of distribution. The pamphlets are distributed among members of His Majesty's Forces by methods such as I have described. They are thrown over the barrack railings, or pushed into the hands of soldiers or sailors in places or refreshment or in music halls; and it is estimated that in each of the last two years something like 50,000 copies of these subversive pamphlets have been produced and attempted to be distributed for circulation among members of His Majesty's Forces."

Sir, I have no desire to tax the patience of the Honourable the Home Member of those sitting opposite. I am not reading these passages because I approve of them or because I approve of the methods. What I want to impress on this House is this, that there is much more vitriolic, poisonous and combustible matter in circulation in England than here. Yet do the English people ever think of putting restraints like these on their Press? Has it ever occurred to them that they should do anything of this sort? The other day I was surprised to hear from Mr. Griffiths that there is no difference between the censorship of the cinema and the control of the Press. So far as my Honourable friend, Mr. Morgan is concerned, if he had said so, it did not very much matter, but when a gentleman in the position of a District Magistrate, one belonging to the Indian Civil Service, who has to try and dispose of cases of this sort shows such a confusion of thought, that is a conclusive argument as to why the executive should not be vested with these powers. Does he not know, Sir, that the cinema is regulated and controlled all over the world? Does he not know that in England, in France, in Canada, in Australia, in tha United States and everywhere the cinema is subject to censorship? Does he not know with it that it will be against the Habeas Corpus Act, it will be against the Bill of Rights, it would be against the

Magna Charta, if any Bill of this nature were introduced in the British House of Commons or the House of Lords for restraining the liberty of the Press? Does he not know that it is against the fundamentals of the American constitution, and the House of Representatives or the Senate cannot pass any law that would interfere with the liberty of expression or freedom of association. (Hear, hear.) Does he not know that the Free State constitution contains laws of that type? Does he not know that even in the Canadian constitution, you have laws of this nature? Does he not know that these are fundamental rights to which greater value is attached than to anything else? Does he not know that in the case of the cinema the criterion is simple—if the thing is obscene and vulgar, one can at once notice it? If there is an objective standard of measurement and scrutiny, it is easy for people to arrive at right conclusions. I admit, that so far as India is concerned, even the regulation of the cinema is governed by political considerations. We know that here even the cinema is used or abused for political propaganda and as an aid towards the perpetuation of foreign rule. The cinema containing the pictures of the Bombay Congress was actually prescribed! I ask the Honourable the Home Member, I ask those sitting on that side under which law, whether local or international, it is permissible. What was obscene, demoralising or vulgar in the pictures of the Bombay Congress? Can anybody justify it? Is that not proof positive of the fact that the executive at least in this land as it is constituted today does not deserve any exceptional powers?

Sir, I am aware even at this very moment of how the executive are behaving against the rules that they have themselves framed although they find a solemn place in their own manuals of Government orders. In my province, the elections for the district and municipal boards are in progress and the Congress has set up candidates. There is a rule in the manual of Government orders that no Government servant should take any interest in the elections so much so that none should even indicate his preference for any particular candidate. In flagrant contravention of this rule there is a regular conspiracy and crusade on the part of officals all over the province to shut out Congressmen and to put up and extend support to rival candidates. I know, Sir, even today efforts are being made to organise all the reactionary forces in almost all the provinces and certainly in mine and to recruit to the bureaucratic army the lame, the blind, the halting and the cripple, whose docility and subservience is not open to any doubt. Sir, that is what is going on under our very eyes today, and yet we are asked by the self same executive to have implicit confidence in them, so much so, as to surrender all our liberties to them.

Sir, let us look at the other pamphlet now. It contains the statements that were given in reply to Seth Govind Das' question. We find from this that security was forfeited in 17 cases, and Mr. Griffiths laid great stress on this Well, Sir, what does it prove? Out of 4,600 publications security was forfeited in 17 cases. May I know what is the proportion? I think it comes to about 1.7 for 500 or about I for 300. Now, Sir, is there any profession anywhere in the world, is there any community, is there any class however noble and faultless it may be in which the number of defaulters and delinquents does not come at least to that limit? Look at the Honourable Members opposite; let them recall to their minds the Back Bay muddle of Bombay, the Lloyd Barrage scandal of Bombay, the Munitions Board scandal, the Mesopotamia muddle, and the like? Is it not a fact that even amongst the holiest of the holy there are people who have been found to be guilty, in a much higher proportion, of offences much more reprehensible? Then, Sir, why should not there be a law requiring every member of the Indian Civil Service to deposit a security of Rs. 10,000 for good behaviour and honesty? We have just before us the Benda incident which happened but recently and we know other cases in which the soldiers of the army have been held to be guilty of violent offences of a very serious type, and their proportion is much higher again than that of the newspapers whose securities have been forfeited. Why should not there be a law then requiring every soldier who is imported into this country to give a security of his pay at least for a year so that he may be kept in good behaviour? Sir, I think it is implicit in the terms of the engagement of the Indian Civil Service and other Imperial Services that they will be faithful to the interests of this country. Yet many of us do not believe that all of them always behave accordingly. Then, Sir, if difference of views does not matter, why not appoint a Standing Commission consisting, for the matter of that, of Sir, Zafrullah Khan, Kunwar Jagdish Prasad and Sir Nripendra Sircar, who will impose a fine or forfeit the security of those members of the Indian Civil Service who, in their opinion, are definitely proved to have been unfaithful to the interests of this country? Just as members of the Indian Civil Service and other services are free to determine whether their critics have or have not excited disaffection or hatred towards them and will sit in judgement on us, why should not they trust their own colleagues of tried loyalty in the services and in Government to decide matters pertaining to them in relation to their loyalty to this country? Are they prepared to do that? If they agree I will be prepared to reconsider my position. But even the suggestion is giving offence to the Honourable the Home Member. He is tolerating it because he is in this House, otherwise, the idea that three Indians, brown in colour and belonging to those races about which a very apt description was given by another fellow European, Mussolini, it is intolerable to him that we should ever think of these people sitting in judgement over him. Then, Sir, what can they expect from us? After all, are we not human beings? Have we no sentiments? Sir, the Honourable the Home Member told us the other day that all murders were alike. I do not know, Sir, but does he exercise the power of reprieve? Does he grant pardon in some cases? If he does, does he make any distinction between one class of murder and another? Otherwise how are these petitions of mercy disposed of? And does he after all see no distinction between Kharag Bahadur murdering a rake with a view to protect the honour of a family and a rake murdering another person with a view to ravish his wife? Would both stand on the same footing? So far as my attitude towards terrorism is concerned, I do not want to make any declaration of faith, specially after the vulgar manner in which the statement of Mr. Asaf Ali was received by some of the Members opposite. I belong to the Congress: I have signed its creed, and those who do not believe my word receive from me nothing but contempt and I do not worry about what they think of me. But I should stress that there should be a sense of proportion, there should be a sense of proper perspective, which should never be lost. After all, even in the eye of the law, are all culprits alike? Is there the same procedure for the trial of Europeans and Americans as for the trial of Indians? Have we all forgotten the scandals that occurred about the rupture of spleen cases in the old days till the electric fan came to our rescue? And I remember a typical case, a case which, whenever. I think of it, causes me immense mortification. Sir, in 1924 there was a case of rape in Tundla. Some Anglo-Indian lads belonging to the Railway Department ravished some Indian girls. They were convicted and sentenced to whipping. Sir Henry Gidney, who is unfortunately not here today, then made a representation to Government, and to what purpose and with what end? Not with a view to obtain their release, but his representation was to the effect that these meanest and most wretched miscreants should not be whipped by the Indian who normally performed that duty but by a non-Indian. (Cries of 'Shame, from the Congress Party Benches.) And what happened? That representation was accepted and accepted by whom? By one who had been the Lord Chief Justice and Lord Chancellor of England, the Viscount of Reading who was the then Viceroy of India. (Cries of 'Shame' from the Congress Party Benches.) Sir, with this attitude of the head of the executive towards these matters, to dangle before us these things and to tell us that there is no danger of discrimination, that there is nothing, but unadulterated justice to be the guide of their conduct, is to tell us something which our experience belies and which we know is not true. Now, Sir, with these experiences, when even a man of that position, with that training, with that knowledge of law and justice can behave like that, how can you ask us to surrender our liberties and our cherished and valued rights to the minions of law who do not know law and who indulge and revel in lawlessness? Sir, how can that be done by us or with our consent? How can we voluntarily commit suicide?

I have given you 17 as the number of cases in which securities have been forfeited. Along with that I will give you the other side of the picture. Even in this year, according to these figures, security was demanded from 71; end out of these only 15 could find security and 56 papers had to go out of publication Similarly we find that 448 other papers went out of publication. What do we infer from this? That this is a most repressive and oppressive law. And how? Even according to the executive judgement, of those who had been running the presses, only 17 were found to be guilty; but there were more than 500 who were throttled, practically strangled at the outset and were not even allowed a trial. That is the greatest mischief of the repressive law. It falls more heavily on the innocent than on the guilty. There is no doubt that most, if not every one, of these, 500 would have been helpful to themselves and to others had the road not been blocked against them at the very beginning. The other day, the Honourable Member from Midnapore told us that the methods of the government were humane and that they wanted to protect the young men from the snare and the net of terrorism. Is this the way to achieve that end? Just see. You have deprived 500 men who were going to adopt an independent vocation for earning their livelihood of what was perfectly legitimate. If these 500 persons had been allowed to work, there would have been work for at least five more in each press and you would have encouraged the employment of at least 3,000 men if these presses had not been prescribed and if security had not been demanded. I remember what I read some days ago and again something over which my heart wept. There were seven vacancies in the cadre of constables in Patna and there were 2,000 applicants; and how were they treated? There was such a scramble that the crowd of applicants were subjected to a lathi-charge. That is the state of unemployment in this country. Seven posts of constables draw 2,000 applications, and instead of giving them bread you give them stone and something worse than that—Lathis. On the other hand people try to find out careers for themselves and where 2,000 men would have been engaged and would have been in a position to earn their living for themselves, you stand in their way and these 2,000 are thrown on the streets and on the lanes and on the by-lanes. Is it a surprise that some of them should take to methods that are desperate, howsoever harmful, howsoever injurious they may be to the larger interests of the country? I am one of those who feel that methods of violence should not be encouraged directly or indirectly, not because I have any tenderness for this Government, which if I could I would break to pieces this moment, but because I feel that in the interest of my country, situated as we are, if the cult of violence spreads, we will be nowhere, and there will be no end to it and things will go on from bad to worse and from worse to worst. Therefore I would not be a party to anything that encourages such a thing directly or indirectly. But the etiology of the disease should be dispassionately studied in a detached spirit and if you want to root it out effectively.

The Honourable Mr. Griffiths told us that he was anxious to help the youth of the country. I do not at all doubt the sincerity of his declaration; he also told us that his methods and the methods of this Government were humane. I was reminded of what I read the other day, that an internee had been sentenced to five years' rigorous imprisonment for having written an innocent letter which contained nothing objectionable, but because he had not obtained permission of the jailor for writing it. These methods are humane par excellence; but we on our part are unable to appreciate their humaneness. Has it ever occurred to Mr. Griffiths as to why there is so much of discontent in this country? He must be knowing what Becon said about the cure of sedition; he said: "the cure of sedition lies in taking the matter out of it, and the matter consists of much poverty and too much of discontentment." I think he knows that. Has it ever occurred to him why he is there? Has it ever occurred to him as to what had been the role of the service to which he belongs? Does he not know that more than 40 years ago a resolution was passed in the House of Commons in favour of simultaneous examinations for the Indian Civil Service in India and England? But why was it not put into practice? Does he not know that even today out of 2,500 in the superior Civil Services occupying the higher posts, and 5,000 holding the King's Commissions, the Indian is not one in five or one in six? Does he not know that if foreign recruitment were stopped even today, many of those who find a blind alley facing them wherever they go will take heart again and be restored to the ways of peace and prosperity for themselves as well as for this country? I would appeal to him to work towards that end and join hands at least with those who want to put an end to foreign recruitment to all the services in this country. Even if that much is done and it alone, which does not ensure Swaraj, I assure him that he will be providing an effective remedy towards ending terrorism in this country.

Mr. Griffiths has a fine name: it reminds me of Mr. Arthur Griffith, the founder, the father of Sinn Feinism, the first president of the Sinn. Fein Republic, the leader of the deputation that went to Downing Street to hammer out the Irish Treaty in collaboration with Michael Collins, with persons as proud as Lord Birkenhead and persons as powerful, mighty and celebrated at that date as Lloyd George; and Griffiths succeeded in doing wonders. I hope Mr. Griffiths will take a lesson from the name which has much to inspire and will do something to help the lot of the people in this country in reality; and for that we will ever be grateful and thankful to him.

Sir, Mr. Griffiths told us that it was but logical that when an association is declared unlawful, then its funds must be forfeited. Well, Sir, I was reminded of the logic of some of those pastimes with which Nero used to beguile himself in olden times. There were people known as gladiators in those days. Sometimes Nero used to apply a fixed number of lashes to the gladiators. If he died, the logical end was to throw him to the wolves, if he did not die but blood came out of his nose, it was to set the wolves on him, but if neither of these two things happened but only his skin was split, then the logical treatment accorded to him was to strip off the skin with the knife, and Mr. Griffiths wants to see things to their logical perfection. But has it not occurred to him that even an unlawful association may have lawful activities? Has it not occurred to him that there were and are Congress institutions like the hospital at the Swaraj Bhawan in Allahabad and the Prem Maha Vidyalaya in Muttra and Brindaban and various other useful institutions which did no more than humanitarian and constructive service? So, it is not inconceivable that even unlawful associations may have activities which are beneficial to all classes and devoid of political taint.

Sir, I have taken much longer time, than I had intended and I shall now make only a few remarks as to the provisions of this Bill. As Sir Lawrence Jenkins said, human ingenuity has never hit upon anything more comprehensive than this, and he said that, Sir, about the Bill of 1910, and not about this Bill, which is much more wide and much more comprehensive in scope than the Bill of 1910. This is what Sir Lawrence Jenkins said about that Bill:

> "The provisions of section 4 are very comprehensive, and its language is as wide as human ingenuity could make it. Indeed, it oppears to me to embrace the whole range of varying degrees of assurance from certainly on one side to the very limits of impossibility on the other. It is difficult to see to what lengths the operation of the section might not be plausibly extended by an ingenious mind. They would certainly extend to writings that may even command approval. An attack on that degraded section of the public which lives on the misery and shame of others would come within their widespread net. The praise of a class might not be free from risks. Much that is regarded as standard literature might undoubtedly be caught."

Sir, the other day Mr. Morgan told us that we were irresponsible and lacking in a sense of reponsibility, because we do not always see eye to eye with the Government. May I remind him, and may I also remind the Honourable Members belonging to the celestial service, as to what attitude they and the press they patronise adopted towards Lord Ripon's Government, when Sir Courtney libert's Bill was on the anvil? May I know what was their attitude when Sir Bamfyde Fuller submitted his resignation and when it was accepted by Lords Morley and Minto? May I ask them what was their attitude when Mr. Montague censored General Dyer for what he had done in Jallianwalla Bagh? May I ask them what was their attitude even when Lord Irwin, was conducting negotiations with Mahatma Gandhi which culminated in what is known as the Gandhi-Irwin Pact? But, Sir, we are small men. I will not depend on myself, but I shall read out for the benefit of Members opposite the opinion of one who has been for seven or eight years the foremost man in the British Cabbinet either singly or jointly or in the alternative, with Mr. Baldwin, I mean the Right Honourable Ramsay Macdonald. This is what he said:

> "The English-owned papers in varying degrees of aggressiveness are pro-English in the sense that they maintain the British ascendancy with all its privileges and are vigilantly anti-Nationalist."

Mr. F.E. James

What is the date?

Pandit Govind Ballabh Pant

Of course, before he became the Premier of England. Has wisdom dawned on Europeans since? Then I congratulate my friend and I hope he will support us:

> "They attack the administration with candour when it seems to be yielding to nationalistic claims, and carry on an anti-

Indian propaganda which causes much offence and which frequently, in the case of some papers, oversteps the bounds of public policy. In a land subject to severe press law, these papers ought to have been dealt with, for their tone and temper have undoubtedly added to that feeling of resentment which has been played upon by the agents of disorder and political crime. Their criticism too often takes the form of insults, and Indian papers pursuing the same recklessly mischievous course would undoubtedly have had the law applied to them."

Sir, we are said to be irresponsible men. I will again venture to bring to the notice of responsible Members opposite, whether official or non-official, the unambiguous opinion of the same great man who was Prime Minister for a series of years and is now holding a position second only to that of Mr. Baldwin about the Press Law and Criminal Law Amendment Act:

"Here lies the fault of the Indian Government. Its Press Act of 1910 and its Criminal Law (Amendment) Acts of 1919 are contrary to freedom of people and responsibility of Governments, and ought to appear on the Statute-books of no country.

In the first place a power of repression habitually enjoyed tends to develop a habit of mind in the Government which regards all effectively troublesome criticism as sedition, and it allows a Government which is always partly responsible itself for seditious conspiracy to avoid its own share of the blame and impose the whole upon the shoulders of its opponents......The power and policy of repression do not make for tranquillity, but for repression and nothing more... Every foolish Government would like to be able to exercise absolute authority when, in its own opinion, it thinks it ought to do so, but no people with any regard for liberty will give its Government such power."—I wish to bring the last few words to the notice of the non-official Members of this House,—"but no people with any regard for liberty will give its Government such power"—"Governments should be compelled to meet the growth of sedition by political wisdom and not allowed to burden other people with their mistakes, as the Indian Government does when it seeks to maintain order by its Press Laws and Rowlatt Acts."

I will now read just two or three sentences from a speech delivered by Mr. Sheridan in the House of Commons as to the potency of the Press. He said:

"Give me but the liberty of the Press, and I will give to the Minister a Venal House of Peers. I will give him a corrupt and servile House of Commons, I will give him the full swing of the patronage of office. I will give him the whole host of ministerial influence, I will give him all the power that place can confer upon him, to purchase up submission and overawe resistance; and yet, armed with the liberty of the Press, I will go forth to meet him undismayed—I will attack the mighty fabric he has raised with that mightier engine. I will shake down from its height corruption, and bury it beneath the ruins of the abuse it was meant to shelter."

Sir, one word more and I have done. These are the last two sentences from the Chapter on the Press from Mr. Ramsay Macdonald's book:

"The last chapter in the history of bureaucracies is repression. They pass away like on old monarch driven from his throne, hurling accusations of sedition against his approaching successor."[19]

INDIANISE INDIAN ECONOMY[20]

Sir, I have listened to the speech of the Railway Member with undivided attention. It was lucid as usual, but what struck me most was its sophistry, the inconsistency of his argument and the delusion...

Sir Muhammad Yakub

On a point of order. Before the Honourable the Railway Member got up to speak, closure was moved, and it was expected that the Railway Member's speech would close the debate. How can another Member speak now?

Mr. Deputy President (Mr. Akhil Chandra Datta)

Technically the position was this. Although the closure was moved, the question was not put to the House.

The Honourable Sir Muhammad Zafrullah Khan

May I submit that I personally have no desire to shut out the Honourable Pandit Pant from making his speech. A request was made to me by the Party, to which the Honourable speaker belongs, that the debate might now be closed and that I should get up as they were anxious to close the debate, and then the formal request that the question be now put was made to the Honourable the President. He observed that one member of the Opposition was still anxious to speak. That Honourable Member said he would take only two minutes, and when he sat down, I accepted it as a ruling from the Chair that the debate was now to be closed, and I must get up to make my reply.

Mr. Deputy President (Mr. Akhil Chandra Datta)

The position is that the Chair has already called upon Pandit Pant to speak. He has begun. Under the Standing Orders and Rules, the Honourable Member in charge of the Department can speak again. That is the Chair's impression about the rules. (Some Honourable Members: "He cannot.") Technically, the question was not put, and, therefore, the Chair would like to stick to its ruling.

Pandit Govind Ballabh Pant

I do not see why the Government should be so nervous.

The Honourable Sir Muhammad Zafrullah Khan

I have not the slightest desire to prevent the Honourable Member from speaking. I was merely explaining what had happened.

Pandit Govind Ballabh Pant

It is just like him,—he does not want to prevent discussion, but he does not want it to go on. (Laughter.)

The Honourable Sir Muhammad Zafrullah Khan

I did not take objection.

Pandit Govind Ballabh Pant

That was my commentary on your remarks.

Well, Sir, that is just on all fours with the trend of his arguments on the main motion itself. As I was observing, his speech was a patchwork of sophistry, inconsistency and delusions, I will not say hapocrisy. He has again dangled before us the old slogans which have been repeated from that side,—of trust and trustees, of our unduly importing racial and political prejudice, and of our introducing sentiment where reason alone should be allowed to have its play. Well, in fact I would not have got up but for my impression from the way he made his speech that the real issue was being left out and he was concentrating on mere words and the formal part of the subject, instead of going into the matters of substance and the questions really in issue. He made a passing reference to the decision of the Public Accounts Committee, and, then played upon certain words that had been used here and there by other speakers. The question before the House is this.

This Committee had been asked to survey the entire field of railway administration. It had been appointed with a view to framing proposals that would place the railway administration on a sound and stable economic basis. Whether, a Committee, consisting of strangers imported from abroad, can do justice to the national interests that are involved in such a survey—that is the real problem, and I ask the Honourable the Railway Member to answer the question straight,—whether an issue of such a far reaching character, which requires a study of the entire Railway Administration in all its aspects in order that a remedy might be devised by means of which the Railway Administration will be permanently placed on a sound economic footing, whether such an inquiry can be conducted by strangers imported from aboard, and whether such a Committee can do justice to the various conflicting interests that must necessarily come in for consideration and examination.

Sir, too much has been said as to the expert character of this inquiry. I do not understand what is exactly meant. Is this inquiry being held with a view to devising the form in which the balance-sheet should be cast? Is this inquiry being held with a view to devising a formula as to how the depreciation charge should be calculated? These are matters more or less of expert accounting and auditing; but here we are concerned with the human factor, and political and racial issues do come in. What is, after all, the main problem of our Railways? We have a top-heavy administration. The men at the top are imported from abroad, and they are given salaries which are entirely beyond the reach of the average passenger who travels on the railway trains. We have been told that the railway rates are low. I want to put the other question—what proportion do the salaries of the men at the top bear to the passenger or the goods rates in other countries? Do they bear the same proportion here? If they do not, is it not necessary to bring them down? We know that many of our woes are due to the foreigners being in charge of the administration in this country in every vital department. Here we know that the question of the Lee privileges does come in. The question of the far salaries given to foreigners does come in. The question of Indianization does come in. If you want to put the Railway Administration on a sound basis, you have to run the railways economically. If you run them economically, you have to cut down salaries. If you want to cut down salaries, you must withdraw the Lee privileges. If you want to cut down salaries, you must replace the foreign agency by the indigenous agency, as it is only in this manner that you can make the railways work economically. Then, does not the political or the racial issue come in? If it does come in, then can foreigners do justice to the Indian interest? That is what my friend has to answer.

Then, there is another question. It is mentioned in the terms of reference that this Committee will deal with the problem of rail-road competition or rail-road co-ordination. It is one of the most intricate issues, but it has been handled in different countries by the people of those very countries. If you import more of motor buses, more of motor cars and these things, there are interest abroad which are interested in the export of these things. There are similarly others interested in the import or export of engines, boilers and wagons. Do not these issue come in, and do not thus foreign interests come in for consideration in a matter of this sort?

Then, there is the question of the manufacture of locomotives in this country. It does react on the manufacturers of locomotives in other countries. Will this Indian question be properly tackled in this manner? And can they do justice to it? And I ask—can he draw a picture ignoring the background? Can anybody go into the question of the Railway Administration in this country if he is unacquainted with the ways of living in this country, if he does not know the standard and level of living of the people of this country? Sir, unless one is familiar with these basic fundamentals, it is impossible for him to arrive at any sound conclusions that would place the Railway Administration on a sound, economical basis.

Then, again, the question of railway rates is equally important. So far, the Railway Administration has followed a policy by virtue of which the export and the import trade has been encouraged and the inland trade has suffered. The time has come when the entire rate policy should be re-adjusted and modified in the light of the requirements of the country so as to encourage the inland trade and the movement of goods within the country. Thus the question of racial and political prejudice againcomes in. Are not other people interested in facilitating the export and import business and in keeping out the inland business? If they are, then, who is there to safeguard the interests of Indians in this country on this Committee, and to see to it that justice is done to Indian demands and Indian interests? Does not the Honourable the Railway Member know that during the last twenty years, while the railway expenditure has mounted up at a geometrical pace, even while the railways were working at their best the railway income went up only by an arithmetical scale, with the result that, during the twenty years that preceded the year 1933, the railway income went up by only about 110 per cent, while the railway expenditure rose by 230 per cent? Sir, the crux of the problem of Indian Railway Administration, in reality, is, how to reduce the expenditure. If you raise the railway rates, you thereby handicap the movement of goods and thereby prejudice the progress of trade. If you raise the salaries of people when you import, then you add to the expense. The other day, certain figures were given. What do we find? We find that the pace of Indianization is so very slow that it does not go beyond two to three per cent a year so that it must take another fifty years to replace Europeans by Indians even in the railway services.

Then, again, we find that during the last ten or fifteen years, the interest charges have gone up by about 70 per cent. The capital at charge has mounted up, and the income has gone down. You have all these things to solve. Every one of these things does involve a political issue, and there the rub comes in. It is not a mere academic question. These are vital issues which have to be tackled by this Committee and on which findings are expected from this Committee. When these findings will be placed before us, they will come with the weight of an expert Committee of people imported from abroad because of their special knowledge, and then we will be told that these are the only sound conclusions on which a sound railway policy can be based, and this House will then be confronted with a fait accompli which will be the result of the machinations of this Government. So, I say it is not a question of mere form; it is a question which involves fundamental issues of a far-reaching character.

Then, Sir, may I know if South Africans and Europeans were imported in other countries? Does not the Honourable the Railway Member know that there are other countries, such as Bolivia, Paraguay, and Argentine and several others in which the railway traffic had to be suspended completely for three or four years, because the railways could not pay their way, and yet these people did not invite their neighbours from South Africa though they were close by? It is only here that we have considered it necessary to import these people from such a long distance to tell us what is wrong with Indian railways. It has been said that no experts could be found outside South Africa. Well, we have know South Africa as an expert in so far as the heaping of humiliations, insults and effronteries on Indians is concerned. I do not know if it possesses any expert knowledge or tendency in any other direction. He said, you are importing sentiment. Yes, we are importing sentiment inasmuch as we know that national self-respect is the key to the solution of national economy. Persons, with a perverse outlook, cannot give you a sound decision even on matters of scientific interest. And it is not a scientific problem. The question of Railway Administration is a human problem. The question of efficiency is a human problem, and here you have to see how best to promote efficiency in this land; how best to encourage economy in this land. Then, the Government have been following a perverse policy. They have been raising the rates during the last few years, and they have been raised in spire of the fact that the prices have gone down. And what is it that we have observed? We have observed that the rates charged for same distance for goods taken from one place to another inside the country as compared with the rates charged for goods exported to the ports or imported therefrom are almost double. All these political questions face us; to tell us that we are importing political or racial prejudice, while political prejudice has been imported by the Government in deliberately excluding Indians, is a travesty of truth. I say, Government have been guilty of grave political and racial bias and they have been swayed by political and racial considerations alone. It is not only in this case, but that has been the way of this Government all the time. You imported people from abroad to deal with the question of income-tax...

Mr. Deputy President (Mr. Akhil Chandra Datta)

The Honourable Member has got two minutes more.

Pandit Govind Ballabh Pant

That is enough for me. They imported people from abroad to deal with the problem of income-tax. Was there nobody available in this country conversant with the subject of income-tax? They imported people from abroad in order to study the question of education of our children. Was there no Indian available to help them in this matter? They imported people from abroad to deal with the question of the Indian agriculture. Was there no one available in this country to help them in this matter? They imported people from abroad to deal with the question of financial administration and adjustment of relations between Burma and India. There is not a single problem for which they can find a suitable Indian in this country, and that is the state to which they have reduced this country after 150 years of their administration. The railways in this country have been in existence for about 100 years, and we have got a larger network of railways than many other big countries, and yet we cannot find a single Indian in this country to be included in this Committee. The Honourable the Railway Member told us that he had brought into this Committee other people as there were various matters to be considered, and he wanted to give this Committee a long rope. I hope the House will not be misled by the Railway Member's remarks.[21]

We are here to serve our country according to our lights. If the (British) Government is prepared to give priority and precedence to the interests of this country as against every other country, including the United Kingdom if they behave as the true and faithful servants of India and choose to promote the interests of India even when they happen to be in conflict with the interests of the United Kingdom, I think the occasions for clash and conflict will be diminished to a great extent.[22]

We are prepared to do the best we can only with one dominant and sole objective before us and that is the moral and material welfare of this country, and the acceleration of the day of independence and complete freedom for this country. Whoever is prepared to help and cooperate with us in that respect will receive our hearty response; but if there be any reserve in any quarter, if the desire be not to promote the interest of this country but to use this country as a tool for promoting the interests of any other country, then we will not be to blame for the consequences.[23]

So far as we are concerned, we are determined not only to win independence for India but also to make the world safe for democracy. A bountiful providence has provided enough for each and all, and we must shed petty prejudices so that there may be ample opportunity for self-realisation, peace and prosperity for every country and for every individual. Let the reign of reason be restored. Let unreason, suspicion and distrust disappear. Let political reconstruction be founded on freedom. Let freedom he our object and let us achieve it without delay. We are determined to achieve the aims which we have set before us and we are prepared to adopt every honourable course to put an end to the process of suppression which is in alliance with the forces of reaction and is responsible for the moral anarchy which is prevailing in the world so that humanity may go on advancing till it secures material, intellectual and spiritual realisation, through liberty, equality and fraternity.

The Congress wants the democratic system, wants the popular voice to prevail, not the voice of any one individual, but the voice of all communities and of all interests so that a constitution consistent with the independence of India may be evolved by the people of this country. Any reference to internal difficulties is really irrelevant. Independence has to be determined vis-a-vis Great Britain.[24]

The freedom of India is bound to come and it must come within a short time. But the question is not only of the freedom of India but of the peace of the world and making the world safe for democracy and saving Great Britain and France and Germany and Italy, the United States and every other country from future temptations which may again upset peace, throw all that may have been achieved through ages into the boiling cauldron. It is for this that we insist on the declaration of Indian independence. This would be in the interest of Great Britain and France also. This will be equally in the interest of Germany. We have no quarrel with any people, but we are determined to put an end to systems and arrangements which are a perpetual menance to peace and which at any time may bring about political disequilibrium. It is in the interest of England that she should realise this as the sands of time are running fast. She has already generated enough of bitterness against herself in this land and it will not be to her advantage if after becoming free India carries with her bitter memories of her association with England as is the case with Ireland.[25]

Nazism and Imperialism are twin brothers, the aggressive savagery of the one being only surpassed by the insidious suppression and exploitation of the other. So long as a nation is held in subjection by another the prospect of an abiding peace is remote. Domination of one country by another incites the greed and avarice of other powerful nations, who in their turn want to extend their dominions at the cost of the weaker people. There can be no equilibrium in the international order so long as a country like India with a population equal to one-fifth of the entire human race is tied to the chariot wheels of another. If you want the principles of democracy and freedom to prevail and if you are really sincere about your desire to found a new world order on a moral basis and if you want to end war for ever and to remove the causes which lead to upheavals and periodical convulsions in the international world, Indian independence must be accepted as the condition precedent to the fulfilment of this noble purpose.[26]

The people of India, as has been abundantly made clear by the Congress, are interested in the suppression and elimination of all those systems and methods which result directly or indirectly, in human degradation and the imposition of alien will and domination on any people, since such activities tend not only to the impoverishment, demoralisation and weakening of the victims of such methods of violence and oppression but ultimately recoil also on the aggressor. Humanity eventually becomes the poorer and tends to descend to the level of brutes by resort to such methods, by the employment of force and violence and by the suppression of individual national freedom. Let us then fully appreciate the character and implications of the malady which has gripped the world and from which it has to be saved. Let us also take note of the objective which all those interested in establishing genuine peace and preserving human dignity and freedom desire. India shares the views and the aspirations of those who are so interested and it is the duty of us all to determine how this objective can and should be achieved.

India has been re-born in the midst of travail and turmoil but today we are observing the dawn of a new era. Everything should change now and the change should be for the better. The old order must yield place to the new and to a better one. The fight against foreign domination is over. We have still to carry on a ceaseless and organised struggle against poverty, illiteracy, disease, and superstition. Healthy democracy can function only with the active and conscious cooperation of every citizen. All our people have to be roused out of their placidity so that their talents and energy, skill and resources may be mobilized for the progress and advancement of this ancient race and the world may witness the flowering of the genius of India and the fulfilment of our great mission.[27]

Our cultural heritage is rich and varied. We have every reason to be proud of it. It has not received the attention it deserved under foreign rule. It will be our privilege to foster the cultural renaissance of which we see signs all around us. We have to regain our soul in its pristine purity and fulness. Outlandish features which owed their existence to alien support cannot thrive in the refreshing breeze of freedom. All that is a misfit will have to give place to what accords with the genius of the people. Our language, our ways of life, will have to be in tune with our traditions and our innate culture.[28]

Democracy and totalitarianism, whatever their shape or name, cannot go together...A system which stifles individual freedom and reduces all men to automatons cuts at the root of real human progress. Everything should be done for creating conditions of expanding welfare but the spirit of man should not be crippled. Democracy believes in conversion. It wins over people through argument. Its appeal is to reason. There can be no true democracy and no real human progress through violent means. It is impossible to separate means from ends and it is a delusion to think that any right purpose can be achieved through wrong means.[29]

References

1. Debates, U.P. Legislative Council, 8 September 1924.
2. *Ibid.*
3. Debates, U.P. Legislative Council, 19 December 1924.
4. *Ibid.*
5. Debates, U.P. Legislative Council, 3 July 1926.
6. *Ibid.*
7. Debates, U.P. Legislative Council, 25 February 1928.

8. *Ibid.*
9. Debates, U.P. Legislative Council, 18 September, 1928.
10. *Ibid.*
11. Debates, U.P. Legislative Council, 20 February 1935.
12. *Ibid.*
13. *Ibid.*
14. *Ibid.*
15. Debates, U.P. Legislative Council, 6 March 1935.
16. *Ibid.*
17. *Ibid.*, 10 September 1935.
18. *Ibid.*
19. *Ibid.*
20. *Ibid.*, 24 February 1937.
21. *Ibid.*
22. Speech in Legislative Assembly, 23 April 1936.
23. *Ibid*, 28 April 1936.
24. Speech in U.P. Legislative Assembly, 27 October 1939.
25. *Ibid.*
26. *Ibid.*
27. Speech delivered on 15 August 1947.
28. *Ibid.*
29. Convocation Address at Aligarh Muslim University, 27 February 1950.

3

Social Philosophy

Govind Ballabh Pant always supported social measures which were in favour of several development scheme in our society. Indeed it was the mission of his life to see that the weaker sections of our society was the gainer and could reap the rich dividends provided with his as well as his Party's efforts. He pleaded for the encouragement of nationalism and social service, vernacular as medium of education for the development of the proper mental faculties of the students, representation of labour in local bodies, improvement of rural areas, improvement in the administration of jails in U.P., salaries and allowances of Indian and British soldiers, abolition of salt duty, relief to Indians in zanzibar and several other measures during the long-drawn political struggle in our sub-continent.

ENCOURAGEMENT OF NATIONALISM AND SOCIAL SERVICE[1]

I think we owe an apology to the Hon'ble the Minister of Education and to his chief assistants in this matter for the series of resolutions we have been bringing up from day to day relating to the subject of education. Perhaps we have been influenced to a certain extent by the hope that the discussion that these resolutions may lead to will enable us to hear the lively utterances of the Secretary of the department or the exquisite speeches of the Director of Public Instruction.* But apart from that, there are other reasons which have led us to refer to the subject of education again and again. For a weak spot in the social system has a cerresponding spot in the educational system. Whenever people have thought of bringing about any change or any progress, they have referred to education as the lever or fulcrum through which one can uplift society in a civilized State. As was remarked by Mr. Fisher when he was the Minister for Education the future welfare of a nation depends upon its schools. Whenever we look to the advent of a better day or to any scheme of large social reconstruction we look to education as the means through which to achieve that end. All the evils of society seek the panacea in education. So it is with this conviction and faith that we have concentrated on the subject of education and we have made it a principle to bring forward the vital subject of education again and again before this House. From the moment some sort of constructive efforts started from our rank we have tried to approach the subject of education according to our humble lights. It is on that account that this question has been raised today. In making criticism of, and asking for a change in the present system of education, it is but fair and necessary that I should admit that the present system has given us some advantages. It was of more than ordinary utility situated as we were at the time this system was introduced. Much of the awakening that is in the country can very well be traced back to the day when Lord Macaulay first of all wrote the minute on the basis of which the policy of English education was introduced by Lord William Bentinck. So while making our criticisms of this system we do not mean to suggest that no good has come of it. We know that we have reaped certain advantages, but at the same time one should realize that there is nothing perfect in the world. If we say that the system of education, as it is, is imperfect, we are perhaps not asking for an unqualified censure on the department or on the system as it is or as it has been. Our ideas grow with times, our needs change with times, with experience we come to see that things we designed for one purpose have ceased to serve that object or that times have changed and new agencies are necessary. So from whatever standpoint one may look at it, the reasons for asking for a change, for a further adjustment, for further development, for the introduction of new appliances, are perfectly justified. I think that in this one particular respect the system of education has been woefully lacking from the outset. The resolution which I am moving today consists apparently of two parts. The first one contains the substantive proposition and the sub-clauses contain the illustrative parts of it. In a way I should say that the body of the resolution is followed by its tail. I hope there is no sting in the tail and nobody will fly away from it. So far as the body is concerned, I think in spite of bad workmanship, everybody will love it. I will for the main part confine myself to the first portion of the resolution which covers the main proposition. As I just submitted the sub-clauses follow by way of corollary. The first thing that I have perhaps to bring to the notice of the House is the necessity for such a resolution. The reason for my coming forward with such a proposition is, I think, plain enough. I just submitted that we could trace back the history of the present system of education to Lord Macaulay's famous minute. Its rhetoric, its sincerity, though at the same time I should submit its one-sideness are still ringing in the ears of many of us. It was followed by the determination that controversy which had been going on for a long time between Anglicists and revivalists as the protagonists on opposite sides were then called. Western knowledge and sciences with English as the medium of instruction was then determined for this country. After that there have been a series of Commissions beginning with Lord Ripon's and ending with Sadler's and at the same time there have been a number of committees. I need not go into their reasons or objects and assume that all of them thought in their own earnest manner, made an endeavour to improve the system of education, suggested such means as they considered necessary to bring about men better equipped and better qualified but I maintain that they—one and all ignored one of the most essential elements of education without which education cannot be perfect. I speak subject to correction, but it is my conclusion that in spite of all that has been written, the correct ideals of education in regard to the social or communal spirit have not yet been determined by the educational authorities. The question which I am bringing today relates to the relation of the individual to the society in so far as the educational field is concerned. Of course it goes without saying that every endeavour towards improving the individual reacts on society, so every efforts made with a view to perfect the system of education in order to turn out men of better culture and better talents does in a way react on society and leads to its improvement, but I submit that the public purpose of education—the idea that an individual is educated with a view to raise the society to which he belongs, that the individual exists on the earth only when his services are conducive to the welfare of the community to which he belongs—has not been put forward at all, and certainly not with that prominence which it deserves. It is with that object and with that view that I am putting forward this resolution. Even if the idea has been expressed incidentally, I feel sure that so far full emphasis and sufficient stress has not been laid on it. Naturally the system of education that was introduced here was inspired by a number of reasons. There was the utilitarian aspect, there was the necessity of turning out a class of people in the country who could be more conversant with those ways of life with which the rulers were, there was the necessity of introducing that language which could be easily made intelligible to them and which could be the means of communion between their servants and themselves. I do not think, in spite of what Lord Macaulay said, that the main, or even the subsidiary object in introducing this system of education was the emancipation of this country. It might have been lurking somewhere in the background, perhaps it was there in spite of the wishes of those who pioneered this system, but even today I could refer the Council to the recent authority who has been admired in some of the highly cultivated circles, the author of the "Lost Dominion" where he expresses a pang of regret for having introduced the English language here. It is plain enough that the system was introduced with a view to facilitate the working of the administration in this country and the public object of education was not kept in view. Even to this day it has not been given due importance and I am not surprised that it was so in pre-Reform days, though I take note of the fact that the new angle of vision has not affected and inspired the department yet in this respect with genuine regret.

The idea of the Brtitish administration in this country in those days was one of extension of its territory which was followed by that of consolidation. It is only recently that we have for the first time got a definite expression of the policy which must inspire the activities of British rule in this country. So, so long as the Government itself had no objective to guide it in its activities in this country one need not wonder if the Education department, which was only one of the fractional portions of it, and that, too, a very neglected part of the administrative machinery, did not consider it necessary to frame a more lucid, more clear and more definite goal for itself. Consequently the system of education was carried on in a haphazard manner. It was carried on with a view to bring out such men as would be most helpful in doing the humdrum everyday administration work. It was that basis, I submit, of the system of education which affected the output of that education. Naturally the effect followed the cause and the men who were turned out of those educational institutions naturally contracted the infection while receiving the education that they were meant only to work in office as clerks, in villages as patwaris, in the Secretariat (which has now a bit changed its former ways) as superintendents and registrars and as deputy collectors and later on as collectors. Well, that was then the aim and that was one of the basic causes on which the educational system was based. Naturally it could not serve any high purpose. It had not before it that vision which alone could maintain it high up with an apex in the clouds. So the system of education generally was, as one of the eminent members of this House has described rural education, cold, lifeless, and artificial. It is with a view to introduce a bit of warmth, a bit of full-blooded vigour in it that I am bringing forward the resolution which I have put before the House today.

Of what use is education if it does not in any way tend those who receive it to devote themselves, of course ordinarily consistently with the satisfaction of their own common material wants, to the service of the community? That is after all the objective of education in all those places where modern education has received encouragement. But apart from that there are other reasons why nationalism should hold the first place and a prominent place in the system of education as it is today. Those who have compared the state of things as it prevailed under the Oriental system of education and as it prevails today must have been struck with the distinct cleavage that marks the two. Whether you look to the old Rishis or whether you look to Plato or Aristotle, according to them education was meant only to serve a spiritual purpose. It was not as extensive as it is today, but those who received education were expected and designed to devote themselves selflessly to the service of the community, to meditation, to the researches in the domains of the mind and of all that is high and noble. That was the one object for which education existed. That was the one purpose which those who received education served. But what do we see so far as the present system of education is concerned? The most prominent objective of education is individual materialism, if I may so call it. Those economists who have inspired the philosophy of education of modern times have placed before themselves the ideals of "survival of the fittest", of "struggle for existence", of "every man for himself" and for the rest the noble-minded say "God" and the worse-minded say "Let them go to the devil". Well that is the system of education under which the educated classes have been manufactured. Then it naturally led to its own consequences. It made man think of himself. I do not say that a man can help thinking of himself, but it became his main object to enrich himself, to enrich his own material existence. He was every day thinking of increases in population and the law of diminishing returns. All this led to a false theory of individualism. This led everyone to think that his main object in life was to fatten and pamper the body and those high and noble objects resided into the background. Glory to those Indians who, in spite of all this have done so much for us. The theory did not end on what I have said, in fact men like Nietzsche and Treitsche developed the theory further—they brought forward their theory of the superman—they said mercy, kindness, love, all these should be squeezed out of this universe and those only who can work as machines be preserved and developed. These are the theories under which this system has been working and naturally we see there was no correlation, there was no co-ordination, between the head and the heart, and consequently we do not find a similar amount of selfless energy in those who are turned out by the present system. In other countries the antidote was equally strong. In other countries nationalism has been the main living force. In England, a boy from the time of his birth thinks of his country, of the traditions of his country. We, too had our own ideals, we lived for our religion—when Hindus and Muhammadans came together either of them looked to the country as his own and lived for that country, but with the introduction of this new system those ideals disappeared, new ones took their place and under their influence we become more self-centered. So I submit, that unless and until nationalism is given a proper place, an adequate place, a prominent place, an all-absorbing place in the system of education, the purpose of education, which is service of the community through the individual, the attainment of self-fulfilment for the country through the actions of the individual, will not be attained, and if that object is not attained then all effort is vain. You may make men better animals, but that is not the object for which humanity exists. If education does not in any way inspire in us a longing for a higher life a desire to live for out country, a desire to die for our country, it is education that has lost its main object. I submit that it is in that sense I am using the word nationalism. It has been the subject of various citicisms and as many controversies but still I think the definition as given by John Stuart Mill in his book on Representative Government holds good to this day. We ask for true nationalism, for the acceptance of that spiritual principle which leads to a greater sympathy, to real co-operation in the service of the country for self-effacement in the service of the community and that through regular endeavour and not by spasmodic effort only. It is with this sense that I am using the word here and I expect the Government will have absolutely no objection to the resolution that I am moving. I have given you a general idea of the subject. But look further at the state of our educational outlook, at the men who are turned out of our schools and colleges. You will pardon me for saying that all there is in our society indirectly reflects on the system of education. We were talking the other day of corruption, that corruption was rife, that society is still so low. We were told it is a social vice. But these social vices are traceable to the weakness of educational inspiration. If it was a social vice, who is to blame for it? Is it the educated men in the higher grades, or the lower, or both. Why do they do so? Simply because we have not instilled in them the spirit of service for the community. We want a spirit which will induce a man to join Government service not with a view to sustain himself alone but with the main object of serving his country through that means. We want a man to enrich himself through trade or industry with a view to enrich his country, to lead to its further progress. That is spirit that we want. Then go further and we see that there is a strong aversion for manual labour. Where is the recognition of the dignity of man as man, where is there that desire to serve humanity for its own sake, where is there that love which inspire one to carry on life-long work day and night not with a view to staisfy oneself but to serve others? I do not mean to suggest directly or indirectly that any one who occupies these benches possesses these qualities, but that is the ideal, that must be one's vision as to what education ought to be. After all, we were talking the other day of the unemployment problem, we see that our sense of social responsibility does not come up to our social requirements. How does that disparity come in? At the root it is the same thing. Why should a man who receives such education only think of enriching himself? Because you have never asked him to devote himself to anything higher or instilled into him a higher vision. He cannot dream dreams, and if he does he is regarded as an offender. The mind within me and the man within me is killed outright, and unless and until education places before us an idea, and an ideal, on its programme of daily activities, it cannot attain the high aim to which all true education should be directed. So far I have devoted myself to one aspect of the question, and that is training them in such a manner that they may regard it as the ambition of their lives not to stand for themselves alone but to serve others. I do not say they are to wholly forget themselves. I do not expect that virtue in the ordinary world, but I do expect some higher and nobler and wider outlook. It is that which is saving the western countries from falling into the mire. If they had all that individualistic economy and politics, without the corresponding, saving, protecting safeguard that the spirit of nationalism provides every family, these would have gone to the blind alley and the western world would have been ruined by this day.

It is the salt of nationalism which is saving it in the face of all these attacks which are being made by this individualistic political and economic system. When you have just that alone when you have not given place to nationalism in the educational system as it obtains in this country, it is no wonder that even our Oriental method of thinking, even our Oriental view of life, does not permit us to withstand the effect of that system effectively and completely.

Then, Sir, education has another aspect about it and that is the fire, the flame to be free. A self-centred secular system of education makes the people so very cowardly and so very timid. Where self-reliance is lacking in everything, there can be no enterprise and no manly co-operation, these things come out of men who are born with a sense of national dignity, with a sense of national self-respect, with a faith in their national glory and in their future and with reverence for the past; when none of these exists how can you expect that spirit of enterprise, how can you expect that backbone on which alone national life grows? If education has any use it is to create those ideals for which humanity, for which man, should exist, and one of the noblest of those ideals is freedom for the country, the desire to live in a free country. If education in a way leads us to conceal our little life under the shell, to acquire the habit of concealing the truth and not telling that which we feel, how can you expect that education to solve the larger problem which humanity expects from every individual? Education has its object, and that object is the promulgation of right ideals of living. With that object is needed the real, genuine ideal of fredom for the country, the emancipation of the land. Those who have read the history of France must have noticed the nationalism as it existed in that country after the year 1870, that nationalism which does not acquiesce in foreign rule, which burns out of education—I do not say it should lead to a conflagration, but it should lead to a constructive, and selfless effort to be in one's land what others are in theirs: it should lead to the desire to attain one's full stature in one's own country; it should resent every obstacle, everything that is done to put down man from attaining the highest position in the land; it is that which can inflame an Indian to be a Napoleon Bonaparte; it is that which can inflame an Indian to be in his own country what the greatest statesmen have been in theirs; it is that which can make an Indian feel that there is a day when he can be a Gladstone, when he can be a Wellington, when he can be a Lord Reading in his own country. Until and unless you can put education in such a form as to lead man to think that the highest is attainable by him you are stifling the essential object of education. It is that what I mean by "nationalism". It is the substratum, it is the basis on which all that is good, all that is desirable grows, has its being and is bred. So, when I ask for nationalism I am not asking for anything that is undesirable. If even this is denied let us wipe out the lessons of history and let us say once for all that education in India means nothing more than making the beast a better beast than he has been so far. If it means in any way giving full scope to the humanity in the India then education severed from nationalism is a meaningless dogma without any purpose whatsoever. So, I submit that nationalism is an essential part of education. It is not, I assure you, in a spirit of resistance or resentment that I am making this suggestion. It is only on the lines of constructive effort that I bring forward this suggestion. It is combined with the very essence of social services nationalism which manifests itself in the service of society from day to day with the real object before it of living for it. That I want to be inculcated, to be imbibed, in the educational institutions.

The State when it spends money over the individual has a right to expect service to the State from that individual. I am using the word State in its real sense, and not in the morbid sense of subjection. Education which does not lead to the attainment of the real object of education fails at the very outset; and if education is to attain that ideal it should be through a direct effort, through a realization of the true aim and object of education, and everything else should be subordinated to that one object. It is, as I submitted, necessary for all countries and for all communities. For ours there are special reasons why we should attach that importance to education on the social side for encouraging and for strengthening the community spirit. We are often told that we are on the threshold of responsible government and our feet, we are told, have been securely laid on the road that leads to responsibility. If that is true, much more is the reason why the community spirit should be strengthened in every member of the society. As I have submitted, in the olden days men lived for the corporate life and not for the individual personal satisfaction. They may not have been aggressive, as aggressiveness is of recent growth, being necessary for the present-day system of politics and economics. In their own way they served society and community spontaneously without ever feeling that they were rendering any service. That was the beauty of it in the days gone by. Now, if responsible government is a reality, then the first fundamental condition, as we are told often and often, is the realization by the individual of the duty that he owes to the State. Responsible government is government by public opinion. Public opinion in order to be sound must be the opinion of individuals who have acquired the habit of subordinating their individual interests to the interests of the State and communtiy and the larger world to which they belong. If you want responsible government to be a reality then it becomes all the more necessary to introduce and strengthen the spirit of nationalism in the people. If the angle of vision has really changed then let it manifest itself in our educational institutions. These are the bases on which the fabric of self-government can be built up. If those gentlemen who come out of our schools and colleges were not possessed of the spirit which demands from them the best in them for the country, which demands from them, the subordination of personal interests to the welfare of the larger whole, then, I submit, you cannot expect correct public opinion from them, you cannot expect to form that right basis of self-government which can be formed duly on the realization of national ideals. It is therefore all the more necessary that in the present circumstances, on the threshold as we are said to be of responsible government, nationalism should be given a full-blooded and virile life in our schools and colleges in which education is imparted. In the book that has been recently published with the names of His Excellency the Governor and an American writer much stress is laid on the necessity of going instruction in schools and colleges on civic science and constitutional government. Well, there I have the authority on which I rely. I say that if society is to be formed, then civic sense must be developed. It must be developed, it must be a true civic sense, which takes into account all parts of the country, has faith in its glory, and inspires its vast masses to look to the future with hope and with faith. When I talk of nationalism I do not exclude any particular community; be he a European or an American. If he finds dignity in the name of an Indian I should not exclude him. But everyone is free to choose and if he shinks from that, if he considers it beneath his position to identify himself with this placid mass of humanity, which is downtrodden today, then I say he is not' an element which should be included. So I submit that these are the ideals which I want to place before the boys in the schools and colleges. These are the objectives which, I think, should be placed before every boy.

With this object in view I have placed before you a few items which I think can be taken up at the outset in order to encourage such a community spirit. What is the use of a school or a collage if you do not allow, if you do not require, the boy to think of the country, to think of the people from whose contributions that school or college is maintained, at the very outset of his studies every day. He should be made to realize that whatever facilities are being granted to him have been provided for him by the community or the society and that it should be his duty to pay back all the benefits that he is receiving to that society or community. It is with that object that I want certain things to be recited every day. I know that it can be said that it is a mere formula, but formulae have worked wonders and especially a Hindu has much faith in mantras. Then, Sir, I want the use of swadeshi goods to be encouraged. The Government says that it wants swadeshi goods to be used by all Indians. Let the boys from the very day they enter the schools until they come out of college, realize that that is their duty. Then I ask for a simple mode of living. Those who have noticed the vast gap that obtains between the vast illiterate masses, between the larger community, and the few educated classes, must have seen that one of the greatest dangers to the community lies here. Those who have studied the history of Italy and France must have seen that success in the cause of freedom has been followed generally by further inter-community struggles, because the larger mass has not been moving in unison with the smaller educated class. If you want real progress, then it is absolutely necessary that the educated class must breathe in unison with those who are not educated. In this poor country nobody ordinarily has the right to live much above the level which is generally attainable. Apart from other things, so far as the educated class is concerned, it must set an example and that makes it all the more desirable that they should live a simple life for their own sake. It is absolutely necessary that a simple mode of living, which has been the characteristic of the inhabitants of this land from time immemorial and which is today demonstrated and symptomized to us by the spirit of India in Mahatma Gandhi, should be the thing which should inspire and determine the everyday life of an Indian who is receiving education here. That is again the reason why I want manual work to be included in the curriculum. Those who have read the inspiring and ardent words of Mazzini to the working classes should know that this is absolutely necessary in order that things may go on evenly and there may not be any disturbance hereafter. The rest is about Scout troops, and Sewa Samitis. I think the Government has already accepted the principle and all we want is that steps be taken to suit our needs. As to the last clause we had very recently the very sad epidemic of communal strife and no apology or argument is necessary. I do not in any way insinuate against the educated class. By educated is generally meant "politically-minded". Well, men are entitled to their own views and this is not the time to enter into a discussion upon that subject. But I say that even those who have been educated in the villages and primary schools should have to bring about a spirit of unity between the races, should develop the spirit to help every man according to their lights, be he of one race or of another, be he of one creed or another; and I do think that if education had put proper emphasis on this, if the boys trained in the village schools, in the primary schools, in the secondary schools and in the colleges, had been inspired with that vision and told that they should live for unity, for the sake of their country, there would never have occurred those heartrending disturbances which have occasionally disfigured this land to the mortification of many of us though to the malignant jubilation of some others. So I submit that from whatever aspect we may look at it, my resolution is most momentous in the consequences that it entails and in the remedy that is provides, but it is most simple in the method which it proposes.[2]

VERNACULAR AS MEDIUM OF EDUCATION[3]

When before this we made attempts to offer our advice to the Board of High School and Intermediate Education or to other educational bodies I could see the annoyance that we caused to the Director of Public Instruction by infringing upon what he held to be his exclusive field. Perhaps they were the questions of policy in respect of which we may had the temerity of offering our humble suggestion to the Director of Public Instruction, but in matters of the sort that is before the House, of an educational character, as the subject has been described by one of the members of the Board of High School and Intermediate Education whom I regard as a better judge of the problem of that nature because of his association with the Board than anyone else amongst us here. I think there is much more reason why, if a suggestion is made which is inconsistent with the views of the Board, the Director of Public Instruction should resent such an attitude on our part. Happily for me today I am strengthening his hands as president of that Board—a fact of which he has reminded us as often as he has referred that subject of encroaching upon the province of that Board. I am in a happy position of strengthening his hands so that he may be strong enough to carry out the wishes of the Board of which he is president and chairman. I hope he will thank me for the position I am taking for giving him assistance in the matter so that if there are other busy bodies standing between him and the Board he may meet them with greater force because of the assistance that we are lending him. Coming to the subject of the resolution, Sir, the question seems to me to be a very simple one and we have to take into consideration two or three simple points. The first one is this —what is the desirable and the wholesome medium of instruction? What is the natural method of imparting instruction? What is the natural method of instruction for every community and for every class of people? As to that I think there can be no two opinions. I do not think that the honourable the Director of Public Instruction had the privilege of receiving his education in the Russian of the Japanese or the Chinese language as the medium of instruction. He had not, I hope. The point is a very simple one and I think it is being unnecessarily confused. The position is equally simple. We want a sound knowledge of English. At the same time we want as sound knowledge of the subjects that are taught to us. Above all, we want to fulfil the object of education. Now, what does education aim at? I should think education aims in a way at the enrichment of the personality as it is sometimes called. it aims at drawing out of the inner senses of a man through observation of facts and collecting information so that he may apply his mind to those facts and arrive at inferences and conclusions and act accordingly. It is after all setting up in motion the motor nerves of a person so that he may make use of information and make observation through his senses. The question reduces itself to this—whether a man is better able to serve and fulfil the purpose of education when he receives education in his mother-tongue. I submit that when he receives education through the medium of a foreign language, the whole object of education becomes the acquisition of certain acquaintance with the medium itself rather than the subject that is to be learnt through the medium. The question is, whether we Indians in lower classes should receive education in the subjects which are taught to us or whether all our energy should be devoted to the acquisition of a certain amount of knowledge of the medium itself rather than of the subject itself? There is another important question—whether any language can be the means of bringing knowledge to a man when he has no knowledge of that medium itself—whether a man can be taught a subject through a certain language when he does not know that language itself. It seems to me a simple proposition. There cannot possibly be two opinions. If a boy up to the intermediate or the high school standard has not the capacity to understand English, has not the capacity to express his thoughts in English, it naturally follows that he cannot learn any subject through English. As I have just said, no language or vernacular can be the medium of instruction so long as you do not know that language or the medium itself. I submit that in order that a boy may benefit by the instrnction that is imparted to him, it is absolutely necessary that he should possess some sort of acquaintance and familiarity with the medium of instruction and that, too, to a degree which will help him in thinking and expressing his thoughts. Where the system of education is reversed, what is the result? The result is that a boy never masters his subject. He can never apply his mind to it, and being overburdened and overworked, he cannot even learn the language through which he is expected to acquire a knowledge of the subject. I need not labour the point any further. I shall refer the honourable members to Chapter XVIII of the report of the Calcutta University Commission, where this subject has been discussed at considerable length. There we find it stated—"Boys begin to learn English as a language, and also to learn other subjects through the medium of English, long before they are capable of understanding it, and in the lower classes are taught by ill-paid teachers, who have no claim to be regarded as qualified to teach the language. Faults acquired at this stage are seldom completely eradicated, and even when a boy reaches the higher classes of a high school, he is generally taught by a teacher whose vernacular is not English and who is wanting in the capacity to teach the language properly. Numbers of students reach the stage of Matriculation without ever having heard an Englishman speak, and incapable of understanding English as spoken by those whose mother-tongue it is." Further, in the Government of India Resolution of 1913 it was stated that "there is much evidence to the effect that scholars who have been through a complete vernacular course are exceptionally efficient mentally." Again, when the question of the medium of instruction was raised in the Imperial Legislative Council in 1915, that eminent educationist admired by the Education Secretary, Sir Harcourt Butler, said that his own experience and that of many competent educationists there was markedly greater intelligence in the boy whose education had been conducted through the medium of the vernacular until the highest classes of the school were reached than in the boy who had had his education conducted in English in what used to be called in some provinces the upper middle school. Again, in Chapter XIII, in paragraph 26, the Commissioners put the question, "Do you hold that English should be used as the medium of instruction and examination at every stage above Matriculation in the university course?" The replies have been analyzed, and an overwhelming majority of them point to the conclusion that the vernaculars should be adopted as the medium of instruction. A further question will, however, be raised as to whether imparting of education through vernacular is practicable. Personally, I do not find any difficulty in such a course. The point that we have to bear in mind is that in all countries education in all subjects is given through the vernaculars. If you want a national system of education, then vernacular should be the medium of instruction. The gulf between the educated classes and the un-educated classes cannot be bridged unless the educated classes begin to think for themselves and that too in their own mother-tongue and to express themselves as well in that. It is absolutely necessary for national interests, differing though I happen to be from Thakur Hanuman Singh in the matter, and for political progress, that the medium of instruction should be the vernacular. The next question that arises is this: Whether the present system is conducive to a sound knowledge of English? Whether the fact that instruction is imparted through English makes the boy better acquainted with the subjects than he would otherwise be? My submission is that the present system is defective in that respect too. The boy begins to make a wrong use of English from an age when he does not know English. Naturally he acquires the habit of making a wrong use of English which tenaciously sticks to him and which cannot be given up later. Moreover, the boy has to make more than ordinary efforts in picking up the knowledge of various subjects. When you introduce such system of education for the boys which deprives them of the faculty of intelligence, then they can never acquire any knowledge in a sound manner. So, I submit, that for the proper knowledge of English, for the correct use of English we should acquire our knowledge in other subjects through such medium in which we are not bound naturally to make as many mistakes as we have to make when English is the medium of instruction at a time when the boys cannot possibly make a proper use of it. Moreover, the boy will have more time to devote to the study of English when he can learn other subjects through the vernacular than he has at present. In that way he will be able to get a better knowledge of English. I do not know what the Education Secretary meant when he put the question whether you want English to be used only as the second language. It may be the first, second or third language, I do not mind. But we want to have a sound knowledge of English in our schools and for that I consider it absolutely necessary that the medium of instruction should be the vernacular to let the boy acquire the habit of intelligently, idiomatically, and grammatically using words in the vernacular and thereby to make a proper use of English and to get much more time to devote to the cultivation of English than he gets at present. Then, I submit that for all the objects that we have in view the vernacular medium of instruction is very necessary. We have been told about the different vernaculars and the analogy has been given of the Central Provinces and Bihar and Orissa. It does not apply to our province. So far as the High School stage is concerned, there is absolutely no reason to fight shy of a proposition which is sound inherently and feasible in practice. So far as these subjects are concerned, so far as the subjects of History and Geography are concerned, so far as Mathematics is concerned, so far as other subjects in school are concerned, except English itself, which is a different matter altogether, so far as the question of the nature of medium is concerned (we have used very simple words), we can easily adopt in all schools simple words which are in vogue among all classes. It does not even require a number of text-books in Hindustani. The teacher can very well take up a book in English and give instruction, using simple words and I hope the Hon'ble the Director of Public Instruction is in fact aware of the practice that obtains even today under which teachers in various classes do give their lectures in Hindustani because they themselves are nervous of using English and, on the other hands, they have hopelessly failed in their effort of driving into the heads of their boys whenever they have made an effort to use English in the usual manner. So I submit that unless you want to have a greater mockery of the Baboo-English repeated every day, as most of us have a meagre knowledge of English, I do not think there are many Indians who can use English fluently. I myself am always very nervous whenever I have to stand up to speak in that language in the Council. So, I submit, that it is very improper, it is unnatural, it is simply dwarfing the intelligence of the boy from his earliest age. It deprives him of the habit of intelligent thinking and intelligent application. Hindustani, I submit, can very well be the medium of instruction. Every teacher can easily express himself in that language on all the subjects in school in such a manner as to make himself perfectly intelligible to the boy; every boy can very well appear in the examination and use the language in such a way that every teacher would understand it. There is already the necessity, I understand, of every boy learning both forms of vernacular now, so that so far as the script, is concerned Nagri and Urdu are known to every boy. There should not therefore be the least difficulty for teachers whether the answer is given in Hindi or Urdu. The only difficulty will be about the script, and that is in my opinion not such a very great difficulty as to drive us away from what is fundamentally sound and what is absolutely desirable in the interests of educational growth and progress of the Individual as well as of the community. I think Pandit Nanak Chand was on surer ground when he said that the department ought to have accepted the resolution of the Board of High School and Intermediate Education. It is certainly very improper that, having set up a body like the Board in which there are experts, their opinion should not be accepted. The Curriculum Committee had considered the question and the views of the Director of Public Instruction having been fully expressed before the Curriculum Committee, the question having been reconsidered by that Committee which, I believe, consists both of Hindus and Muhammadans as well as of Christians, Indians, and Europeans, the question came back to the Board of High School and Intermediate Education, of which the Director of Public Instruction is so zealous a

President, and it was certainly improper for him to have thrown that recommendation into the waste-paper basker or to have mutilated it in such a manner that there is a difference of opinion between the Director of Public Instruction as to what was communicated to him and the Educational Secretary as to what was the recommendation of the Board and between the President as to what was really decided by the Board. Well, confusion worse confounded is seldom seen like this. I think, therefore, that with such expert educational opinion before them and supported by the analogy of the countries which are said to be most civilized and to whom we look for our guidance and for our further progress, the department will have the fairness to accept the resolution as it has been proposed. We do not want the vernaculars to be adopted as the medium of instruction up to the Intermediate stage all at once, but it cannot be denied that the Intermediate standard has now been made a part of the school course; classes up to XII are common, they are a homogeneous body under the same bond, and it should be so devised that the vernacular should be the medium of instruction up to the Intermediate standard. We will not quarrel if for the present it is immediately introduced up to the High School stage. I hope the Hon'ble Minister will give us a lead in the matter and let us know his own views before the question is put to the House.[4]

REPRESENTATION OF LABOUR IN LOCAL BODIES[5]

This resolution is very simple and I never expected that it would give rise to the prolonged debate that has centred round its simple terms. I have noticed that the Hon'ble Minister is in agreement with the principle of the resolution, but still there are certain features of it in respect of which he wants some further light. One of the criticisms that have been made relates to the very elastic character of the terms used in the resolution. I personally thought that, if given a wide latitude, the Government's difficulty would be minimized; as sometimes it is on account of the strictly precise language of the resolutions and the rigidity of their terms that the Government finds it difficult to accept them, even while agreeing with the underlying principles. I had thought that if the language were wide enough and if the Government were given sufficient latitude, they would feel it easier to accept the resolution, especially if they agreed with the principle of it. The resolution only wants adequate representation, and that only, in local bodies, and again only for factory workers and again only in those areas where the factory workers form an appreciable proportion of the population. It has been said that the resolution does not deal with the ordinary labourer who is to be found everywhere. I am prepared to accept that the scope of this resolution is restricted and that it is confined only to factory workers. But that is not in any way incompatible with the views of those who may desire special representation for ordinary labour. It is for them to make an effort in that direction and then it will be time for us to consider that representation on its merits. As it is, this resolution applies only to factory workers, and the reasons are simple enough. As gentlemen are aware, there are some peculiar problems which should be faced along with industrialization of cities and towns. There are certain statutes which apply only to factories and factory workers. It is because of these problems that it is considered necessary to recognize their position in local bodies also. Those who are acquainted with the social problems obtaining in factory covered areas, must have heard of questions pertaining to over-crowding, housing, slums, the growth of depravity and demoralization and so on, from time to time. These are the peculiar problems which arise out of the growth of factories and some of them are very closely connected with the work and the service and the functions that have to be performed by local bodies. For example, the provision of good houses, proper sanitiary arrangements, and so on, falls within the scope of municipal bodies. There is no doubt that these questions cannot receive sufficient attention from those who do not live in the midst of the environments under which the factory labourer has to suffer all the pains and all the difficulties which are generally heaped upon a poor man with very small resources, especially in big eities. So, it is obviously necessary that there should be representation of this class of people in the areas where they form an appreciable proportion of the population. The question was put as to what we meant by the word "appreciable." We could have very well defined it if we wished, but we thought that if we left it to the Government to decide whether a certain proportion of the population, in a certain municipal area, is or is not appreciable so as to come within the definition of this word, there would be a very much Better chance of their accepting the resolution. If the Government find it difficult to accept the resolution on account of this elastic adjective that we have used, I am ready to make it more rigid.

Hon'ble Rai Rajeshwar Bali

I raised no objection to the use of the word "appreciable".

Pandit Govind Ballabh Pant

Then, the other question was, "what is the meaning of the phrase 'adequate representation'?" Here, again, we thought that instead of saying that labour should have a certain fixed percentage, it would be better to say that they be provided with adequate representation, so that the Government might have a free hand in the matter and the request contained in the resolution on behalf of the factory workers might be more easily accepted by them. Adequate representation only means representation of such a character as will enable the factory workers to realize the presence of somebody in the local bodies, whom they can claim as theirs and whom also they can approach to ventilate their grievances, in an adequate and satisfactory manner. As to who the representative should be or what should be the number of such representatives depends on the circumstances of a particular city or town. So far as Cawnpore is concerned, I understand the municipal board of that city passed a resolution last year unanimously to the effect that labour or factory workers be represented in the municipal board by three members. I hold that municipal board of Cawnpore are in a better position to understand the requirements of labour or factory workers than we are in this assembly, belonging as we do to different parts of the province. Personally, I would take their decision as final on the point. If, however, I were asked what is adequate representation for Cawnpore, I would say that in accordance with the resolution of the municipal board it would be three representatives of the factory workers. Sir, we were told that the municipal board of Cawnpore had never felt any difficulty on account of the absence of representatives of labour from the board, nor had the labourers felt aggrieved on that score. I do not think that this statement is quite correct, for when the municipal board passed a resolution that labour should be represented directly by three members in the board, they accepted both the propositions, namely, that labour stood in need of representation and that the board stood in need of their cooperation. In the circumstances it is not necessary to labour the point any further. I may further point out that the Mazdur Sabha wanted a certain site in order to erect a building for the factory labourers where they might assemble for the purpose of refreshment or other social amenities; but it was not granted by the board. Again, I am told that the Mazdur Sabha wanted to open a library for the labourers of Cawnpore, and with object they approached the board for a grant, but it was refused. Honourable members will, therefore, see that if there had been representatives of factory workers in the board, they would certainly have pressed for such a reasonable request as a grant for a library for benefit of the labourers. I am further told that the representatives of the Upper India Commerce opposed that request of the Mazdur Sabha and that they were also opposed to representation being granted to labour. That shows that there is no identity of interest between the Chambers of Commerce and the labourers. If it were so, they would not have opposed a request of that character. From that one can safely conclude that the representatives of the Chambers of Commerce do not represent the interest of labourers. Then the phrase "adequate representation" gives even further latitude to the Government. They may either allow the labourers to elect their own representatives, or they may nominate such gentlemen as they think will safeguard the interest of labourers, or they may use, wherever there are societies consisting of labourers and of their sympathizers, these societies to recommend people to them and approve such of them as they consider suitable and fit for the purpose.

Sir, we were told that there was no need for any specific provision for facory workers, as their interests were adequately represented by other people, but in the same breath we were told that even those who were expected to support the cause of labour and the cause of the depressed classes had resiled from their position. Taking that into account the labourers cannot hold a secure position, unless and until some definite provision is made for them.

There is one other important principle of representation which should also be borne in mind, and it is that certain interests may receive sympathetic attention from persons returned by general electorates, but in order that there may be a living link between the representative and the particular class concerned, there should be some one who is specifically returned as their representative. Assume for a moment that there is a conflict of interest between the general electorate, and the labour class as such. Those gentlemen who have been taking a sympathetic interest in the cause of labour will certainly not be able to uphold their cause when they find that it is against the interest of general electorates. In our own Council you see we have a representative of the University. All of us are certainly for the encouragement of education. Still, it is considered necessary to have a representative here of the educated classes to be returned by graduates. Then, again we, have here a representative of the Upper India Chamber of Commerce. Of course all of us here are interested in the growth and promotion of industries and trade. Still, it is considered necessary and desirable to provide some sort of special representation of the trading and commercial interest in this House. It is quite true that a single individual or two or three cannot carry any proposal by themselves, unless they get the support or the co-operation of other members, but they can espouse the cause for which they stand and it also leads to a certain enlivening of social and political consciousness in the group whom these particular individuals are returned to represent. There is a sort of reaction in the class to whom such representation is granted. I submit, therefore, that the fact that there are other persons interested in the cause of labour is absolutely no argument why labour by itself should not be given some special representation. The honourable members should be aware that in the Legislative Assembly Government has nominated Mr. Joshi, and I think he was there also during the first session of the reformed Assembly, to represent labour, and he has been nominated again to represent labour there. Of course Mr. Jinnah and others who are in the Assembly do espouse the cause of labour but still it is considered necessary to nominate some gentleman there on behalf of labour specially wedded to cause of labour. Similarly in these local bodies we must have some one who can represent the interests of labour. Then we were told that there should be some connection between taxation and representation. I fully accept that proposition and when you are told that in a place like Cawnpore there are about 50,000 labourers out of a population of 196,000, and when these labourers make a contribution in various forms towards municipal funds, while the number of electors from them is very small, there is an unanswerable case for their special representation on that board. In Cawnpore we have got house tax. Apart from that, we have terminal tax. So that every article that is consumed has to pay a certain tax and the consumer has to bear it in the end. Now, as these labourers must be consuming something, they should be contributing towards the funds that are spent by the municipality. So they should be represented on these bodies. We were told that some of the office-bearers of the Mazdur Sabha are at present members of the municipal board. I have only to say that the office-bearers of the Mazdur Sabha are not there as the representatives of the Mazdur Sabha not are they there as the representatives of labour, and just as Mr. Hafiz Hidayat Husain had once been an office-bearer, but who gave it up when it did not suit his interests, in the same way when other office-bearers of the Mazdur Sabha will feel that the Mazdur Sabha is carrying on certain activities which are not in the interest of their general electorate, they may give up their position of office-bearers. In that case the labourers will not be represented there at all, though even the representative character of the Mazdur Sabha has been doubted in this House. In the circumstances much importance should not be attached to that objection. I will not take more time of the House over this resolution and I will say that we must understand that we have to move towards democracy. That interest should be represented specially in the case of the poor who are an uncared for and unlooked after class. It has often been asserted by those who want to stand in the way of our progress towards democracy that in our country the interest of poor classes and masses are not properly looked after and there are special electorates ro represent those classes who can very well take care of themselves. Well, it is a question which may or may not be looked upon with the same view-point or with equal concurrence by all parties concerned, but, we have to grant that in the case of the poorer classes there is much greater need for adopting such expedients as will safeguard their interests and that will at the same time quicken the sense of citizenship and of social consciousness in them. In the circumstances it does not suit us, who for the time being happen to occupy, socially and educationally, a position better than theirs, that we should not help such special electorates. If we do not want to help them it is open to us to drop them off wherever we are deriving any benefit from them. But in the case of other interests to use such an argument only looks a selfish way of getting more for ourselves. So, I submit as a representative who happens to be educated that we must pay great attention and we must deal with this question with great tenderness. These poor people are gradually acquiring some sort of consciousness. There is awakening all over. If we do not make direct provision for them, it will not be a good thing. So I make an appeal to the honourable members of the House to accept the resolution which is elastic enough and under which the Government will have sufficient latitude, but which still will enable the Government to make adequate provision for those classes who are not adequately represented on local bodies today.[6]

RESOLUTION REG. IMPROVEMENT OF RURAL AREAS[7]

I

The resolution I have the privilege to move today is of a comprehensive character; there is nothing original or novel about it. I had opportunities of raising a discussion on the subject of rural development more than once during the last three years. If I refer to the subject again today it is because it is one of those matters to which I attach great importance. It is one of those problems on the solution of which, I believe, the future progress of this country, its capacity to govern its own affairs, and its right to stand on its own legs, depends. The question of rural development is in a way very comprehensive. In a province like ours, where 90 per cent of the people live in villages, even a little progress, a little advancement, a little addtion to the amenities and the comforts of life in those parts would benefit about forty millions of people. So, considering the great good that can accrue from a proper solution of this problem, I beseech the attention of this House and expect that this resolution, which is of a non-contentious character, will be passed by the Council unanimously, by the officials as well as the non-officials. I do not think it is necessary for me to paint the picture of the very deplorable state of things that prevails in rural areas before the members of this House, a goodly number of whom are people hailing from the villages, and who have a direct personal knowledge of the difficulties, of the privations, of the miseries and the hardships which are borne by the people living in those parts. Being fresh from the recent elections, I trust every member of this House must carry the recollection of the state of things actually observed by him in the course of his election campaign. I venture to remind honourable members also of the promises and the hopes that they must have held out to the electorate in the course of their election campaigns. Sir, I referred just a few minutes back to the gigantic nature of the problem which faces us. I have referred to the large number of people living in the villages. I do not think it is necessary for me to remind the honourable members of the large number of villages scattered over this province. We have to deal with not only about as many people as there are in England and Scotland, but they are scattered over about one lakh of units, which is the number of villeges, roughly, in these provinces. The appalling state of ignorance, poverty and misery of the villagers should not be further dwelt upon. We are here concerned with the solution of the problem and we have to take note of the fact that this is the state of things after 150 years of British rule. We have to take note of the fact that, at present, the proportion of illiterates in our provinces is almost equal to the proportion of literates in advanced countries. We have also to take account of the fact that the slow progress that has been made so far, even if it is maintained, will require hundreds of years to cover the ground that has yet to be covered. There is large leeway to be made up and we have to see how we can do so. Sir, I believe we are all aware of the low vitality of India. We must be conscious of the fact that the expectation of life in our province is not even half of that which a Westerner expects in Europe or in America. While there the average expectation of life is about 45 years, here it is said to be something between twenty-two and twenty-four years, and what is the most discouraging feature of this is that, as time advances, we are being told that this expectation is likely to go down. While some years back the expectation of life in our province, according to some economists, could be fixed at twenty-four years, it cannot be put now higher than twenty-two. We also know that the death-rate in the province is almost double that which we can find in any country which can boast of any sort of civilization. Epidemics are one of the inalienable features of this province. You may open any is issue of the Gazette and you will find some portion or other of the provinces suffering from some epidemic disease or other. There is no part of the year when the province can be said to be immune from epidemics for even one week . While in other countries the population has been growing by leaps and bounds, and, taking all the provinces into account, in India too, between the years 1890 and 1920, there was an increase of about ten per cent, in our province there was an actual decrease. It again goes to show how very poor is the vitality of our people and how inadequate are the resources. It proves conclusively that there is a real lack even of creature comforts and of those things which are necessary for the bare maintenance of life. I may also remind honourable members that if they will look at the decennial figures they will find that very little progress has been made, and if that speed is maintained it will require many centuries to reach even the stage that prevails in the backward countries of the West today. I will not talk of our agricultural backwardness. I will not talk of the regular flow of our people from the cities to villages. That is the natural consequence of the destruction of industries, whether the artificial means or whether the decay be due to natural causes. The only thing on which people have to fall back is land, and naturally this leads to very severe pressure on the land. Further pressure without adding to further proportionate production leads to further weakening, to the distribution of almost constant quantity of produce among a large number of people and consequently to deterioration in every direction. The little creature on whom this superstructure of Government is based, from whom everybody derives nourishment and who pampers the man in the palace as well as in every profession in this country is entitled to some sort of regard and tenderness from those who pose to be his representatives in this House. It is, as I said, a problem which surpassed everything else in its importance and which claims an urgent solution. On the other hand, the financial resources of the provinces cannot be unlimited. During the last six or seven years there has been a considerable increase in the provincial revenues. It should be roughly put down at something like 35 to 40 per cent at least of what it was prior to 1919. Some effort has been made to improve the lot of those who are steeped in misery and ignorance. Still, if you look at the expenditure and the results that have been attained, one can say without entering into the question whether full value has been earned for the money spent or not, that this scale, if maintained will require millions and millions; at the same time it will require a long period to attain that normal strength to which the people of this country are entitled to look forward. In these circumstances, it is necessary that the whole question should be examined, it is also necessary that progress in these directions should not be of a spasmodic character, but it should be in accordance with a systematic scheme formulated for that purpose and it should not vary with the freaks of the monsoon or the viscissitudes of the finances of the provinces. I claim that it is necessary to borrow one crore of rupees for police buildings during a period of three years, it is much more necessary, and an investment which is more profitable and more useful ultimately—it is much more necessary to frame a definite scheme for the development of rural areas with the definite understanding that in case the income in any particular year from the current sources is not enough to meet the expenditure in that year, then Government will borrow to meet the expenditure in the year. What I am suggesting in my resolution is that there should be a definite scheme. This scheme should cover all those subjects that have a direct or indirect bearing on the life of the ordinary villager; that scheme should be financed and that there should be provision for a graded scale of expenditure. In case the money is not sufficient to meet the expenditure in any one year, Government should borrow as much as may be necessary to meet the deficit. I also suggest that the scheme should, in the beginning, be formulated for a period of three years. There are reasons why I do so. The life of the Council is normally three years. The Hon'ble Ministers when they are installed in their chairs normally look forward to their life for this period. So it behoves us, at the very outset when we are entering into our duties, to determine in a distinct and definite manner what we are going to do during the next three years. I may correct myself and say, to find out what those who are in power are going to do for the next three years. It will, enable us either to look forward with hope or to suffer disappointment at the very outset. It will enable us to see if the results that are attained thereafter are in accordance with the hopes that were held out to us, at the beginning. There is one other reason why I want such a scheme to be framed. The Hon'ble Ministers have not so far given us any scheme which they mean to work. They have not given us any time-table. We do not know whether it is the intention of the Minister of Education to double the number of schools, to treble the number of students and scholars that are in them today, to make it possible for the boys to be retained in the schools up to the upper primary stage at least, whether he intends to prepare a scheme for vocational education and whether he has any definite ideas for the next three years which he means to put into effect year by year, so that at that time his life is out as Minister with a hope of resurrection I am prepared to admit, by that time he may show us the results which he intends to attain in accordance with the scheme which may be published today or within a short time. Similarly, we do not know what the Minister of Industries proposes to do, whether he stands for industrial concerns or for a network of small cottage industries, what are the particular subjects on which he means to concentrate his attention, how he proposes to finance them and how, year by year, he intends to tap the resources of the province and to redress the natural conflict and competition between the various portions of the province from north to south and from east to west. Similarly, we do not know how the local bodies are to be treated during this interval. They cannot frame any scheme for themselves—any scheme for expansive development unless and until they know that they are going to have something by way of additional grants during the next two or three years. I will no develop the point further. It will appear to the honourable members of this House that unless and until we have a definite and clear scheme before us we cannot earn full value for the money that we may spend. A policy of drift cannot lead to results which can be attained economically from a system based on scientific methods. So I propose that some scheme should be prepared for the next three years.

I will now turn to the other points which I have raised in my resolution. I have confined the scope of this resolution to rural parts and have not touched the urban areas. The urban areas have their needs, and I am prepared to accept that they have a right to look up to the Government for generous treatment. But I feel that the rural areas have been more or less neglected. I feel that the men in the villages are not as vocal as those living in other places and are not as well organized or equally powerful. In these circumstances if they had not received an equitable share of the attention or of the financial expenditure incurred by the Government for beneficial purposes so far, there is nothing strange about it. There is one more special reason why I want the Government to concentrate over the rural areas. The Improvement Trusts have spent lakhs and lakhs over cities, and I am told that the expenditure there is going to be of an unproductive character except in a few places. Indeed, the Government have already wiped out or deferred the realization of instalments which were due from the Trusts. I further understand that the universities are getting a goodly share out of the public revenues. When I say so I do not mean to suggest that they should not get more, nor even that they do not deserve more; but I do demand that the poor man should have his full share of education, at least in the primary stages. I am prepared to accept that a university is a place for those who want to obtain high education and to conduct researches. I am prepared to accept that thinkers can be produced only in universities. I am prepared to accept that the science of physical culture can be studied only in well established gymnasia. But what I want is that the man who is starving and dying today should get at least one little slice to fill his empty mouth. I am not prepared to accept the world is meant only for those who have, and that the have-nots should be condemned for good. It is because I claim justice for those who are not in a position to assert their rights that I beseech the sympathy and support of every just-minded member of this House.

There is one more reason, and it is this. The income of the

muncipal boards, though they are concerned with not more than one-tenth of the population that lives in the villages, is almost equal to that of the district boards. While the incidence of income per head in a district board is about 6 annas, in a muncipal board it is about Rs. 4-8, so that in a municipal board the resources per head are twelve times as great as they are in the area comprised in the district board and because the men who are in a position to look after themselves through their own resources should not be subjected to the demoralizing effect of receiving doles and help from others. I think it is morally sound and just that those from whom we have squeezed everything that we could receive such assistance as they are entitled to.

There is a further reason, and it is this. In other countries all rural local bodies look to the land for financing measures for rural relief. It is regarded more as a subject for local taxation than for central; but in our country more than half of the central revenues are derived from land and so nothing is left for the poor man to contribute towards his own local needs and requirements. As therefore, he contributes the greatest share of the provincial revenues, he is entitled to alion's share out of them; but, alas, he has not been so treated. How many lakhs of rupees have been spent so far over water-works in big cities? How large are the obligations which the Government have undertaken for supplying electric power in order to light the streets in a few cities only. Just compare the expenditure which has been undertaken year after year in order to increase the amenities of there cities, and then compare the population which lives in them with the vast population of the province; and what is the proportion? It does not affect 3 per cent of the people, if you take the population of these few cities which between themselves have consumed several crores. In these circumstances it is just and fair that these people should get a reasonable share for their development. It is because I consider that their needs cannot be postponed any further and it is because I feel that it is the moral duty of these who are in a position to take account of the requirements of those on whom they live and who feed them, that I appeal to every section of this House to take up the cause of the downtrodden in this province and to look after their interest with sympathy and understanding. If you will be pleased to look at the additions that have been made to the district board grants during the last three or four years, it will be apparent that there has not been such an addition as we are entitled to claim.

During the last two years the province has received remissions in the provincial contribution to the tune of about a crore of rupees. I had moved a resolution in this House to the effect that all amounts that are received by means of this remission should be devoted to the development of the rural areas. Whether that resolution was in consonance with the canons of finance or not is not the point at issue. What I desire is that, so far as this one crore of rupees is concerned, the Government should have a definite scheme of rural development and this amount should be devoted exclusively to that one purpose. What is the condition of sanitation in our villages? Who does not find it necessary to stuff his nose in order to avoid the stink while passing through the village lane? Just imagine how you drive over these fine roads in your motor cars and consider and compare the stage of village paths over which even carts can be carried with very great difficulty in the months of July and August. Are we to have such an iniquitous and unfair division in life all through? Will the man in the village be allowed to suffer and will we have all the things to enjoy? Such a division of labour, however flattering, however profitable and however useful it may be to us, will certainly recoil and will bring Nemesis down on us some day sooner or later. The condition of the man in the towns is not ideal. If we compare how we live in the towns and how the people in the Western countries live in the towns and even in the villages, we feel the agony of subjection. But when go beyond that and see the condition prevailing in the villages, then we find ourselves on a plane which is outside the pale of humanity. It is because every human being is entitled to be treated at least with creature comforts that I claim that, according to the recognized notions of social and political sciences today, it is the duty of the Government to provide for their elementary needs.

I will not develop any arguments beyond what I have said. To me it seems that the subject is very simple and every member of this House should be fully conscious of his own duty in the matter, of the responsibility that he owes to his constituency and, above all, of the moral duty that he owes to his poorer countrymen to give back to them what they have been giving in order to enrich the life of others. It is because they are entitled to claim compensation and because it is time for us to give back to them the capital—not only the capital but also the interest—that I propose this resolution.

II

The various Secretaries to Government, I hope, will thank me for once for having given them a legitimate opportunity for making a display, by means of glorified narratives, of the activities of the various departments. I think we were never under the delusion that every department had not been trying its best to keep up appearances or doing something to justify its existence. I never questioned that the departments had been doing something. They would not have been here and perhaps even they would have felt some little difficulty in issuing their Annual Administration Reports with fine photos, as is it the fashion now, if they had not got something to say; and I find the reports as interesting as a little boy will find the teaching of the alphabet by means of the modern Montessori method. So there is much in the reports to enlighten us, at least to interest us, to give us some zest.

Coming to the resolution itself, I fear no direct answer has been given to any one of the many questions that I put. I am not concerned with what the departments have done, except in so far as it is necessary to find encouragement or inspiration or not to lose hope. What I am really concerned with is the future. I am not here to look back; I want to look ahead, and for that none of the various statements made by me has so far been questioned by anybody. The facts that I gave are practically admitted, I think. That we are in the lowest rung of the ladder of literacy in the Indian chart is not denied. That we are in a state of abject poverty is not disputed. That taking the economic and vital factors into account our position is most unenviable and unedifying is not disputed. Taking all these factors into account and also bearing in mind the further fact that this is our condition after 150 years of British rule, are we to be satisfied with the rate of the progress that we have been making? If we have got all the schemes that the collective wisdom of trained experts could produce, and it there is that able and judicious guidance which the heads of the Government should possess, why is it that our condition is so very deplorable? That is the simple question that I put to the occupants of the opposite benches. If schemes are there, if funds have been properly utilized, and if, as has been suggested by some of those who are responsible for the running of some of those departments they have never felt any paucity or want of funds, then I put it to them why has there not been adequate or reasonable progress? Even during the last five years it will have to be admitted that much more has been done in the neighbouring province of the Punjab in the matter of primary education, co-operative societies and cottage industries than has been done in these provinces. Why is it so? I was not concerned with the reports and achievements for the last three years. It was perhaps assumed, and perhaps not very justly, that we are not at all acquainted with the glorious achievements of the various departments, for even they should concede that if anything tangible has been achieved by them it could not have escaped our notice and it should not be necessary to make a display of it on the floor of this House.

Now, of all the speeches that were delivered here the most amusing speech seems to me to be that of the Director of Agriculture. From what he said I conclude that the Agricultural Commission has been wasting all its time in making any inquiry at all in order to frame a scheme for agricultural development in this country. He seems to hold that the last word on the subject has been said, he has got all that can possibly be had and that no further word is needed from any quarter. Well, I congratulate him for all the knowledge that he possesses, and in so far as he has indicated the futility of any further endeavour in that direction, I can only tell him that that opinion is not shared by other members. He says that they have started some more institutions and that they have been doing so many things in so many directions. But the simple question that I want to put to him is this. He says he spent Rs. 26 lakhs last year and has got that amount now. Can he tell me to what extent the agricultural problem of the vast magnitude which has to be faced in these provinces has been affected by the expenditure of Rs. 26 lakhs? Can he tell me that the amount he said has been distributed by way of seeds in these provinces is not even an infinitesimal portion of the seeds that are needed for a single harvest in one division? Can he tell me what is the output of the agricultural instruction and education which is being imparted through the institutions that are maintained by the Government? Does he mean that the college at Cawnpore and the newly-started school at Bulandshahr are sufficient to meet the requirements of 40 millions of people? Does he not know that most of the people in these provinces do not yet know that there is anything by the name of fertilisers or artificial manures or improved implements of agriculture? I wish to inquire whether during the year 1926 any single demonstration farm has been opened. Honourable members will remember that a question was put in the House today whether any experimental farm has been opened or whether any experimental farm has been converted into a demonstration farm. The answer was that no experimental farm has been converted into a demonstration farm, which means that not single farm maintained by the Government has during the year proved more profitable than in previous years, or even has been able to pay its way. So far as my own division of Kumaun goes, I know that since the

Reforms constitution the activity of the Agriculture department has been manifested there in two directions. The jam factory at Chaubatia and the demonstration experimental or miscellaneous farm (I do not know which it was) at Jeolikote, which used to remind us of the existence of this department, have been effaced from the surface of our division. So that is the achievement of the Agriculture department in my part of the province. Still, if the Director of Agriculture tells us that nothing more is needed, that all that could be done has been done and all that is now wanted is expert guidance—not money mind you, but trained staff—I wish to ask him to make a comparison and to find out if even a thousandth part of the agricultural needs of the province has been met by the expenditure of 26 lakhs over agriculture. If such is not the case, it is time for him to revise his opinion and to frame a project for the next three years to come. He should in the first instance put down how many farms he is going to open in the various parts of the country in order to demonstrate to the stupid villager the benefits of the improved system of agriculture; and further to consider if it is not possible to find out some useful channel for the activities of students who might be trained by the establishment of another school besides the one at Bulandshahr. I think it will be possible for him to imagine in a charitable and generous moment that if another school for agricultural training were started, its output too might do some useful work. I have no mind to develop the argument any further. I hope he will be pleased to consider the possibility even now of doing some thing more by means of a programme of systematic and progressive expansion for the improvement of agricultural methods and also by inculcating such methods in our rural population. I will not give figures as to our backwardness in this respect for they can be seen anywhere.

Turning to the Department of Education, the modest head of the modest department had the pleasure of informing us what vigorous methods have been adopted by his department for the expansion of education. Well, I do not deny that in the Education department an earnest effort has been made to tackle the problem. Here again I find no answer to the questions put by me. The Director of Public Instruction says that a scheme has been prepared, and it makes provision for a large expenditure, with the result that he expects that in five years about four lakhs of students would be put in the primary schools. I want to know definitely if the Government intend to make provision for the admission of this number of students during the next four years. If the Government is determined to finance such a scheme, I want to put a question to it. What is the number of schools that it means to open next year? I want to put it definitely to the Government—What measures it is going to adopt in order to induce students to continue their studies beyond the preparatory or the lower primary stage? The Hon'ble Minister thinks that it is not only a question of money, but also of men. I entirely agree, but both of them have to be found by those who are by Providence or by accident placed at the head of constructive opinion of the province. It is for them to enthuse people for the constructive activity. They are here not only as heads of the bureaucratic departments, but they are here as leaders of public opinion and have taken the responsibility of running the departments in an efficient manner. While, therefore, the Hon'ble the Finance Member may find shelter under that argument, it is not open to the Hon'ble Minister to say that while funds are available men are not. I humbly submit that it is his business to find men to create enthusiasm in the non-official public. The Hon'ble Minister are here as representatives of the public. They are not sun-dried bureaucrats, though in this country it is not very difficult for men to contract certain habits by close association with those who possess this strong qualification and who are members of a steel frame. But apart from that, I think they cannot take shelter under that statement. If men are not available and if district boards are not functioning properly, what have they done so far in order to enthuse people and to put the district boards in a vigorous frame of mind? If they say that they have failed in doing so, then perhaps that will not be a laudable commentary on their own vigour of mind and their capacity of influencing others. I submit that they will kindly bear this fact in mind.

The next item related to the department of Local Self-Government which is under the Secretary, Sir Ivo Elliott. He has told us that he had a scheme of communications ready some eleven years ago, which was put in the pigeon-holes of the Secretariat and which has evaporated therefrom. I really feel that the present condition of roads and of bridges is simply deplorable. I am aware of a road in my own district in the construction of which something like a lakh of rupees were spent only eight or nine years ago, and today it is not possible for even a human biped to pass over it. All that money is being wasted. The district board has perhaps made certain suggestions to the Government and has been sending reminders after reminders, but no reply has so far been vouchsafed. So again the question comes in the same light, and I put it. You say communications have to be set right, and I put it to the Government whether they are going to have a definite and elaborate scheme showing that they will put in order at least 1,000 miles of metalled road, 10,000 miles of unmetalled road and 20,000 miles of some other sort of road. I am simply giving an illustration without knowing the financial commitments of it. I want a definite time-table for all these things. I know that it may be necessary to make certain modifications in the light of experience. All the same, there must be a definite and determined resolution to give effect to the scheme in its fullest details. It is the primary duty of Government to make provision in these directions. If it cannot find money, whether by loan or out of its recurring income, then it must admit its financial bankruptcy, which in a case of this sort means moral bankruptcy. When a Government cannot even cater for the barest requirements of the people whose responsibility it has taken upon itself voluntarily, then it has no moral right to sit on the hedge and to run about in a dignified manner. It has to carry the burden on its back. If it fails to discharge its elementary obligation, then the Government which exists only for the preservation of law and order by means of ordinances or repressive law is entitled to nothing but opposition, which, if necessary, can be even of a violent nature. The only justification that a Government can have for its existence at any place is the discharge of all its duties which conduce to the real welfare and progress of the people that are committed to its charge. Just imagine what Philippines have done in a few years and how Japan has achieved eminence in a few years. And you cannot get over the charge that this Government have failed in the discharge of its elementary duties. My friend, the Director of Industries has reminded us of the purchases that he has been making for the Government out of cottage industries. I want to know whether he has started a single cottage industry in single village of these provinces. There are 1,04,000 villages in the United Provinces; in how many have you cottage industries?

I put another question—What proportion, whether infinitesimal or fractional, of the total imports is bought from local manufacturers in these provinces and for what portion of these manufactures his department can take the credit? Can he say that even one rupee worth of goods out of Rs. 1,000 that are imported from outside, whether manufactured outside these provinces or outside India, are manufactured in these provinces, because of the activities of this department. This is after all the crux of the problem. It is high time for us to have a definite project even for industrial development. Can his department tell us what sort of cottage industry would be congenial to a particular locality?

The Hon'ble Lieu. Nawab Muhammad Ahmad Sa'id Khan

Yes.

Pandit Govind Ballabh Pant

If that is the answer I go a step further and ask what methods have been adopted in order to encourage the improvement of these cottage industries in these particular localities? Have experts been trained to work in that direction? Have these industries actually been revived, and have they been adding to the industrial output of the province? If not the answer does not help us. We want practical and solid results, and if they have not yet been achieved, then the mere fact that our archives are full of schemes does not help us. I admit that the Government is as scheming as any Government could be. We do not deny their resourcefulness, but what we feel and what we realize from our experience is that results that have been attained do not in any way justify the course on which the Government has relied so far. I assure the honourable members of this House that I never meant to move this resolution in a spirit of carping criticism, and that I did not mean to cast any censure on the various departments. I simply wanted to place before the House what I and most of us have been feeling most strongly. We are holding such an unenviable position in the ladder of human hierarchy today that it is time for us to reconsider our plans, to take stock of the position and to see what we can do. I do not deny that the local body has a certain responsibility in the matter; but what can the local body do? You cannot get oil out of stone. When you have squeezed a thing out and there is no substance left in it no amount or rubbing will produce any oil. The point is this, whether the villager, that emaciated skeleton who has nothing but bone and skin to connect its bones together, can be further squeezed, and can you get anything more out of him, when there is nothing left in him? Then why put off the performance of that which is absolutely necessary in order to enable him to give you something, at least for this object and motive, if not for any other, that you may get something more out of him hereafter. It is the best investment that a State can make even for purposes of taxation. Of course the Government which may be afraid of their existence after a few years may not feel personally interested in the matter, but so far as the State is concerned, they cannot make any better investment than in the improvement and progress of the human source of all that is good and of all that is worth having. We are told that district boards can add to their resources. Some questions were put on January 24, and I have got the answers.

The answer was that eight boards had been trying to impose new taxation, and it was also said there that some had imposed taxes, and that the actual yield of taxation in 1925-26 was: Moradabad Rs. 9,820 and Lucknow Rs. 6,323. Let me assume that other boards were either induced or coerced into imposing these additional taxes. But will that make any great difference? They may give you all that they can get, but still by far the largest portion has to be contributed by the State, and it must be admitted that in advanced countries the State has admitted its responsibility in this matter, that it is their primary duty. So even if Moradabad had not been able to collect Rs. 9,820 which it has got by taxation, would that be a pretext for withholding from it what is absolutely necessary for its progress? I say these few thousands cannot make any material difference. Ask the boards to make additions to their resources somehow or other and they will do it. Moradabad might have raised these Rs. 10,000 by means of subscription, if not by means of taxation; but the point is whether you are prepared to admit your responsibility for meeting these charges primarily and saying that the boards might pay what they can, but whether they do so or not, we owe this solemn responsibility to the people of these provinces and we will discharge it to the best of our power, to the best of our capacity honestly and conscientiously.[8]

ADMINISTRATION OF JAILS IN U.P.[9]

This motion was at the outset confined to one particular issue that arose out of the appointment of the Jails Inquiry Committee by the Government, but almost everything pertaining to the jails has been brought within its compass. I am sorry that on that account the issues have been jumbled up and it must necessarily lead to an amount of overlapping at the way the matter has been treated and the course that this discussion has taken, I think it is desirable that I should submit a few words for the consideration of this House pertaining to matters connected with the administration of Jails.

I am sorry that the question of the Jails Inquiry Committee has again taken a prominent place in the discussion that took place yesterday and again today. To me it looks like flogging a dead horse. Whether we are satisfied or not, I think nobody who has eyes to sec or ears to hear can have any doubt about the fact that, whether our reasons are adequate or inadequate, those who hold opinions against us are not in a mood to be influenced by any more of reasoning. But I certainly feel aggrieved when some of the honourable members here find fault with us for having kept away from a committee which was designedly formed with a view to exclude us from it. When the Government non-co-operated it cannot possibly accuse us of reciprocity on our part. They wanted us to do so and we carried out their wishes. Not only this that they did not want our assistance but contrary to the convention which prevails in all countries and in all governments in matters of this sort they designedly, and deliberately slighted those people who had espoused the course to which they ultimately acceded by scrupulously excluding everyone of them from having any part or share in the affairs of this committee.

Having pursued this policy it is not open to them to say now that we have been unfair to them or we have been in any way unjust to them if we have just followed their wishes and carried out their designs in having allowed ourselves to be the willing victims of their policy. I have nothing to say about the individual merits of the respected members of that committee. The whole question is one of outlook and view-point. Some of us feel that if some other people who have so far openly expressed a different view about jail affairs had been given a place in that committee, its recommendations would have been more comprehensive and probably more suited to the present tendency displayed all the world over. I do not claim a monopoly of knowledge about jail affairs on this side and I do not claim that we alone know about them and others know nothing, but I do think that it is highly desirable in such cases that people holding different views should combine together if best results are to be attained. Government, however, think otherwise. They believe that they have a monopoly of wisdom and of knowledge in this world and I am not surprised at the display of conceit which is one of their main characteristics. I, however, believe that the very fact that we have kept away from this committee with and must have set the members of the committee a thinking. The question was about the attitude and about the mentality of the members of that committee. The line which we were expected to follow and to support and advocate before them would have been discouraged and disparaged by them if we had appeared before them, but the very fact of our abstention has probably aroused their interest in matters which if we had appeared before them they would have regarded as our special concern. So far as the ultimate result is concerned the course of self-denial which we were constrained to adopt will be more to the benefit of the public at large than our crossing swords with the committee. I, however, wanted to say only one word in this connection and it was this, that the graceful tribute which the Hon'ble the Home Member has paid to Pandit Jagat Narayan will, I hope be remembered by him when he comes to deal with the people who assaulted a number of public men in Lucknow at the time of the visit of the Simon Commission. He probably knows what Pandit Jagat Narayan publicly stated about this matter, and as he has publicly testified to his impartiality, wisdom, public spirit and legal knowledge. I hope he will be guided in his views in the matter and will consider it a sacred duty under the circumstances to take action against those people who were guilty of those assaults. I want to invite the attention of the Hon'ble the Home Member to some of the prominent features of jail administration which he may have noticed already, and which call for very urgent treatment having not received all the attention they deserved so far. One of the most disquieting features of jails today is the progressive increase in the number of inmates in the jails. Though the number of persons sentenced to imprisonment during the last year was a little less than what it was during the year before last the average jail population was the largest during the last ten years since 1919. The question is very important and I think it is necessary for the Government to devise some measures to relieve this pressure in the jails. It is due partly to the detention of long-term prisoners in this country and those who were formerly transported, but other causes which can be easily removed are equally responsible. Even during the last year the number of prisoners who were below 16 was almost double of what it was during the year before last. Even during the last year the number of prisoners who were sentenced to a term of imprisonment below one month was 1,600 roughly, and these sentenced to three months and less was more than 5,000, and those who were sentenced to six months and less were about 5,500. I think the Government should make it a definite rule for the guidance of the judiciary that first offenders should not be subjected to a term of imprisonment of less than six months. It is only when the offence seems to be so reprehensible that it is absolutely necessary to sentence a first offender to a term of imprisonment and when the court thinks that that term should not be less than six months, it is only in those cases, if at all, that first offenders should be sentenced to imprisonment. It is very dangerous to condemn as many as 13,000 persons to terms of imprisonment of below six months as such sentences are likely to demoralize them and to produce a tendency of an undesirable sort which unnecessarily goes on adding to the strength of the jail population and complicates a problem which is already complicated enough. So I suggest that it must be an invariable rule that no first offenders, unless they have committed an offence for which the court considers that they should be sentenced to imprisonment for more than six months, should be condemned to imprisonment. Government has not yet introduced the Borstal system. I think it is high time now to introduce these methods. It would lead to further relief in the jails and the tension will cease which exists today. It is now a recognized system in all countries that offenders who are brought before the courts for the first time should invariably be released on probation or should be treated in accordance with what is known as the Borstal system, which system has already been introduced in several parts of this country. I think Government should resort to these measures for the relief of the jail population, for the sake of economy in the growing expenditure in jails, and for avoiding such a colossal expenditure as 23 lakhs for the proposed Meerut jail. I think, Sir unless these measures are adopted it will be very difficult for the Government to find all the money which is being unnecessarily wasted over measures which are not only of a doubtful but of an undesirable character. I hope the Government will consider it necessary to do things of this sort at least for their own protection and for the relief of their own finances if not out of regard for the humane principles which are at present in force all over the world. The Hon'ble the Home Member must have noticed that as many as 3,000 persons were sentenced to imprisonment during the last year who were of an age below 21. And again I think it is desirable that Government should issue a circular to the judiciary and to the magistrates asking them to refrain from condemning people to imprisonment so far as possible except in very reprehensible cases where the age of the culprit is below 21 years. I am as I said at the outset advocating these measures in the interest of economy at present, apart from other things. And in this connection I would again urge, in case it is permissible to do so, that the gigantic undertaking connected with the construction of the Meerut jail should not be taken up. The Government should at least wait for the recommendations of its own Jails Committee. It must see whether their recommendations will not result in a substantial reduction in the average population of jails in these provinces after those recommendations have been given effect to. If the recommendations of that committee proceed on the lines suggested by me, as is not unlikely, then there won't be as much pressure in jails after these recommendations have been put in force. And in that case a jail in Meerut will not be necessary. It is too much to ask even the credulous members of this Council to believe that an expenditure of Rs. 23 lakhs on the Meerut jail in the present state of our finances is an absolute necessity or is one to which they should submit. Sir, I presume that the Hon'ble the Home Member has seen the statement relating to punishments in the jails in these provinces. I do not want to compare the figures in our own province with those in others; but there are certain very interesting features of the statement to which I want to invite the attention of the Hon'ble the Home Member, as they deserve his consideration. If he has cared to scrutinize these figures he must have noticed that there is a very strange contrast between the methods adopted in the various jails. Let us take for example the Bareily Central Jail. It has almost the largest population in the province—more than 2,000 inmates—and yet not a single person in this jail was flogged during the last year, and not a single person was given the punishment of being located in what is called separate and cellular confinement, and only twelve persons were given the punishment, of hand-cuffing and link-fetters. As against this, in the Lucknow Central Jail there were 696 major punishments of hand-cuffing and link-fetters. Similarly separate and cellular confinement accounted and otherwise shows 55.8. Then, in the Sultanpur District Jail the mortality even in the case of under-trial prisoners is very high, being 47.6. It may be due partly to the fact that the prisoners are placed in the Jail which is meant for tubercular patients. If that be the reason, I think the Government should pass orders for segregating under-trial prisoners from the ordinary jail in Sultanpur so that the mortality may not be as high as it is. Then, Sir, when we go to the average expenditure per head of the jail population we again find a similar disparity. I think it is necessary for the Government to make an inquiry why in certain jails the average expenditure per day is so very high. For example, in certain jails the average net expenditure per prisoner goes to Rs. 331, in some places it goes to Rs.230 while the average is only Rs. 48 for every prisoner. I see on reason why it should be so high as that in some of the jails. In this matter again I think we have so far allowed ourselves to be led away by the general provincial average without looking into the condition of various individual jails. It is necessary that wherever the general average is exceeded in a manner which cannot be rationally accounted for, an inquiry should be made with a view to bring about a reduction in the expenditure incurred in that particular jail. Similarly, in the matter of the income earned by the prisoners in various jails there is a vast amount of disparity. This can be explained in various ways, and perhaps it is, to a certain extent, inevitable. Still I think that if proper steps are taken it should be possible to have a more uniform evenness in the jails than what exists at present.

Sir, I will not try to prolong my observations as this debate has taken very long. But there are certain matters to which I particularly want a reply. I have more than once brought the case of Shatrasudan of Bareilly shooting case to the notice of the Hon'ble the Home Member. He is a young man, one of the young flowers in this country who has been suffering from tuberculosis and from a long-standing lung disease, which he contracted after his incarceration. It would perhaps amount to a reflection on the judiciary if I said anything about his being guilty or not guilty. That perhaps is a question into which we cannot dive and peep. But considering his age, his condition and the miserable plight of his wretched young wife, who has herself contracted tuberculosis since her husband's incarceration because of the misery which she has been suffering on that account, it should be possible even for a cruel and brutal and heartless Government, such as that sitting outside, such as that represented by some of the members on the other side, to cultivate a feeling of commiseration for such persons as Shatrasudan. At the worst he can be said to have been a victim of circumstances: he cannot be called a felon, he cannot be said to be one who by nature belongs to a criminal tribe, but one who, owing to the infatuation of the time was at the worst incited in such a manner that he happened to do something which legally was an offence. Is it too much to expect that a man like him, who has been admitted to have lost his weight considerably and who has again and again been sent to the Sultanpur jail, should be let off and released on such conditions as the Government consider necessary out of regard for his health only? I am not pleading his cause on any political ground. Otherwise I would not have said "on such conditions as the Government think fit." I say that merely on humanitarian grounds he must be released, and I think it is high time that the Government should see that he is set at liberty. Even if the Government is devoid of live human element, the Hon'ble the Home Member must not after all forget that he is an Indian.

The other question to which I wish to invite the attention of the Hon'ble the Home Member is the treatment meted out to the Kaori prisoners. This is again a question which must be considered from a human standpoint. Whether the Kakori prisoners did anything that was wrong or not is, I think a question which hardly admit of any two opinions. There is no person in this House who would go to the length of saying that if a man has committed an offence of the nature which these men are said to have committed, he is innocent. But at the same time nobody can assert that persons who according to the judges themselves had no selfish and personal ends in their pursuits, however undesirable misguided their activities might have been, belong to a plane quite different from that of an ordinary prisoner or culprit. If this is accepted, I think they are entitled to some sort of consideration, and they should be treated in as kind and as humane a manner as possible considering all the circumstances. I have been informed that a number of them have been again and again complaining about the treatment that is being meted out to them. Honourable members must have seen the letters which have appeared in the press form the parents and guardians of some of these young folk, lovable and fine as they are and with whom for a very considerable time I was in close personal touch when the case was under trial. I hope Government will consider their case sympathetically.

Next, I wish to inquire what the existing practice of supplying fans in the jail is. It is one of the subjects for which I have disclosed a particular hobby of mine more than once. I want to know whether any Indians got the fans during the course of the last year, and if so, what their number is? Again, out of the total number of Europeans, how many got the fans and how many did not? Further, what is the proportion of those who got fans to the entire European jail population and what it is to the entire Indian jail population? I also want to know if arrangements have been made enabling an Indian, who has been used to a certain standard of living, to have the same amenities of life as are provided to Europeans. The latter enjoy these even as culprits and offenders, because they happen to hold a dominating position in the country. Of course Alexander was once told that there is hardly a difference between a robber and a king; so perhaps the lesser of these people is entitled to as much of the good treatment as the better ones among them whose traits have turned them into administrators instead of villains.

In future, Sir, I beg to suggest that a statement should be attached to the jail report showing the total number of European population in jail (by European I mean the Anglo-Indians too), and the total expenditure on them. The jail report already analyses the figures regarding Hindus and Muslims, and I see no reason why it should not henceforward give similar information in regard to Europeans also. So I suggest that in future in the jail report there should be a special page allotted to the information I have referred to, so that honourable members can see at a glance what is the expenditure incurred per head on Europeans as against Indians. Only then will it be possible for us to make a comparison.

There is a further point which has been brought before this House more than once and in regard to which I wish to make an inquiry. Has the practice of converting men into bullocks for working the oil mills been discontinued or is it still in force?

Then I wish to inquire of the Hon'ble the Home Member whether the practice of midnight parades, which means that every prisoner should come out of his cell between 11 and 12 and remain standing in the yard for at least half an hour every day, whether that practice is still in force or whether it has been abandoned. I further want to know whether the practice of incessant shrieking and howling throughout the night by the warder saying, for example, "Block No. 2, resident 45, lock and barrel, lantern and bar all right," is still in force or whether it has been discontinued. I have been told by a number of friends that nobody can sleep throughout the night inside the jail because of this continuous howling outside the cell which does not stop even for a single minute.

Sir, I should also like to know from the Hon'ble the Home Member whether he has ever received any report from any jail saying that the allotment for grain in that jail has not been appropriated during any month, and whether there has always been this strange coincidence of the allotment made under the rules being always found sufficient and never a bit less or more than what has been ordered for. I mean that under the rules there is a provision that a prisoner should have, for example, twelve chataks of *ata*, one chatak of *dal*, one-quarter chatak of something, and so on. It is possible that in certain cases the whole thing may not be used and I want to know whether in any case it has been reported that there has been an excess of provision. My suggestion is that in fact there is no legitimate consumption of all the grain that is provided in the jails. But these artificial rules are enforced in such a manner that whatever is left is taken away by somebody. If it were not so, there must have been at least some cases in which reports like this should have been made. I will refer the Hon'ble the Home Member to an interesting case which is quoted by Mr. Dange in his book "Hell Found." The Hon'ble the Home Member may not feel any curiosity in the expression because he might have found the hell for himself inside the machine in which he is working at present. It says: "The Deputy Commissioner, Sitapur, Mr. A.G. Shirreff, on his visit on May 7, 1925, said in his inspection note: "The Inspector-General of Prisons has noted that under-trial prisoners are to have *dal* with their morning diet, as suggested by the non-official member, and so on." The *dal* was issued. Again on January 18, 1926 he said: "Jailor will please explain why the order regarding the issue of *dal* to under-trial prisoners attending the court is not being carried out daily." Further, he said: 'I am not satisfied with jailor's explanation and shifting the responsibility on the two warders.' Then the writer says:

"Every day nearly thirty to forty under-trials attend the court and stay the whole day there on mere dry bread and a few grains of salt, and this state of things existed long before the Deputy Commissioner ordered as quoted above, and continued to exist in flagrant defiance of orders for over eight months without being detected. For all this time where did the share of the undertrials' morning *dal* ration go?" A pertinent question in this connection is where did this *dal* for eight months which was not given to undertrials go, and who made use of it, and if it was somebody other than the prisoners, what action was taken by the Government against the persons who surreptitiously made away with this *dal*? Similarly, I want to know the Government have issued any orders prohibiting the giving off *dal* is out of jail produce to jail superintendents and other officials, whether any orders have been issued that the jail produce should not be shared by jail officials. It leads to many scandals and it gives rise to a lot of trouble in the jails. All that is good and all that is worth taking is taken away by those who are in power in jails for their own use. I might illustrate this—let us take, for example, *mooli*. The *mooli* itself is taken by the sahib and the leaves are given to prisoners. Similarly in the case of matter. The peas must go to the sahib and the rest to the prisoners. So in almost every case only what cannot be used by any decent person is left for the jail prisoners. In this book there is an interesting account of the sort of food that is supplied to the prisoners. Mr. Dange is a very decent man. He has got sufficient information and is a man who has written the book from his experience inside the jail. Here he says: "The food supplied to me as an undertrial was of the worst quality. The breads given to me were pure *ata* and water mixed together, and it would have required a great analytical process to find out the components of the *ata*, so black, so rough so full of grit it was. And the thing that went under the name of '*dal*' would have horrified and taken away the hunger of the hungriest of Oliver Twist's companions in the poorhouse, and I was sure the guardians, who were horrified at Twist's 'asking for more' would never have been faced with that calamity if only they had indented the services of Khan Sahib Amanat-ullah Khan, the jailor of Cawnpore, a century earlier from the dispensing courts of *Allah* and made him their guru. The wastery soup of the morning was followed in the evening by cooked vegetables termed '*zhalara*' in prison phraseology. Pen and decency refuse to describe this edible. Black buckets full of rust, small pices of hard wood and black leaves of I know not how many kinds presented the appearance of being drawn fresh from the city sewers and emitted a smell which, if whiffed in a concentrated form, would have put to flight the strongest German cavalry if only the War Ministry had knowledge of this recipe in war time. Horror possessed me and I began to wonder how hundreds of human beings lived that life without revolting." That is what he said at one place about the diet which is given to an under-trial prisoner and I will not take much time of the Council by reading this paragraph further. At another place he makes pointed observations of the same type as to what happened after he had been admitted to the jail as a prisoner. "I took my bath and prepared myself for what is called 'dinner' in a civilized tongue and '*roti* parade' in jail parlance. When I received my share of '*roti* and *dal*' I was surprised to find the similarity in dirt and bad cooking it bore to the Cawnpore preparation. (I hope the honourable member from Cawnpore would like Cawnpore mentioned specially as he is a member of the Jails Committee.) It seemed as if the bread, the '*dal*' and vegetable for all the prisons was distributed from a central kitchen of a cook-in-chief or was prepared from some common recipe, in the discovery of which all available scientific skill had been employed in making its produce the blackest, dirtiest and most uninviting. The Cawnpore and Sitapur products were as much identical as the same edition of one and the same paper sold in different places can be identical. This wonderful ability of kitchens in different jails to prepare like bread and vegetable without any under-ground, aerial or earthly' communication with each other is superior to that of the electric wave of a wireless which produces identical impressions on all receivers within its range." This is the sort of food which is supplied to prisoners. I will next invite the attention of the Hon'ble the Home Member to the question of riots in the Allahabad and Benares jails. What action did he take in accordance with the recommendations of the courts to the effect that a special inquiry should be held in these cases? Further, I find from the jail reports that a certain person, who had taken a big contract for the supply of grain from the Jails Grains Committee, committed a breach of contract I want to know whether the Jail department recovered any compensation from him? If so, what was the amount and, if not, why did the Government not care to do so? I want further to know who are the members of this Jails Grains Committee. How many times do they meet and what were their activities during the last year?

In the end, I wish to invite the attention of the Hon'ble the Home Member to the existence of a number of practices in jails which do not see, the light of the day and which cause an amount of hardship to the inmates of the jails. I will refer only to two cases which are mentioned in this book of Mr. Dange:

> "On the morning of June 9, 1925, a convict officer, who is as much a paltry animal as a simple convict, was received in the hospital, black and blue all over. He was beaten by a head warder over some tobacco affair. When examined he was found to have the following injuries:—
>
> *True copy*
>
> (1) A patch of bruise $13'' \times 6''$ on the side of back extending below from the shoulder.
>
> (2) Bruise $1\frac{1}{2}'' \times 1\frac{1}{2}''$ over the lower part of left shoulder blade.
>
> (3) Bruise $1\frac{3}{4}'' \times 1\frac{1}{2}''$ upwards and inwards of injury No. 2.
>
> (4) Several other small bruises $\frac{1}{2}'' \times \frac{1}{2}''$, each above

No. 2.

(5) Bruises (two) $1\frac{1}{2}'' \times 1\frac{1}{2}''$, each in the right buttock.

This convict lay in hospital for these injuries from 29-6-'25 to 6-7-'25.

I should like to know if this case ever came to the notice of the Hon'ble the Home Member and whether any action was taken for this extremely cruel manner in which the prisoner was treated.

There is another case here. I will not refer to it at a greater length than is necessary.

"On 29-5-'26 a prisoner, named Hussaina, No......... was hauled up before the jailor at the time of the morning count for not increasing his output of labour. He asked for forgiveness and said he would do it next time. This was not accepted. A convict warder was asked to beat him. Two hundred shoes were counted on him. Then three warders and two convict officers hammered him with sicks. His legs were lifted up and blows of a truncheon were given on the soles of his feet, which disabled him from walking for a week. After this the prisoner was sent to the factory. This took place at about 6 a.m. At 7 a.m. the superintendent came and on his rounds espied the prisoner groaning and crying. He was questioned and he related what had happened.

"The superintendent ordered the convict to hospital. The following note of injuries was taken:

Patch of bruise $5\frac{1}{2}'' \times 5''$ bruise $2\frac{1}{2}'' \times 1\frac{3}{4}''$, bruise $3'' \times 1''$, $3'' \times 1\frac{1}{2}''$, $1'' \times 1''$, and so on........."

This covers a number of pages. He states further that the jailor got up a serious case against the prisoner concerned. All this came out and still the Inspector-General of Prisons, against the recommendation of the superintendent, did not take any action against the jailor as he thought it would be harmful to the discipline of the jail.

The Hon'ble Captain Nawab Sir Muhammad Ahmad Sa'id Khan

Which was the jail?

Pandit Govind Ballabh Pant

The Sitapur jail, I should like to know had or had not the superintendent recommended very strongly that action should be taken against the jailor and whether the Inspector-General did not like the jailor to be punished in any way. I should like to know further whether the Government approves of the policy of a few petty warders being punished in such cases departmentally and of the case not being taken to the court whether the prisoner is liable to be hanged even if he commits an assault inside the jail. Whether he is satisfied that that is the proper way of dealing with such cases which can come to light only on very rare occasions. Departmental action alone should not be considered sufficient and the wrong-doers should be committed for trial to court. In the end I want to sound a note of warning and to tell the Hon'ble the Home Member that from some of the speeches that have been delivered here and from what one occasionally learns outside, there are indications to show that efforts are likely to be made hereafter to add to the cost of the officers who superintend the jails or who are otherwise employed there. While we are prepared to allow money to be spent in dietary, in clothing and in decent arrangements for the benefit of the prisoners, we will very strongly protest, if we cannot do anything more effective, against the application of a single shell towards increasing the pay bill of the jail staff or towards the multiplication of the officers who are in charge of jails. Already the bill is too high and it is being increased from year to year. Even this year there are a number of increases which, if we had persisted in a systematic way, we should have been able to avoid. I hope the Hon'ble the Home Member will bear this in mind that while he may expect serious opposition to any proposal for raising the standard of comfort of prisoners, there will be strong opposition to any sort of increase in the jail staff.[10]

SALARIES AND ALLOWANCES, ETC., OF INDIAN AND BRITISH SOLDIERS IN INDIA[11]

Pandit Govind Ballabh Pant

(a) Will Government be pleased to lay on the table a statement showing the comparative emoluments, including salaries and allowances, etc., of Indian and British soldiers in India?

(b) What is the total number of officers holding King's Commissions in the Indian and British forces in India and how many of them are Indians in active command?

Mr. G.R.F. Tottenham

(a) The pay and allowances of the British private soldier amount at present to about Rs. 850 per annum, while those of the Indian sepoy amount to about Rs. 285. These figures include, besides basic pay, messing, kit and clothing allowances and proficiency and deferred pay.

(b) The total number of officers holding the King's Commission in the Army in India (other than medical and veterinary officers) is 5,773, and the number of Indians on the active list other than Medical is 195.

Pandit Govind Ballabh Pant

Is the cost of maintaining one British soldier equal to that of maintaining three Indian soldiers?

Mr. G.R.F. Tottenham

The Honourable Member's mathematical calculation appears

to be correct.

Pandit Govind Ballabh Pant

Will Government devise measures to replace British soldiers by Indian soldiers?

Mr. G.R.F. Tottenham

That, Sir, is a very large question which I can hardly be expected to answer in reply to a supplementary question in this House. If the Honourable Member wishes to raise the whole question of the number of British soldiers in this country, the procedure of the House is open to him, and I would ask him to bring a Resolution on the subject.

Pandit Govind Ballabh Pant

Is the British army including British soldiers maintained here as a counterpoise to the Indian army consisting of Indian soldiers?

Mr. G.R.F. Tottenham

That, Sir, does not arise out of this question, and it also asks me for an expression of opinion.

Pandit Govind Ballabh Pant

How long will the army of occupation be retained intact in this country?

Mr. G.R.F. Tottenham

I do not quite know what the Honourable Member means by the army of occupation. In any case, I could not give him an answer to that question.

Mr. S. Satyamurti

May I know what are the reasons for a British soldier, who costs three or four times the Indian soldier, being kept here? What are the military, economic, or State reasons as to why Government spend so much money on British soldiers, when they can get four Indian soldiers for every British soldier?

Mr. G.R.F. Tottenham

Those who are at present responsible for the defence of India consider that it is necessary to maintain a certain number of British soldiers in this country. Those are the reasons.

Mr. S. Satyamurti

What are the grounds on which they consider it so necessary?

Mr. President (The Honourable Sir Abdur Rahim)

Next question. The Chair thinks the House had a sufficient number of supplementaries on this.

Pandit Govind Ballabh Pant

Does the defence of India means the defence of Indians in India or the defence of non-Indians in India?

No answer.

ABOLISH SALT DUTY[12]

With your permission, and with the indulgence of Sir Cowasji Jehangir, I have the honour to move this amendment No. 4:

"That for clause 2 of the Bill, the following be substituted:

"2 Despite the provisions of section 7 of the Indian Salt

Act, 1882, the Governor General in Council shall not impose any duty on salt manufactured in, or imported into, any part of British India other than Burma or Aden during the year beginning on the 1st day of April, 1935."

Sir Cowasji Jehangir

I can object to it, if I want to.

Pandit Govind Ballabh Pant

That is why I said, "with your indulgence". The motion that I have made before the House does no more than fulfil the intention of the Mover of the preceding amendment, and we are in perfect agreement. It is no more than a matter of form. I have chosen to achieve the same object in a more legal, and to a certain extent, more effective manner, as, even if the amendment moved by the Honourable Member from Jubbulpore is carried by the House, it would still leave a loophole. I do not say that the Governor General in Council will have recourse to it, but all the same it would be a clumsy method of dealing with the matter. If, in reality, we do not want the salt duty to be imposed, then our purpose should be expressed in an unmistakable manner and we should not leave room for confusion because of the form in which the motion is made. Sir, to me it is a pity that there should be any form of taxation in any country under which an almost negligible amount has to be distributed over millions of people. If one were to speak in America of a tax of this type, even in this age of chaos, the people there would be almost amazed.

The Honourable Sir James Grigg

Planning?

Pandit Govind Ballabh Pant

In a day or two, I will have my turn to speak about planning, and I hope that my Honourable friend will appreciate if

I do not digress now. On the question before us, I feel that this salt tax is associated with the inconceivable poverty of our people, and that is exactly the reason why we are objecting to the existence or continuation of this tax. If we were a rich people, no Government would have imposed a tax which, according to them, amounts to an incidence of less than four annas per head over 280 millions of people. If, on the other hand, we had been rich, we would not have minded a tax which in effect did not entail a burden higher than three annas ten pies as we were just told by Mr. Lloyd. Sir, it is only a commentary on the economic destitution to which this country has been reduced. About three or four years ago, I was travelling by train, and I met a party of enlightened Americans who had been touring round this country in cities and who had also taken the trouble of visiting a number of villages. I asked them as to what in this country had struck them particularly, as to what it was that they had found remarkable no notable. Unanimously they all told me that what had struck them was the colossal, the inconceivable and the unimaginable poverty of the people in this country. They said that they could not possibly conceive or imagine how any biped on earth could drift in the manner in which men and women had been managing to breathe and to move in this vast land. Sir, that is the background on which this picture has been painted, and that is the background which you have to place before yourself in order to judge as to the nature of the burden and the incidence of the salt tax. In other advanced countries, as I submitted, it would be unusual for people to object to a tax of this sort, but unfortunately, situated as we are we have to face the deplorable situation in our own country. Does not even the Honourable the Finance Member accept that the tax does bear heavily on the people? If not, may I know why he favours the withdrawal of the import duty on the salt that we import from abroad? That is much less than this. It amounts only to two annas six pies per maund. He thinks that he will be giving distinct relief to the people of Bengal, Bihar and other places by withdrawing the import duty. Sir, whatever be our differences in other matters, I think the Honourable the Finance Member will agree that Rs. 1-9-0 is certainly bigger than two annas six pies. There perhaps he will concede this point. So, Sir, when even a withdrawal of two annas six pies per maund can afford appreciable relief, undoubtedly the reduction of Rs. 1-9-0 must go much further than two annas six pies. Sir, it is not absolutely correct to say that this tax presses equally and evenly on the rich and the poor. In fact, Sir, the tax presses with much greater weight on the poor than on the rich, and, in fact, the poor consume a larger quantity of salt than the rich if they can afford to do so.

Sir, salt is one of the indispensable, essential ingredients of human life, but the rich men can manage to get their quota of salt out of fruits, out of vegetables, out of several other things which have the chemical ingredient of salt, but, so far as the poor are concerned, they have no other alternative, they have no other option (Hear, hear), and they can use nothing except natural salt in order to get the minimum of chemical salt needed to preserve and maintain their existence So, Sir, in fact, the poor, if they can afford, consume a larger quantity of salt than the rich, and consequently, the salt tax is borne to a greater extent per capita by the poor than by the rich.

Sir, in the opinion of experts, who have made an inquiry into the matter, the salt tax is an oppressive tax in this country, and the salt tax, in fact, from the days of Fawcett has always been regarded as an undesirable type of tax. I think the Honourable the Finance Member remembers Fawcett's dictum that water and air and salt should be free. (Hear, hear.) He laid it down that no man should have to pay anything for fresh air or for fresh water or for his salt. So, it is one of those bounties that Nature has provided for every individual, and which it is a crime against God and man to keep away from any individual. In the circumstances, salt must be treated as a commodity which must be provided by the State to every individual, and, in respect of which, the State should not at least embarrass anybody who stands in need of it. Sir it has been proved again and again that the reduction of the salt tax serves a as stimulus to greater consumption. I ask Mr. Lloyd if he does not accept that proposition; and if he does not, I can remind him of a statement that he himself made some time back. Sir, Mr. Lloyd said, what he does not seem to remember now, on the 17th March, 1925:

> "When the salt duty was Rs. 2-8-0 a maund in 1902-03, the average consumption of salt per head of the population was five seers. When it was at rupee one a maund ten years later, the average consumption was only six seers per head of the population. Some increase in consumption must be allowed for."

I hope he will revise the statement that he made in the course of his speech, and, he will concede that he was labouring under a mistake when he made certain remarks which do not tally with the statement relating to facts—not to matters of opinion—which he himself had made previously. I wish the Honourable Members of Government had a tenacious memory. Sir, we on this side may easily and even without reason be taunted and twitted with short memories, but they are expected to guide us at least in matters of fact, and we are, I think, entitled to refer to them for facts, and to a certain extent, they are entitled to ask us to accept their facts, but if there are lapses of this type on the Treasury Benches, then, naturally, their statements about facts lose the weight and value to which they would be otherwise entitled.

Sir, I have got a statement before me of the salt duty for a series of years from 1899 to 1925, and another for still later years, and both lead to the same conclusion. These figures of the gross revenue, expenditure, net revenue and consumption, are interesting as affording evidence of the influence of a lower rate of duty in stimulating consumption and consequently adding to the total revenue, and so on. Sir, the same conclusion is borne out by other facts. The consumption of salt per head in England amounts to forty pounds, while in our country, it comes to only ten pounds. Obviously our people are not getting as much salt as they need. I concede that in England this figure goes up also, because, perhaps, it includes salt used for other purposes, but we could as well make use of salt for our cattle, for industrial development, for manure and for many other profitable objects. We are not able to do so......

Mr. A.H. Lloyd

May I say, Sir, that much salt is issued for these purposes from the Government factories. I have left all such figures out of account in the figures I gave.

Pandit Govind Ballabh Pant

I am not unaware of that fact, but the concession is illusory. It is fantastic to expect the poor villager in the remote corner of this country to send a direct order to the Salt Department or to the Central Revenue Department for a duty-free consignment of salt. How does he benefit by this rule on paper? It is utterly ineffective and futile. Sir, every single tola that is used pays the duty so far as the really poor classes are concerned, on whose behalf I am making this proposal on the floor of this House. Then, there are other ways of arriving at the same conclusion. There is a higher allowance for salt per head in the army, and there is a higher allowance per head in jails than the average consumption per capita in the country. What is the result of that comparison? The figure that we reach is higher in the case of jails and much higher in the case of the army. What does it show? Does it not show conclusively that the amount of salt that the average consumer can manage to secure for his urgent necessities falls far short of what his system needs; and, then, I am reminded of another fact which may not be within the knowledge of many Members here. We in jails, Sir, had our usual allotment of salt, and this, as I have told the Members of the House, is much higher than what the average Indian consumes, but even that was not enough, and we used to spend some annas every month out of our own pocket in order to obtain for ourselves the necessary quantity of salt; and, Sir, salt is really regarded as a boon inside the jails. Ordinary prisoners always feel the want of salt. All these circumstances go to establish that, on account of this duty, people are unable to enjoy, to utilise one of the most primary necessities of life. In these circumstances, the salt tax is certainly uneconomic, the tax is certainly un-social and this duty is oppressive.

Sir, the Taxation Enquiry Committee report shows that at least one of the Members, Dr. Paranjype, was of opinion that in normal years the duty on salt should not exceed eight annas pe maund: And there is another important feature of the present situation which has also to be taken into account. During the last five years, the prices of agricultural products have gone down almost by 50 per cent. The crops that were sold for five rupees are now yielding no more ordinarily than two rupees; while everything else has fallen in value, the only oasis in the desert is this salt which retains its old index and which continues to be as costly as it was when agricultural products were fetching double their present prices. There is only one island above water, viz., the safe island of the salaries of the Government servants, and only one oasis, that of salt, in the desert in which everything else has been reduced to sand. Sir whatever might have been the case in normal years, is it not strange, is it not queer that salt, for which Government hold the monopoly, should be doubly as costly at present as it was five years back? Salt even now sells ordinarily at the rate of ten or eleven seers per rupee. The average villager could get ten or eleven seers of salt formerly by parting with five seers of wheat, but today he has to part with about 14 seers of wheat in order to get 10 or 11 seers of salt. It shows how callously the Government have been moving in this matter. No other Government dare retain the original rates in the face of the slump in respect of everything else. After all, the prices generally have to be co-related to the prices of other articles, especially to the prices of staples in the country. So when the price of everything else produced in this land has fallen, that salt should still continue to be as dear as it was five years back, especially when it is a monopoly of the Government, is indefensible. The salt tax is no less than a poil tax, and a poll tax which has to be paid inversely in a higher amount as the income of a man declines, the smaller the income, the higher being the poll tax, and the larger the income, the smaller the poll tax. We were told by Mr. Lloyd that the proportion of direct taxes in this country has increased considerably. I do not know where he formed that impression. He must remember that in England, since 1916, the increase in direct taxes has been about 700 per cent., while the increase in the indirect taxes does not exceed one hundred per cent. In our own country, if you remember, up to 1916, the income from customs was almost nil. We had only the revenue tariff between five to ten per cent, at the most; but, during the last ten years, the direct taxes have increased by a much smaller amount, while the indirect taxes have gone up enormously, with the result that today indirect taxes yield a proportion of about 77 per cent to the revenues of the Government of India. In England, the indirect taxes do not go beyond 40 per cent. In other countries, they are equally low. So, in these circumstances, Mr. Lloyd was perhaps a bit careless when he made that remark, and I submit that it is high time that we revised our Schedule and Scheme of Taxation. I believe in this matter I have the sympathies of the Honourable the Finance Member.

An Honourable Member

Revise which Schedule and how?

Pandit Govind Ballabh Pant

Revise the Schedule so as to reduce the incidence of indirect taxes, and, to make a beginning, by repealing the salt duty today. The question was put, and not altogether an irrelevant question, that if you want to take away this duty, how is this gap to be filled? I could have met that question with the answer which Mr. Asquith gave to the Prime Minister at that time, "it is no business of mine". But I will oblige the Honourable the Finance Member in spite of our "Bacchanalian abandon", a pharse for which he will be remembered in this House as immortally and for ever, as another Member for his "congenital idiocy", and both of whom have made abiding countributions to the grace and dignity of this House. I, on my part, happen to be a teetotaller and also a vegetarian, and I never worshipped at the temple of Bacchus and never drunk from the fountain. Similarly, I have never gone to Billingsgate market to purchase any fish. So I have the advantage of being a teetotaller and a vegetarian, but here in his House we have the unique opportunity of learning many things from the Benches opposite in which they are experts, about which we ourselves are utterly ignorant. So I am prepared to learn these words, these expressions, these beautiful epithets from the Benches opposite. I had said, Sir, that I am prepared to offer certain suggestions as to how the gap could be filled. May be, I made these suggestions in a mood of "licentious abandon", I will not use the other adjective. I had said then that the Honourable the Finance Member will, I believe, be able to earn a greater surplus than he has budgeted for, and I have given my reasons for that. The Honourable the Finance Member has a very facile way of dealing with things, I will not call him flippant, I will not use the words "flip-flap", he has a fine method of conveniently overlooking hard facts, and if one cannot deal with one's adversary in argument, then either put on the look of anger or try to ridicule him. That is really a useful method by virtue of which one can manage to tide over really difficult positions. After all, he thinks, in a House where argument is the main principle which should guide and determine decisions what does it matter if occasionally one deviates a little from truth? I will not press this further, as, I expect, I will have another opportunity for general observations during the third reading of the Bill.

The Honourable the Finance Member then said that my suggestions, which he analysed in his won inimitable way, were either hollow or perverse or unfounded. Sir, I had suggested that I expected a larger amount of surplus than he has provided for. I have the support of the European Group and of all the commercial bodies, and though the Finance Member has his own ineffable charm in spite of his other frailties, I will not be sorry if I have to be in this larger company than in the unique company of the solitary eminence of the great Finance

Member.

As to the other point, I had said that we are entitled to count upon the railway contribution of 5 crores 20 lakhs which had been fixed in 1924. That is a fixed contribution, and it is the first charge on the income of the railways. Sir, even in the Railway Budget of the current year, the amount has been calculated, and it has been put down here as:

"Net payment due from railways to general revenue in 1935-36, Rs. 5,20, 58,498."

A sum which is given in such detail is not altogether fabulous: it has internal evidence of being a genuine figure. Then, Sir, the description given here, "Net payment due from railways to general revenue in 1935-36", clearly shows that the railways have definitely made themselves liable for this payment of 5 crores and 20 lakhs. I may remind the House of what the Honourable Sir Charles Innes said when he placed before this House his proposal for the separation of railway from general finance. I will read only one sentence though there are many which would be perfectly relevant. He said:

> "The next point I wish to bring out is that the House has got to remember that we have to pay this one per cent on all our capital at charge on commercial lines. I have just referred to the fact that it takes some years before we get a return upon new capital, specially new capital sunk in new lines. Further, we undertake to pay the dividend year by year, and we take the risk of the season. When the season is good and trade is good, our earnings go up; when the season is bad and trade is bad, our earnings go down. But whatever the state of the season, whatever the state of trade, we undertake to pay this dividend year by year."

And the main reason for the separation of accounts in the very first clause of the Preamble ran thus:

"This Assembly recommends to the Governor General in

Council that, in order to relieve the general budget from the violent fluctuations caused by the incorporation therein of the railway estimates...the railway finances shall be separated... and the general revenue shall receive a definite annual contribution."

There are other clauses too which are equally clear, but it is not necessary to read them. In fact, it is admitted that the railways are liable to the tune of 5 crores and 20 lakhs for the current year. The railways have not gone bankrupt; we have not treated the railways yet as a dead weight and lost asset. They may be part of a lost dominion some time later, but, so far, the railways continue to be a perfectly valuable and solid asset. And that is further proved by the fact that we have got a constructive programme, and we are spending several millions each year for these railways. In these circumstances, I want to know what can be the justification for not taking this income of 6 crores and 20 lakhs into account. We, on our part so far as the general budget is concerned, are required to pay interest even on the railway depreciation fund; but, on the other hand, I find that the railways are not charged with this revenue which is certainly due from them under the contract between the Railway Department, and this House. So, I submit that we are entitled to take these 5 crores and 20 lakhs into account. It may be that the railways are not in a position to pay them in cash today. Even about that, I think, they can, for we have taken away some 30 crores in the form of interest. Part of the interest could stand over and the revenue could be paid. The fact remains that the railways have a potential liability of 5 crores and 20 lakhs, and that liability is genuine, real, substantial, incontrovertible and conclusive. In the circumstances, what reason can there be for the Honourable the Finance Member disregarding it and for treating a suggestion to take it into account as a hopeless illustration of "diseased abandon"?

Sir, there was another suggestion that I made, and it was this that the restrictions in the matter of deposits in savings or postal banks should be removed. The Honourable the

Finance Member either misunderstood me or,—I would not say he misrepresented me even if he did. He said I had suggested that the rates of interest on savings banks should be raised. I never said anything like that. My suggestion is a very simple one, and it is this that the savings banks get money from the public and Government have reduced the interest very low. Government may still reduce the interest, and in some cases, cut it out completely,—I do not worry about it. But at present the maximum limit of the deposits does not go beyond Rs. 750 or something like that. Similarly, withdrawals cannot be made except after certain intervals. I want Government to leave it free to the public to make such deposits as they choose, and to give them the facility of withdrawing money from the postal bank freely or oftener than they can at present. In such manner, I think the current rupee floating debt could be almost reduced to an evanescent degree, and there can be a material saving. I do not see what difficulty Government find in it. But that is not my quarrel. I am here as an ordinary layman; the Honourable the Finance Member, in spite of his distrust, if not disgust, of economists, is an expert. And if he does not accept a suggestion, it is open to him not to do so. But to misrepresent that suggestion and then to treat it with flippant frivolity is not just to us here. He is entitled to take decisions, and that is why he is there. But we are similarly bound to make our suggestions and why should he not treat them in a fair and reasonable spirit? Why should he come forward and make a political speech which may suit the Honourable the Home Member in spite of his age (Laughter), but which so far as he is concernd, and holding the office that he does, is altogether unbecoming of him? So I submit, Sir, that that suggestion of mine was worthy of acceptance.

Then, Sir, another suggestion I made was this. Money is cheap, and you have to pay many debts at high rates of interest Money is also lying idle. You could raise new loans, pay away old debts and make a great saving even thereby. So there are many ways and many methods of tackling the finances. Sir, I may be wrong. I do not claim to be infallible, and after all, I do not claim the expert knowledge which the Honourable the Finance Member possesses and is expected to possess, and which, if he did not possess, would give cause for pity. But, for all that, why should he treat our suggestion in a spirit of levity and almost of malicious animosity? Sir, I am using only expressions which he introduced on the floor of the House. Formerly, I used to think that "malicious" was an unparliamentary expression, because it carried with it an implication that a man had intentionally done what is wrong and sinister. But he thinks it is parliamentary, and I am prepared to accept it so far as he is concerned.

Sir, then, there were other suggestions which I made. Though he did dot discard them altogether, he said that others on this side might not agree with the suggestion that I had made as to higher taxes on higher incomes and on unearned incomes. As to that, I can assure him, in case this assurance can be of any help to him, that the Congress in its Karachi Resolution has accepted in clear terms the policy that I advocated. He can very well say that the Congress does not represent the people except when it is leading them on to the goal of Communism: but, for the time being, if he can make use of this proposal, it is at his disposal. I do not want to say more about it. So from whatever point of view you may look at it, I am inclined to hold from the materials at my disposal and from the little light that I can afford to apply to these questions, that the Government can make a reduction in taxation to the tune of Rs. 10 crores this year. It may look a very big figure: it does, on the face of it, look like that; but if you remember that the amount due from railways alone on account of fixed contribution comes to Rs. 520 lakhs, and when you take into account the other suggestions that I have made, I believe there is reasonable ground for the support of the conclusions I have tried to place before this House in a clear and unmistakable manner:

I will not take more time. The House cannot do better than make a beginning with the abolition of the salt duty. The poorest of the poor must have the benefit of the first occasion which we can have, for giving relief to the taxpayer. Honourable Members opposite may not worry about these things, as their cut in pay has already been restored, and they need not bother about other things. But we here, even if we cannot succeed in making economics and in making retrenchments, should certainly press the Government for making a propei use of the surpluses that are and can be made available and force their hands, in order that, those who are suffering, those who are groaning under the weight, those whose life is nothing except a wretched and miserable existence, may have at least a little sigh of relief at some moments in the day and some time in the night in the dark comers of their ill-lit sheds and huts in inaccessible villages.[13]

RELIEF TO INDIANS IN ZANZIBAR[14]

Pandit Govind Ballabh Pant:

(a) What steps have Government taken to secure relief for the unfortunate Indians settled in Zanzibar?

(b) Will Government place on the table a statement showing the action taken by the Government of Zanzibar in accordance with their assurance for the relief of individual cases?

Sir Girja Shankar Bajpai:

(a) Representations regarding the Land Alienation Decree and the connected problem of existing debts owed to Indians have been made. Further representations on the subject of the cloves legislation will, it is hoped, be made shortly.

(b) Government have made enquiries.

Pandit Govind Ballabh Pant

Have the Government of India drawn the attention of

Zanzibar Government to cases of individual hardship?

Sir Girja Shankar Bajpai

What we have done is to ask His Majesty's Government to implement the undertaking to redress individual cases of hardship. When Mr. Tyab Ali was here we also investigated the matter in consultation with him. We have asked for certain further particulars from Zanzibar, on receipt of which we shall address His Majesty's Government again.

Pandit Govind Ballabh Pant

Has any reply been received to that representation?

Sir Girja Shankar Bajpai

I understand that His Majesty's Government have addressed the Resident in Zanzibar.

Pandit Govind Ballabh Pant

His Majesty's Government have not yet communicated any reply to this Government?

Sir Girja Shankar Bajpai

As regards individual hardship they have not yet communicated anything to the Government of India.

EXTENSION OF THE MORATORIUM AND AMENDMENT OF THE LAND ACQUISITION DECREE IN ZANZIBAR

Pandit Govind Ballabh Pant

(a) Is there any substance in the report that the Zanzibar Government intend extending the moratorium till July next?

(b) Have Government impressed upon the Government of Zanzibar the desirability of adopting the recommendations of the Indebtedness Commission?

(c) Have Government of Zanzibar amended the Land Alienation Decree, as was promised by them, so as to remove its features of invidious racial discrimination at least in form?

Sir Girja Shankar Bajpai

(a) The operation of section 19 of the Alienation of Land (Restriction and Evidence) Decree has been extended till the 1st July, 1936, by Decree No. 10 of 1935.

(b) and (c). I would refer the Honourable Member to the first part of my answer to part (a) of his question No. 850.

Pandit Govind Ballabh Pant

Is it a fact that the extension of the moratorium is resented by the Indians in Zanzibar and that it has been the cause of considerable hardship and loss to them?

Sir Girja Shankar Bajpai

So far as the question of hardship is concerned, I think it is indisputable that the fact that Indians have not been able to realise their dues must have inflicted a certain amount of hardship. But I discussed this matter with the deputation which came to wait on us in December last. They said not that they generally were reconciled to the moratorium, but that they would be quite glad if the question of indebtedness were settled before the expiration of the extension to which I have refered.

Pandit Govind Ballabh Pant

Did the Chief Justice of Zanzibar preside over this Indebtedness Commission and did it include one of the African residents of Zanzibar?

Sir Girja Shankar Bajpai

The Commission, as far as I remember, consisted of the Chief Justice of Zanzibar as President, an Indian member, an Arab member and an administrative officer.

Pandit Govind Ballabh Pant

Was their report unanimous?

Sir Girja Shankar Bajpai

The report was unanimous, but there were certain additional recommendations not published with the report which were not unanimous.

Pandit Govind Ballabh Pant

Did the Commission unanimously arrive at the finding that the imputations that had been made against Indians regarding sharp practices were altogether unfounded?

Sir Girja Shankar Bajpai

My recollection of the report is that the Commission did not go so much into the question of the allegation of sharp practices as the allegation that Indians had acquired a disproportionate area of land in Zanzibar and a very large number of clove trees. It is perfectly true that the Commission's conclusion was that this allegation was not justified.[15]

POSITION OF INDIAN NATIONALS SETTLED IN ZANZIBAR

Pandit Govind Ballabh Pant

(a) What action have Government taken in pursuance of the Resolution adopted by this House in September last, urging the Government to take effective steps in the interest and in order to vindicate the position of Indian nationals settled in Zanz ibar?

(b) Will Government be pleased to lay on the table the correspondence which they had with the Government of Zanzibar in this connection?

Sir Girja Shankar Bajpai

(a) The attention of the Honourable Member is invited to the reply given by me on the 5th February, 1936, to part (c) of Mr. Satyamurti's question No. 61. Since then further representations have been made to His Majesty's Government.

(b) Government regret that they are unable to lay a copy of the correspondence on the table of the House.

Pandit Govind Ballabh Pant

Have the Government of Zanzibar, out of deference to the representations made by the Government of India, repealed or amended any of their decrees?

Sir Girja Shankar Bajpai

No, Sir. Not so far.

Pandit Govind Ballabh Pant

Have they extended the period of moratorium since the last Resolution was adopted in the Assembly?

Sir Girja Shankar Bajpai

My Honourable friend has got a question on that point later on. But I can answer it now. Yes, the moratorium has been extended till the end of June, 1936.

Pandit Govind Ballahh Pant

In what respect have the Government of India succeeded in securing relief for Indians settled in Zanzibar by means of these representations?

Sir Girja Shankar Bajpai

So far as the clove industry is concerned, I have already explained the position to my Honourable friend. As regards the debt legislation, the Government of India's representation has only recently been made.[1]

The civilisation of India started in the Sindhu basin and it has its roots in that region. India's cultural centre for centuries before the Christian era, before even Gautama Buddha was born, was situated in that land of the Vedas and there also flourished the celebrated university with more than 10,000 scholars at Taxila in N.W.F.P., near Peshawar then known as Pushpapur.

State is a social organization designed for the benefit of all citizens residing within its boundaries. If territory is its body the individual is its soul. Equality, freedom and justice are the pillars of every democratic State. The individual citizen is the cardinal centre and measuring rod of democracy. The central purpose towards which every polity should function is the welfare and happiness of the people and the constitution must be designed so as to ensure equal opportunity for every individual in the state for full development and self-fulfilment. Self-government can possess little substance unless the dignity of man as man regardless of all other adventitious appendages, is unequivocally accepted. The individual forms the base as well as the summit of the social pyramid. All human endeavour is ultimately directed towards the improvement and sublimation of the individual. The supreme object of life is to live and of living to attain more life—more in quality and quantity. That is the central purpose of all states.[17]

To minimise the natural and essential majesty of a single individual is an outrage on democracy. Democracy demands justice and fairplay for every single constituent. Every good citizen must learn to love his neighbour as himself and in any case not do unto others what he would not like done to himself. More life for one's own self as for one's neighbour should be the doctrine of democracy. Every impediment retarding the way of good fellowship must be removed and its evil influence mitigated so that no individual may suffer in his development. It has to be recognised that an individual citizen is always in a minority—in fact in the smallest minority of one. Progressive co-operation should be the creed of enlightened humanity. Man is not mere animal like the rest. The object of life is not merely more food and yet more of it; but food is only a means, howsoever essential it may be for securing the real purposes of life[18]

Hindus and Muslims and inter-woven throughout the texture of India from one end to the other. It is not easy to distinguish the two strains in the warp and woof of this magnificent fabric except here and there. If all these threads were marked white and green respectively, their preponderance would vary in different parts, but there would still not be a single inch where both did not co-exist. Any attempt to separate them would be catastrophic, as it could not but result in the annihilation of both. Even if these were not completely detached, but were only subjected to undue strain, the result would be equally lamentable. Concord and goodwill between Hindus and Muslims would be equally essential even if India had not been able to maintain its political unity fully and completely.[19]

In India there is, no doubt, a rich multiplicity of physical types, but there is neither antagonism between different sections nor any particularly close affinity inside the same racial group. Religions transcend and act through all racial boundaries, with the result that both Hindu and Muslim communities are multi-racial in composition. A characteristic uniformity runs through them all, although there is a rich variety within each. The Muslims of India represent as many races as do the Hindus of India.

The hideous outbursts of communal frenzy are the result in a large measure of the deterioration that has taken place in the general communal atmosphere which has been vitiated by thoughtless propaganda. This evil seed cannot thrives unless it finds a congenial soil. But once it is let loose like the mischievous weeds it ousts everything else and is carried to every nook and corner by the evil media. It is essential to recognise the unalterable inter-dependency of the two communities so that there may be genuine and honest concerted endeavour to retrieve the lost ground and to restore the normal relations.[20]

Derived from Brahmi, the Devanagari script has some inherent beauties of structure and form. Phonetically it is scientific for it writes almost as it sounds. In its simple variants many of the existing Indian scripts such as Gujarati, Marathi, Bengali, etc., conform to the same form and arrangement. In this script are contained the treasures of our art, literature and ancient civilization. It has its defects too. In the matter of speed in writing Nagari lags behind when compared with some others. The defects are not, however, irremediable. Experts are in agreement about reforms and are alive to these deficiencies and to the need of removing them so that the utility of the language is increased and its potency and powers of growth and expansion enhanced.[21]

References

1. Debates, U.P. Legislative Council, 28 February 1925.
2. *Ibid.*
3. Debates, U.P. Legislative Council, 4 March 1925.
4. *Ibid.*
5. Debates, U.P. Legislative Council, 2 December 1925.
6. *Ibid.*
7. Debates, U.P. Legislative Council, 28 January 1927.

8. *Ibid.*
9. Debates, U.P. Legislative Council, 5 March 1929.
10. *Ibid.*
11. *Ibid.*, 20th February 1935.
12. *Ibid.*, 1 April 1935.
13. *Ibid.*
14. *Ibid.*, 26 February 1936.
15. *Ibid.*
16. *Ibid.*
17. Convocation Address at the Allahabad University, 21 December 1946.
18. *Ibid.*
19. *Ibid.*
20. *Ibid.*
21. Speech at Lucknow, 28 November 1953.

4

Congress Leadership

Govind Ballabh Pant became an active member of the Indian National Congress at a fairly young age and after meeting Mahatma Gandhi, he became his ardent follower. He soon gained the political leadership in U.P. and organised the cadre of the Congress party in a disciplined way. Very often he toured many areas of his province and through his speeches and personal contacts he impressed upon the masses about the efficacy of Gandhian ideology. As he was a very fine orator and spoke the language of a common man, men and women from all walks of life flocked to him and listened to his socio-political view with rapt attention.

He had deep connections with Anand Bhawan, the residence of the Nehru family at Allahabad. Pandit Motilal Nehru liked him on account of his oratory and disciplined life. Pandit Jawaharlal Nehru always considered him as a respectable 'soldier' of Indian freedom movement. Indeed his popularily in U.P. and elsewhere was on account of his unchallenged and deep sincerity in any kind of work assigned to him.

When Simon Commission landed in India, there was resentment and anger all over India. All the political parties joined together to accord a black-flag reception to the members of the Commission. In U.P., Pant organised the people of U.P.

against the Commission. He indeed felt agitated at the appointment of the all-white Commission. He gave vent to his feelings in his speeches at Aligarh and elsewhere and criticised the arrival of Commission in our country. The anti-Raj stance was systematically propagated in all areas of U.P., with the support of Nehru and other leaders. He opined thus:

"To us it has proved a veritable blessing. The depth of feeling roused by the white Commission has revealed a hopeful unanimity among Indians regardless of differences of caste, creed and politics.........The Government have by their calculated insult to national dignity facilitated that task of congressmen and revivified to a certain extent the national movement." Pant made a forceful appeal to the countrymen for the total boycott of the Commission. As President of the Uttar Pradesh Congress Committee he made extensive tours of the province exhorting his audiences to observe complete *hartal* on February 3, 1928, the day the Commission was to land in India. He said that the more idea of one nation judging the fitness of the other was abhorrent. Swaraj is not given but it is always won. No nation could rest content without Swaraj. Swaraj is our birth right without which there is no self-respect or honour. The appointment of the Commission was a clear defiance of the Indian public opinion. Pant made it clear that the country would not tolerate this all-white Commission. He said, "history has repeatedly proved that there is a limit to the capacity for forbearance even of fallen and oppressed people, and when tyrants become too bold and aggressive their victims shake off their leathargy and raise their heads against their oppressors". In this regard he also made the policy of the Congress clear by saying, "so for as the Congressmen are concerned it has caused them neither surprise nor disappointment. The Congress stands for self-determination and refuses to recognise the right of any alien agency to frame a Constitution for India. The Congress claims that it is the inherent right of every nation to frame its own constitution."

On 30 October 1928, the Simon Commission arrived at

Lahore and Lala Lajpat Rai led a huge peaceful demonstration near the Lahore Railway Station. It was severely *lathi* charged and several satyagrahis including Lajpat Rai were injured. Lajpat Rai received *lathi* blows on his chest. This news spread like wild fire not only in the Punjab but in all the regions of India. Prominent leaders of all the parties sent telegrams of sympathy to Lajpat Rai. There was a wave of resentment and anger everywhere.

The Simon Commission was to visit Lucknow on 30th November, 1928. Elaborate preparations for its boycott were made by the local Congress Committee. Huge processions, demonstrations and public meetings were organised much in advance as the part of a rehearsal for the November 30 boycott. Jawaharlal Nehru and Govind Ballabh Pant were at Lucknow. As a precautionary measure the Government prohibited processions and demonstrations. Nehru and Pant decided to take out a procession on the evening of November 29th. Both of them led batches of 16 volunteers each when the mounted police broke up their columns. Many a volunteers including Nehru and Pant received injuries. They were pursued and beaten. But afterwards the officials allowed them to go by their original route under the escort of mounted policemen. Describing it Nehru wrote, "innumerable little processions came from various parts of the city and from the Congress office started the main procession, consisting of several thousands marching in fours.[12] Pant alongwith Nehru was in the main procession. They were stopped near the railway station and immediately the mounted police galloped towards them. Describing the incident Nehru wrote, "we held our ground, and as we appeared to be unyielding, the horses had to pull up at the last moment and reared up on their hind legs with their front hoofs quivering in the air over our heads. And then began a beating of us, and battering with *lathis* and long batons both by the mounted and the foot police. Pant suffered the most and sustained severe injuries. Nehru wrote about him, "many of our companions were less fortunate, and were badly injured, Govind Ballabh Pant, who stood by me, offered a much bigger target being six foot odd in height, and the injuries he received then have resulted in a painful and persistent malady which prevented him for a long time from straightening his back or leading an active life. Pant suffered serious injuries and the only impact of it was to encourage people into Civil Disobedience when the movement begain. The *Leader* wrote, "the purpose of the boycott demonstrations had been more than achieved and the victors are those who carry the marks of police batons on their bodies."

After the Lahore Congress presided over by Jawaharlal Nehru, a new political programme for complete independence of India was placed before the nation. It was decided that Mahatma Gandhi was to initiate discussion with the Viceroy and in case of a failure of dialogue with him, he was to launch the Civil Disobedience Movement which was to be at all-India level. After getting unsatisfactory response from Irwin, the Dandi March led by Gandhi along with seventy-eight satyagrahis was commenced from the Sabarmati Ashram to the Dandi village, on the west coast of India. The Salt Law was broken by manufacturing salt at Dandi, and soon after, at numerous other places in India. As a result thereof several prominent leaders and satyagrahis were put behind the bars.

Govind Ballabh Pant established a Satyagraha Ashram at Krishnapur, in Nainital. He himself led a batch of five satyagrahis on 2 May 1930. He was asserted along with these satyagrahis, but soon after they were let off. Pant continued his peaceful and non-violent satyagraha by asking people to observe *hartal* and also undertake bonfire of foreign cloth every day. People were enlightened about Swaraj and thus a new spirit of Indian nationalism was generated among them. They *en masse* gathered under the leadership of Nehru and Pant and showed their willingness to offer any sacrifice for the sake of the country.

On May 25th, 1930 Pant decided to make salt. He was arrested the following day and was sentenced to six months rigorous imprisonment for defying the Salt Laws. He was sent to Dehra Dun Jail and after some time he was shifted to Bareilly. Before his arrest Pant gave explicit instructions to the volunteers to keep the candle of non-violent resistance burning, "enlistment of volunteers should be carried on incessantly.........Salt should be manufactured at Nainital and at other places.........Volunteers should not yield the salt made by them if attempt is made to snatch it......They must remain non-violent under gravest provocation......A batch of five volunteers with national flags will start at 6 A.M. from the Satyagrah camp singing national songs such as 'Bande Matram' and 'Jhanda Uncha Rahe Hamara' and raising non-violent shouts of 'Bande Matram', 'Mahatma Gandhiji Ki Jai' and 'Swantantra Bharat Ki Jai'.

Pant was released from Jail in November 1930 and he reached Haldwani on the 22nd. He was given a rousing reception by the Congress workers and his admirers. He visited Almora in September 1931, where arrangements for taking him out in a procession and giving him a welcome address were made. Pant categorically announced, "Swarajya cannot be stopped now. I know that Britishers have enough arms but when they could not control the thirty lacs of Irish people so close to them how would they be able to control thirty crores of people at a distance of seven thousand miles away. 'We want Swaraj'."

Meanwhile U.P. had to face the serious agrarian problem which became a glaring phenomenon in 1930-31. The lead in this regard was taken by Nehru, Pant, Rafi Ahmad Kidwai and several other leaders and satyagrahis. The protest at various levels was made in several villages and the poor peasants had to face severe repression by the Raj. The bore all this as they were assured that under Swaraj, their economic condition would be far better than it was under the Raj.

"The Indian peasant has an amazing capacity to bear misfortune and he has always had more than his share of it—famine, flood, disease and continuous grinding poverty—and when he could endure it no longer, he would quietly and almost uncomplainingly lie down in his thousands or millions and die. That was his way of escape."[1]

The peasantry was subject to the revages of scarcity years, without adequate reliefs, and when his *zamindar* or creditor refused to oblige him, what did a cultivator do for grain? He could rob a store or he could riot. Riots were frequent in the "distressed districts" of the Doab during the grain crisis of 1877 and were tackled with vigorous police measures. He could also emigrate, this, in fact, was a common line of action which the farmers undertook in the Lower Doab and Bundelkhand; they made their way to Malwa when they were badly threatened by scarcity.[2]

In their social origin the taluqdars were a mixed lot, being remnants of old Rajput lineages, some court favourites and administrators. They were wholly rent-receivers and did not themselves participate in the cultivation of land. They gained much importance as a result of their revenue functions in the 18th and early 19th centuries.[3]

P.J. Musgrave has given a comprehensive analysis of the status of landlords and the modes of management of their estates.[4] "Many of the landlords never or very rarely saw their estates—some of them even boasted of it; even for the big landlords who spent part of their time on their estates it was clearly impossible to function without some kind of bureaucracy, a bureaucracy which is traditionally called the estate management".

During this period, all the agricultural classes landlords, peasant proprietors and tenants—became victims of the money-lender who played a significant role in the subsistence village economy. As there were very few legal checks on him, he exploited the poverty of the villagers very much to his own advantage and thus gradually the land passed to him, in numerous cases from many of the smaller landlords and the peasant proprietors. The agricultural debt increased to a record figure and the economic situation began to display danger-signals,

In the United Provinces the agricultural slump of 1929 and onwards had come as a climax to a steadily worsening situation by 1931. Evictions of cultivators by landlords in this region had mulitiplied in number and the zamindars' oppression increased.[5] This kind of oppressive behaviour of the zamindar had deep linkage with the rise of world agricultural prices, affecting Indian agriculture in adverse proportions. Besides, the disproportion in the rapid development of industry and agriculture in other areas of the world had pushed up agricultural prices. This upward tendency, by which Government revenue and the landlord's rent went up, hardly profited the actual cultivator.

Rent went up much faster than revenue in the United Provinces, and it so happened that the proportion of the relative increase of these two during the first three decades of the twentieth century was nearly five to one. The results were disastrous for the tenant who remained, as ever, at starvation level. But the Government's income from land increased substantially and the landlord's income increased far more under these circumstances. Despite revenue remissions of Rs. 10.9 million and rent remissions of Rs. 41.4 million in 1930-31, the general economic condition of the rural regions deteriorated and economic distress stalked the helpless peasantry.[6] Between the Viceroyalty of Lord Curzon and Lord Irwin, rents had increased by Rs. 66,900,000 whereas land revenue had increased by only Rs. 75,00,000. It is indeed amazing to learn that between the Government and the cultivators, there was an intermediate class of about 1,60,000 landlords, but the fragmentation of land was such that the vast majority of these landholders paid less than Rs. 100 a year in land revenue.[7]

A few months prior to the historic Lahore Congress in 1929, Jawaharlal Nehru, who happened to visit a few areas of the Punjab, apprised the *Kisans* of their plight, particularly their exploitation by Government agencies and the big zamindars at whose hands they were experiencing all sorts of indignities. He said "the big landlords owned enormous wealth and property and spent their time more or less in idleness, while the poor peasants suffered untold miseries. He asked the peasants to read and write and keep themselves informed of what was happening in India and how crores of rupees out of the taxes paid by them were wasted on new and costly buildings in New Delhi and the exhorbitant salaries of officers...He asked the peasants to assert their rights. The exploitation of India would not cease unless the peasants and workers organised themselves. If they could put up a fight on their grievances like the peasants of Bardoli, they were bound to improve their conditions of life and save themselves from ruin and starvation. Peasants should take to the *charkha* and wear *khaddar*. The spinning wheel would solve the economic problem of this country to a very great extent."[8]

In a major portion of Awadh, zamindars had been taking to *begar* (forced labour), resorting to forcible realisation of rent and numerous illegal exactions. In many villages there was concealment of rents, i.e., the real rent was not properly recorded in the official records maintained by the *patwari*, a revenue official at the lowest rung, but something substantially less. In these villages, no receipts were given to the tenants. On the other hand, the unscrupulous zamindars of these villages were more active against the Congress and the *kisans*, and it was in these areas that the condition of the tenants was more deplorable. The zamindars, having realised *kharif* rent from them without giving any receipts, were threatening them that they should pay the full rent (i.e. including the concealed portion), otherwise "they will wholly deny the payment made by tenants for *kharif* and in this manner get more rent out of them than they should pay legally."

The President of the District Congress Committee, Bara Banki, gave a dismal picture of landlord-tenant relationship leading to numerous illegal and coercive evictions and various kinds of exactions.[9] In fact, there had been an awakening among the tenants since the Congress propaganda in 1930 began, and the Congress work in this district chiefly depended upon the support of the rural population. But in areas where the tenants were most oppressed they dared not join the movement in the beginning for fear of severe oppression by their landlords. Indeed, the confidence of the rural masses in the Congress had increased after the truce in March 1931, and there was a much wider awakening. Besides, on account of partial failure of crops and low prices, there was a big agitation among the tenants for remission of rent, this district being very thickly populated and the most rack rented.[10]

This situation led to the convening of a few Congress meetings, mostly at the invitation of the local *kisans* themselves, and these meetings were more numerous in the Sadar Tehsil Nawabganj, as was quite natural. It was obvious that the zamindars disliked this kind of awakening, leading to serious economic consequences for them, and they tried their best to keep away the tenants from joining the Indian National Congress and seeking its direct support and sympathy. They even did not desist from doing propaganda among the officials by impressing on them that there was a danger of trouble from the tenants, while they themselves had been terrorising and beating the tenants to reailse rents as speedily as they could. The local officials had anti-Congress and anti-*kisan* feelings, because the latter had now allied themselves with the Congress. "From the actions which they—officials—have been taking, it appears that they are in the hands of the zamindars. The zamindars, who have been treating the tenants almost like slaves for a long time, think that they will be nowhere if the tenants are able to assert themselves".[11]

Statement showing ejectments, etc., in the United Provinces:

	Revenue year 1920-30	Revenue year 1930-31
1. Number of arrears of rent suits	340,249	288,465

2. Number of ejectments ordered for arrears	53,421	64,076
3. Area from which ejectments actually took place (in acres)	149,071.254	189,362.960
4. Number of cases in which property was actually sold after distraint	10,897	13,337
5. Number of cases under Section 447, Indian Penal Code, against ejected tenants and number of convictions:		
a. Cases	982	1,054
b. Convictions	267	345

The eight days' interlude in the month of Octorber 1930, during the first phase of the Civil Disobedience Movement, did not abate Nehru's activities in any sense. He made himself busy in meeting *kisans* of his province and apprised them of the tactics they were to use in the no-rent campaign. Besides giving a brief message to his countrymen, he levelled severe criticism against the functioning of the British Government in India. "The success of our movement can well be gauged by the number and variety of ordinances which are produced with regularity in the factories of Simla...Indeed the time has come when, from the point of view of the British Government, every one of us should be a rebel...To-day every man has to choose between the two flags, the flag of Indian freedom and the flag of foreign domination". To achieve this aim, he optimistically remarked: "I am very much alive and kicking. I hope to do my little bit to hasten the dissolution of the British Empire and take part in its final obsequies."

In Rae Bareli, which was one of the prominent centres of the Civil Disobedience Movement during 1930, a largs number of peasants flocked to the meetings convened by Congress. Congress Panchayats sprang up in many villages and performed the functions of the police and magistrates. National flags were hoisted in many villages.

After a few weeks of the Gandhi-Irwin Pact, a shift in government machinery at the higher level occurred when Willingdon replaced Irwin as the Viceroy in April 1931. An official with less flexibility of mind and attitude and with a long experience of Indian administration, he and his colleagues wished "to work the settlement only on condition that they should not again subject the services and their allies to the strain of renewed civil disobedience countered only with the limited weapons used in 1930...A tough line if conflict erupted again was therefore an essential *quid pro quo* for the settlement...".[14]

The U.P. Government realized the gravity of the situation when prices of cereals and cotton continued to fall, "reaching a nadir in the second quarter of 1931". The Government, therefore, sanctioned remissions of about 18.2% or Rs. 68 lakh in the *rabi* revenue demand and corresponding rent remission of about Rs. 2 crores. The Congress leaders were unhappy about it and Gandhi asked Hailey to institute an enquiry in which Congressmen could participate. This kind of demand was unacceptable to Hailey who opined that the delay in payment involved in an enquiry would endanger the finances of the landlords and the Government.[15]

In May 1931, Gandhi met Emerson and Hailey and discussed with them the problems of the peasantry in U.P. However, he was not prepared to accept the plea of Hailey that the Congress had no right to intervene between the Government and the tax-payers and pressed upon its role as the "poor man's friend" in advising the tenant on rent matters.[16]

Nehru's contention was that rents should correspond with prices, viz, that rent should be reduced to a figure which prevailed in the past. Approximately, this was so about three decades earlier, i.e., in 1901. The other point he made in this regard was that the capacity of the tenant to pay should be assessed after making allowances for the cost of production and a living wage.

In June 1931, Nehru found the situation much worse for the peasants who were being terrorised by the police with the connivance of the *talukdars.* At numerous places, Congress volunteers were being beaten up for peaceful picketing, which was permitted by the settlement. He had no intention of submitting meekly to all this and accompanied Gandhi to Simla to meet the Viceroy. They suggested to the Viceroy that the district authorities should fix the amount of revenue and rent to be collected after consultation with Congress workers, but if this were not acceptable to the Government, at least a detailed enquiry should be ordered to enable temporary adjustments.

The U.P. Government set up a committee to consider future agrarian policy and invited Govind Ballabh Pant to serve as a member. This committee recommended a complicated system of reduction of rents on the basis of the fall in prices but never more than 50%[17]. Thus there could be a reduction of Rs. 4.1 crore out of a total rent of Rs. 18 crore. But the process was cumbersome because numerous formalities were to be observed at the level of revenue officials and zamindars. Even at this point of time, evictions and convictions continued, and by August 1931, there were about 5,000 evictions in Allahabad District and 2,000 in Mathura.

Govind Ballabh Pant apprised the Chief Secretary of the provincial government of the depressing conditions under which the tenants were living and asked for some remedial measures in this regard. He complained thus:[18] "...There is a marked tendency to condone, if not to countenance or encourage, coercive and forceful methods in the matter of collection of rents by Zamindars. Tenants' complaints are, as a rule, disregarded and it is a hard fact that some of the cultivators who complained against their landlords' excesses and sought protection against them were themselves actually bound down for keeping the peace. I doubt if any formal or legal action has been taken against any Zamindar anywhere in the province...Proceedings under Section 107 against Congressmen, peasants and their sympathisers and others under Section 144 seem to be the order of the day and many public workers are naturally agitated and distressed on this account...I do not forget that a Zamindar was killed at Bara Banki and I deeply deplore the crime; but I am assured that part of the district where this sad incident happened is outside the zone of the Congress influence and there is not a single Congressman in any of the villages in that zamindari and in its neighbourhood. Molestation of Congressmen in other parts can be no remedy for excess by non-Congressmen in that locality, nor can the atmosphere be clarified by overlooking provocative causes...I have received similar reports about repression on the part of local officers and coercion on the part of zamindars from other places also, but, for the present, I am forwarding with this only those relating to Sultanpur and Balrampur in the Gonda district which is under the Court of Wards...I hope that you will appreciate the urgency and importance of the subject matter, and will be pleased to take necessary action."[19]

On 29 June 1931, about 500 Congress volunteers picketed the house of the Raja of Sheogarh because his manager had instituted attachment-proceedings against the defaulting tenants The Government took action against the leaders of the agrarian movement who, in the eyes of the Government were guilty of exciting the tenants to refuse payment of rent.[20]

Jawaharlal Nehru informed the Chief Secretary on 15 October 1931, and give him the reason for the commencement of the no-rent campaign.[21] "I regret greatly that such a step should be contemplated by them, specially at a time when Gandhiji is attending the Round Table Conference. But the question of payment or non-payment is an urgent issue and cannot await the deliberations of the Round Table Conference, or the return of Gandhiji. We have tried to avoid raising any issue which might lead to friction and we shall continue to do so. But fate seems to be against this". He even went to the extent of saying: "It is war: war now and ever till the end of our lives".[22]

However, the Congress propaganda against the British revenue policy remained unabated. In the month of October 1931, Sunderlal circulated a scheme for a parallel government to be brought into force in the Bara Banki district by November 15. He asked the peasants to turn their women into leaders so that when men were arrested, they could lead the *kisan* movement.[23]

While Gandhi was busy in the Second Round Table Conference, the Congress leadership in U.P., whished to avoid any kind of conflict with the Government in his absence. But when his return was delayed and the agrarian situation began to develop rapidly, Nehru sent him a cable informing him of the latest developments. "Agrarian situation becoming critical. Coercive processes, attachments, forcible collection rent continued right through without interval...Condition *kisans* deplorable. Thoroughly exhausted after past six months' continuous harassment forcible measures. Vital urgent problem for *kisans* admitting no delay"[24] Gandhi expressed his helplessness in the matter but advised him to go ahead according to his lights.

On the same day, Nehru informed the Viceroy that ever since the Delhi settlement, the tenants in the United Provinces had to face a most difficult situation. They had been treated to every kind of indignity and harassment and every device was employed to make them pay the rent which in their state of economic disaster, they had been unable to pay at the harvest time. They were threatened with dispossession of their crops and in many cases they were actually dispossessed. He pointed out that the new scale of remissions for the current agriculture year was inadequate in principle and in its application. Even the nominal were threatened to be cancelled if the tenants failed to pay up their rent in full within a month. Therefore in their sorry plight they were left with no other opinion but to think of withholding payment of rent.[25]

When the negotiations and the correspondence between the Government and the Congress leaders were going on, the collections for the current season were to commence on 15

November 1931. At this point of time U.P. Congress Committee on the advice of Sardar Patel, directed the *kisans* of Allahabad district to withhold payment of rent and revenue.[26]

This kind of direction to the *kisans* by the Congress leadership was seriously noted by the Government of India which directed Hailey to strike hard. "With the conservatives back to power in Britain and the Second Round Table Conference a failure, the Government of India had clearly decided to turn their backs on Irwin's settlement; and the harsh Bengal Ordinance and the drastic policy favoured in the U.P. were both parts of a general return to a policy of repression. Willingdon and Emerson went to Lucknow to speed up matters, but Hailey refused to be hustled...So in the U.P., at any rate, there continued what Jawaharlal described as an impossible situation."[27]

At this point of time, Nehru, who convened a conference of *kisans* at Allahabad on 25 November stated emphatically: "If we are to die, we shall die after a fight. I do not want a half-way settlement or a half-way fight".[28] He had the feeling that the Government would not delay his arrest. The *Pioneer*, a pro-government newspaper, even hinted at his deportation.[29] But this kind of action was not possible, as Willingdon confessed in a communication to Samuel Hoare, the Secretary of State, on 13 December 1931:

> "One thing I do regret very much in all this business and, that is, we have no power of deportation out of India. It would be an enormous advantage if we can get hold of 15 or 20 of these leaders, send them right away to the West Indies or somewhere, instead of having to keep them under surveillance in some province or other".[30]

In December the Provincial Congress Committee directed the members of the District Congress Committees to commence the no-rent campaign in Allahabad, Rae Bareli, Etawah, Kanpur and Unnao.[31] As a result of this action, the payment of rent in these districts came almost to a standstill.[32] Landlords were practically unable to collect any rent in the districts of

Rae Bareli, Barabanki, Luknow, Pratapgarh, Allahabad, Agra and Meerut. The Government ordered the Commissioners to provide police assistance to landlords so that they could carry on the processes of eviction and distraint.[33] This was considered the convenient way to smash the Congress support and sympathy for the peasantry and also to gain the loyalty and cooperation of the *zamindars.*

The Government of U.P. was slightly fearful of the fact that Nehru might precipitate the issue on the arrival of Gandhi. It, therefore, wished to grant some concessions to the tenants in order to strengthen its case. It lowered the water rates, introduced a bill to save tenants from eviction if they paid two-thirds of the arrears due for the previous four years, and also offered early measures to protect tenants against debts.

At the same time, the Government had made up its mind to take action against Nehru and other Congressmen. The new Ordinance had given such powers to the Government, which was now quite sure that the Congress leadership had exploited the economic crisis to its advantage to seek the following and support of the *kisans*, thus violating the spirit of the truce. It also declared that Nehru had preached class warfare. On his return to Allahabad from Bombay, the Government lost no time in serving Nehru with a notice not to leave the city without official permission and, at the same time, the U.P. Provincial Conference scheduled to be held on 26 December was banned. Nehru was arrested on 26 December for violating the order restricting him to Allahabad. On 26 December 1931, the Vicerory wrote to the Secretary of State: "The Delhi Pact at all events is dead gone, murdered by Jawaharlal Nehru and Abdul Ghaffar."[34]

Soon the repressive measures were applied all over India. Gandhi, Sardar Patel, numerous other Congress leaders and satyagrahis were in jail. H.G. Haig, the Home Member opined "Jawaharlal is a fanatic. There are threatenings of an attempt to revive a no-rent compaign in the U.P. Jawaharlal Nehru is the author of that policy and his release would obviously give it a definite stimulus."[35]

Jawaharlal Nehru, however, explained the action of the Government thus: "The machinery of coercion, legal as well as illegal, began to move. Ejectment suits brought against thousands, attachments of cows, bullocks, personal property, beatings of agents of landlords......They came to us in large numbers, complaining bitterly, telling us that they had followed our advice and paid what they could and this was the consequence... The District Congress Committee (Allahabad) office was surrounded all day by a distraught crowd. My own house was equally besieged and often I felt like running away and hiding myself somewhere, anywhere, to escape this dreadful predicament."[36]

Thus the agrarian question in the United Provinces was much more an economic issue than a political one. In this context Nehru was of the opinion that while Gandhi had assured the Viceroy that even if he did not attend the Second Round Table Conference, he would not resume Civil Disobedience so long as the conference was in session. But Gandhi had made it clear that this kind of assurance would not apply to any local economic struggle that might be forced on the Congress.[37]

The no-tax campaign had one significant result in the province. It shifted the centre of gravity of the political struggle launched soon after the historic Dandi March of Gandhi and his 78 associates from its urban base to the rural base and "it thereby revitalised the movement."

There were practical difficulties for the Congress to make this campaign broad-based and spread its objective in a major part of the province. For this Nehru had a sense of confession "Our chief difficulty in those days was one of communication, of getting people to know what we were doing or what we wanted them to do. Newspapers would not publish our news for fear of being penalised and suppressed by Government, printing presses would not print our leaflets and notices; letters and telegrams were censored and often stopped. The only reliable method of communication open to us was to send couriers with despatches, and even so our messengers were sometimes arrested.... It was organised with some success and the provincial centres were in constant touch with headquarters as well as with their principal district centres."[38]

The Congress, however, was cautious to see that the Civil Disobedience Movement did not develop as an anti-landlord campaign. By devising such a measure, it was conscious of the fact that numerous rich peasants participated in the movement and some big landlords had a sympathetic attitude towards the Congress leadership as well as its movements.

Thus the appeal of the Congress leadership had been addressed to both *zamindars* and tenants not to pay land revenue. But this appeal was not very effective, for the *zamindars* and Nehru regretted that most of them did pay their revenue, even some of those who sympathised with the national struggle. It was apparent that the pressure on them was great and they had more to lose by not paying. The movement soon spread to some other districts of the United Provinces. But in many districts it was not "formally adopted or declared, but in effect tenants withheld their rents or, in many cases, were wholly unable to pay them owing to the fall in prices. As it happened, neither the Government nor the big *zamindars* took any widespread action to terrorise the recalcitrant tenantry for several months. They were not sure of their ground, as they had the political struggle with civil disobedience on the one side, and the economic slump, resulting in agricultural distress, on the other. The two merged into each other, and the Government was always afraid of an agrarian upheaval. With the Round Table Conference in session in London, they were not keen on adding to their troubles in India or on giving a still more striking demonstration of 'strong' government".

During this period, the Provincial Government resorted to a novel step which produced much commotion in the rural areas The district authorities issued remission slips in the names of the tenants stating clearly how much remission had been allowed and containing a threat that unless the amount then due was paid up within a month (sometime the period mentioned was shorter), the remission could be cancelled and the full sum realised by legal process which meant ejectment, attachment of property, etc. Nehru called it "...a very foolish threat on the part of the Government or their local officials and it was not, we were told later, meant seriously. But it lessened the chances of a peaceful settlement very greatly and led inevitably, step by step, to conflict."

In the United Provinces, this struggle was centred in the rural areas. The remissions offered to the tenants were not considered adequate by the Congress leadership. The Government was anxious that the Congress should not get the credit for these remissions, but at the same time it wanted to give to the peasants as many remissions as possible to keep them quiet. These remissions, considerable as they were, did not solve the agrarian problem, but they did ease the situation. This struggle brought suffering to thousands of peasants in the province and numerous people were "completely ruined" by it. But the pressure of the struggle brought millions of peasants almost the highest possible remissions under the existing system, though the petty seasonal gains did not amount to much.

The Karachi Session of the Indian National Congress was held in March 1931 under the presidentship of Sardar Vallabh Bhai Patel and passed important resolutions on the Fundamental Rights and the Economic policy. Pant attended this session and apprised the leaders of the lot of the peasantry.

The Government was growing coersive. Even in U.P. an Ordinance was issued on 14th of December, 1931 to empower the Government to realise any arrears from the peasantry as part of the Government revenue. The Government was authorised to arrest any person working against the interests of the Government. In short, the Government was dressed up in absolute dictatorial powers.

The session of the U.P. Provincial Congress was to be held

at Etawah. Pant left by train to take part in it. The Government put a ban on the session. As soon as Pant came to know about it he changed his programme and instead reached Allahabad on 24th of December, 1913. From Allahabad he left for Bombay and apprised the leaders of the Congress Working Committee of the situation in U.P. He returned to Bhowali on 6th of January, 1932. In the meantime section 144 had been enforced in Haldwani and Pant's house was searched there on January 19th. A number of Congress volunteers were arrested. The Congress office was also seized. By a Government order dated 30th January, 1932 Pant was not allowed to go out of the town of Haldwani. The police was after him.

In the morning of February 18, 1932 a sub-Inspector of police accompanied by four constables went to arrest Pant. Pant was taken into custody under section 17(1) of the Criminal Amendment Act. He was tried in the local jail and was sentenced to six months' imprisonment and a fine of rupees one hundred was also pronounced against him. He was later on sent to Bareilly Central Jail and his car was auctioned for rupees two hundred to realise the fine imposed on him. He was transferred to Dehra Dun Jail in April, where Nehru had also been transferred from Naini Central Jail, Pant was released in August 1932. The movement had came to a stand still as most of the leaders were in Jail.

After the Civil Disobedience Movement, Pant got himself engaged in the constructive work, development of educations and several other works having deep linkage with the socio-economic life of the people of his province. As a Member of the Central Assembly, his contribution was unique in several ways.

Pant was appointed as the Chief Minister of U.P. from 1937 to 1939. His other colleagues in the ministry were Rafi Ahmad Kidwai, K.N. Katju, Vijaya Lakshmi Pandit, Hafiz Mohammad Ibrahim and Dr. Sampurnanand. P.D. Tandon was elected as the speaker. During his tenure as Chief Minister, Pant successfully pioneered several developmental schemes which led to the growth of socio-economic condition of the people of his province. He devoted his time for communal harmony, grant of civil liberties, development of education, medical education, agrarian reforms, land reforms, irrigation and transport, release of political prisoners and several other measures. This made a popular Chief Minister.

When the Second World War broke out on 3 September 1939, the Congress leadership felt unhappy about it.

Immediately the Viceroy promulgated an ordinance to provide measures for the safety of British India and declared India a belligerent country. The Congress Working Committee met at Wardha on September 7 and decided that in case the war is "to defend *status quo*, of imperialistic possessions, colonies, vested interests and privileges then India can have nothing to do with it. The A.I.C.C. also approved of this decision in October 1939. The Congress Parliamentary Committee called upon the Congress Ministries in the States to resign by October 31.

The *New Age* and *Independent India* realised about the serious situation created at the commencement of the Second World War. Their comments touched upon the national and international situations which had serious global dimensions. They stated thus:

WAR-CRISIS AND OUR TASKS[39]

September 1939

Once again the Indian people and the National Congress are faced with a War Crisis, which is far more serious and graver than the one in last September. Before these lines appear in print, either the world would have been plunged into a bloody war or the crisis would have been postponed. But the threat of war would continue to hang on the world. The only guarantee to the stopping of fascist aggression—and to the establishment of peace was an anti-aggression peace pact between England, France and the Soviet. Chamberlain and Daladier have betrayed and sabotaged it. The people of France and England have not been able to put an end to the regimes of their pro-fascist ministers. The Soviet has been forced into isolation. The clash of interest between the Anglo-French block and the Axis powers has been intensified. The two war blocks face each other. War may be postponed but cannot be averted unless the people and the proletariat in France and England are able to find the path of unity and action against their pro-fascist Governments. India will have to face the issue, if not today, a few days hence. Now do we tackle it?

The policy of Imperialism is clear, it is determined to tighten its grips over India for mobilising India's resources of men and money, for maintaining 'internal peace' in the country in times of war. During the last six months important war measures have been taken in this direction: The anti-recruitment Bill, the 'War' amendment to the Government of India Act, and the hastening of the federation by alternatively cajoling and coercing the princes. Imperialism wants that the Congress ministries co-operate with them in the tasks of war preparations and in suppressing popular discontent and revolt that may arise during the war. Their game is to utilise the war situation, to split the forces of national struggle, to defeat them simply and then impose upon the people the fetters of the Federal scheme. In the recent war crisis, the imperialist newspapers like the *Times of India* and the *Statesman* urge Congress Ministries and the Congress High Command to come away from the policy of non-co-operation with war measures. They condemn the Socialists, Communists, as well as Bose for their demand for an effective policy of war resistance and for an immediate nationwide struggle.

In the grave emergency that has arisen two alternatives are sharply posed before the nation. Will our National leadership implement the Congress policy of opposing fascism and war? Will it unify all the forces of the people's struggle for an effective campaign of war-resistance and for independence? The time has now come when the struggle against war has become one with the fight against the hated Federation. India's vassalage to Britain, the reactionary and autocratic character of the new Federal centre, would be thrown into sharp relief in the emergency war measures to which our country is being subjected. An effective movement against war, in which the ministerial action is supported by mass action cannot but be at the same time a nation-wide protest movement against the Government of India Act itself.

The other alternative would be conditional co-operation with imperialism or mere resignation and neutrality. In both the cases, there would be no mass action to resist war. In these cases, imperialism would strike mercilessly against forces of unrest and mass discontent. Drastic actions would be taken against socialists, communists, kisan sabha workers and radical Congressmen under the guise that they are endangering peace... Some All-India action is being contemplated to suppress the growing resistance of workers all over the country against the millowners' offensive of wage-cuts and victimisation. The position of neutrality or passivity would give imperialism the best opportunity to divide our forces and defeat them singly.

If we examine the resolution which the Working Committee passed on the issue of war in its last session at Wardha we would find that on the fact of it, it is not inconsistent with the first alternative. The resolution condemned the policy of Chamberlain and fascist aggression. It fraternises with the people who stand for democracy and freedom, but states that it is unable to associate with the movement for democratic freedom which is denied to India. Congress declares its determination to oppose all attempts to impose a war on India. As a protest against the despatch of Indian troops without consulting the Assembly, the Working Committee called upon all Congress members of the Central Legislative Assembly to refrain from attending the next sessions of the Assembly as a first step. The Working Committee further reminded the

Provincial Governments to assist in no way the war preparations of the British Government and to keep in mind the policy laid down by the Congress to which they must adhere. If the carrying out of this policy leads to the resignations or removal of the Congress Ministries they must be prepared for this emergency.

The resolution, which was passed some time before the war situation, can be something more than a 'fighting gesture'. It calls upon the Provincial Ministries to implement the anti-war policy of the Congress and face dismissal in doing so. It characterises the decision of the Congress M.L. As. not to attend the present session of the Central Assembly as a first step. The Premiers Conference which met in Poona just when the war crisis broke out is reported to have taken a decision about the practical steps to implement the Working Committee's resolution. The Ministries are to face dismissal in their effort to implement the anti-war policy of the Congress. But what next? The Working Committee is to meet in Patna to chalk out the complete line of the Congress if war breaks out.

Will it be a line of fight or will it be a line of neutrality? In the imperialist quarters, hope is being entertained that some via media will still be found. Inspired Shimla message for some time spread the rumour that the Congress members of the Central Legislature would attend the session later. It was suggested that the viceroy would make an appeal to the national leaders asking for co-operation and assuring consultation with the Party leaders. The *Statesman* of Calcutta went to the length of suggesting an immediate formation of a coalition federal cabinet with the representatives of the Congress, Muslim League and the States. Even the London press was looking for a statement from Gandhiji which would clarify India's position *vis-a-vis* war.

What is the basis of this expectation in imperialist circles? The clue is to be found in the other resolution of the Working Committee. This same session passed the resolution expelling Bose from all elective posts in the Congress. It hinted that the

PCC's deal with the other 'rebels' in the same way. It had indicated its disapproval of the hunger-strike of the Bengal political prisoners while demanding their speedy release. Since they compelled Bose to resign and formed their 'homogeneous' Working Committee, it was clear that this 'homogeneous' leadership had not its heart on getting a 'homogeneous' Congress. In the Bombay session, they got the Constitutional amendments passed which will have the effect of forcing out the leftists, especially, socialists and communits. By banning individual satyagraha taken without the sanction of the PCC and by taking away the right of the PCC's to criticise the work of the Ministries publicly, they put an effective check on the extra-parliamentary activities, (and) rendered the PCC's subservient tools of the Ministries. Finally, they have begun a campaign of expelling Congressmen who dared to raise their voice or exercise their democratic right to mobilise Congress opinion against these resolutions in order to get them rescinded. This campaign of weeding the Left is now reaching absurd limits. In Andhra, Congressmen are being threatened with expulsion even if they participate in the welcome to Bose. The fighting gesture against war is thus accompanied by a purge against the militants in the Congress, mostly such as are prominently connected with the labour and kisan movements in the country.

Is there any wonder if the enemy did not take our resolution seriously and expects a watering down of the same? Those who want a fight do not begin the preparation by exterminating a part of the fighting forces. Not only is the Congress machinery used to this purpose, but the Ministries continue to carry on their repressive actions against Labour and Kisan movements in Bihar, Madras CP, and Bombay. The latest and the most glaring attack is against the textile workers of Bombay, where the Ministry has arrested the whole executive of the Bombay Girni Kamgar Union on trumped up charges of 'incitement to violence, criminal intimidation etc.'. The purpose is obviously to smash the Communist-led militant union, which is just about to complete its 40,000 membership drive and to win recognition under the Trade Disputes Act. The attack against textile labour is universal. In Madras, Bombay, UP, and in CP, the owners are determined to curtail production, cut wages and throw out thousands of workmen. The owners want to crush the united counter-offensive of the workers, want to cancel even the few benefits which the Congress Ministries gave them. Now the Ministries are assisting the owners in their nefarious object by this sort of repression. In the name of 'creating non-violent atmosphere', the arm of law and police is being used against workers and peasants' awakening, which in reality should be a source of strength to the Congress. Is it any wonder, if after all this, imperialism is sceptic about the fighting gesture materialising?

There is another reason which could give hope to imperialism in this direction. In a recent issue of the *Harijan*, Gandhi discloses that he also submitted a draft to the Working Committee on the issue of war crisis. Gandhiji's draft was rejected in favour of the one adopted which was drawn up by Nehru. Gandhi characterised this as his own defeat. The exact nature of Gandhi's proposals are not known. He himself characterised them as 'out and out non-violent'. Besides, his views, that 'India should not exploit the war situation to win independence' are well-known. One can easily guess what Gandhi's line on the war would be—'neutrality and non-resistence to war preparations'—The fact that Gandhi does not approve of the attitude adopted by the Working Committee, cannot but raise hopes in the hearts of the enemy. It would not take long to convert Gandhi's defeat once again to victory.

There is a great danger that the Anti-War line adopted by the Working Committee would be unperceptibly transferred into the line of neutrality and non-resistance proposed by Gandhi. If resignation and dismissal is not accompanied by a mass-resistance to war measures, the result would be neutrality. This would embolden imperialists to intensify the offensive against a section of the National Movement—especially the Labour and Kisan movements. The consequence would be disruption of our forces and defeat. Gandhi's line—of neutrality and war resistance in the case of war—is the logical conclusion of his whole line which he has been advocating in the *Harijan* and which becomes the practice of the Working Committee in spite of the resolution of the Congress.

At present two political lines are contending for supremacy. The one is the line which found its, more or less adequate expression, in Nehru's presidential address at Lucknow and Faizpur—and in the election manifesto, the Lucknow and Faizpur resolutions on civil liberties, labour and agrarian programme and on war and foreign policy. This line recognises the emergence of the new mass force, the organisation and the struggle of the workers and peasants, a new mass technique of struggle—and the need to shape the Congress a new as the instrument of the United Front struggle, in which the organised workers and peasants play an important role...The emergence of this line in the Congress is itself the reflex of the new upsurge of workers and peasants struggle and organisation, Since 1934 and the rise of the working class and Socialism as a political force, we had reached a new stage in our national struggle in which the working class comes forward as a political force broadening and unifying the national struggle and raising it to a higher level. The policy of strengthening workers and peasants' organisations, their unity with the Congress for the struggle for independence and democracy, the unity of extra-Parliamentary struggle with the work of the Ministries, the unity of states peoples' struggle with that of the general struggle for national freedom, the unity with communal minorities by guaranteeing to them all their minority rights and by drawing them in the joint struggle for national and democratic freedom, and finally, the preparation for a nationwide struggle—this is the policy which logically arises from the Lucknow-Faizpur line. This is the truly national line of unity and advance which socialists and communists fight for.

As oposed to this, stands the *Harijan* line which is sought to be imposed upon the Congress from without. This line is based on the oft-quoted dictum of Gandhi that Swaraj can be won in the present period, through the experiment of office acceptance, 'avoiding violent revolution on the one hand and mass civil disobedience on the other'. For Gandhi there is no extra-parliamentary work except 'the constructive programme' viz. *Khaddar*, *Gramudyog*, and *Harijan* uplift. He looks with suspicion at the rise of the labour and peasant movements. He wants non-violent atomsphere for the success of this 'office assistance' experiment. He is prepared to allow the 'minimum violence' of the Congress Ministries against the workers and peasants. He is definitely of the opinion that no mass-movement of any type can be started now because it would lead to violence. With this argument he justifies stopping of the struggle in the States and also his disapproval of the decision to launch a 'Nationwide struggle to win independence'. Gandhi's political line amounts to simple constitutional reformism. He covers his rejection of struggle, by the slogan of a Utopian and unattainable non-violent struggle based on the theory of change of heart. This can, in practice, only lead to ignoble compromise. The organisational implications of his line is a Congress of tru *satyagrahis*, who have non-violence and trust in God, in their hearts. In practice, this means narrowing down the mass basis of the Congress, isolation of the left and the masses. This means disruption.

The root cause of the present conflict in the Congress is the growing conflict between these two lines. It is no good denying the fact that it is a conflict between 'Contraries'. The *Harijan* line which has been triumphing especially during the last 12 months, is contrary to the line of unity with the new mass force and with its new technique of mass struggle—the line which the Congress turned to in its Lucknow and Faizpur sessions. During the last eighteen months or so, the phenomenal rise of the workers' and peasants struggles have frightened the vested interests. They are pulling the national leadership back from the line of Lucknow and Faizpur. The bourgeoisie, frightened by the rise of mass-struggle, is resiling back from the path of united front. In doing so it is not only harming the interest of the nation as a whole, it is harming its own larger interests...

It is the task of the socialists and communits and *kisan* sabhaites, as representatives of the new mass force and the mass technique of struggle, to fight against this retreat—this effort to drag the Congress away from the path of united front, and a united advance against the common enemy. Socialists and communists must fight to overcome this anti-struggle tendency which has brought the Congress into this crisis, of disruption. Not to understand this political implications of the present crisis, to deny that crisis mainly arises out of the growing constitutionalism and reformism of a section of the Congress leadership, is to forget Socialism. But this is exactly what Ram Manohar Lohia does in 'A call to the Leftists' (Free Press Journal 28 August 1939). Lohia seems to reduce the whole question to a matter of mutual recrimination (The contrary outlook in the Congress have largely been created artificially.' Lohia forgets that the contrary outlooks and methods of work are really tracable to the role of the two most important classes in our national struggle namely the bourgeoisie and the proletariat. What is needed to solve the present crisis is not an 'above the battle' super class stand point but the robust outlook of proletarian socialism. To solve the present crisis says Lohia, all that need be done is to stop 'the dangerous pastime of labelling and characterising each other this or that mentality'—and to turn to individual problems such as Hindu-Muslim unity, war-resistance peasant and labour awakening and so on.

Does Lohia think that these problems can be tackled apart and away from the two 'contrary outlooks?' There is no escape from the basic conflict of political polities, which is raging inside the Congress. The socialists and communists are not bringing in a new policy. They stand for the consistent and further development of the policy adopted at Lucknow and Faizpur. They are opposing the attempts to revise and go back upon that policy. They are not doing it by patiently popularising the positive resolutions of the Congress. They are doing it by organising the National Struggle Week which ended just now in which they attempted to win the masses for a policy of unity in the Congress and advance against the common enemy.

How will the Working Committee handle the question of the war-crisis? We apprehend from the argument advanced at the beginning of these notes that the decision would be in favour of neutrality and passivity. This would be disastrous. It would enable the enemy, as we said, to attack our forces singly and defeat them. We therefore suggest the following line of action: our ministries must function as peoples' ministries They must seek to carry out the Congress mandate positively. They must issue orders to the Provincial and Civil Services under them not to assist the military or central authorities in recruitment, war loans, troop and material transport, or in any other measure of war preparation. This will precipitate a clash between the Ministries and the Governors which will be a clash between the democratic will of the people and the autocratic Government of India Act. The constitutional clash must be the signal for unleashing a mass movement for war-resistance and against the Government of India Act. The mass actions which we must immediately unfold should be as follows:

1. General one-day protest hartal and protest strike against war and against the autocratic Government of India Act.

2. A campaign of anti-recruitment, anti war-loan, meetings and agitation.

3. A campaign to stop export and transport of war-materials through the organisation of Dock and Transport workers.

4. Boycott of British and Japanese goods.

5. Protest Hartals and strikes against repressive actions under Emergency laws.

If our anti-war resolution is not merely to be a threat and bargaining device, we must back the dismissals of our ministries with such concrete mass action. Only in that case would we be able to exert maximum pressure on British Imperialism and preserve our fighting forces from disruption and defeat. A mass struggle at such a time cannot but open up new possibilities for us to win our final battle for independence.

DOWN WITH WAR
DOWN WITH THE CONSTITUTIONALISM
UP WITH CONSTITUENT ASSEMBLY.

Independent India
10 September 1939

The British Government has declared war. As a port of the British Empire, India is involved by the declaration. War has been imposed on her. Imperialism has flouted the repeated resolution of the Congress 'to oppose all attempts is to impose war on India'. The leadership of the Indian nationalist movement represented by the Congress, is put to the crucial test. The country is anxiously awaiting a fateful decision on the part of the supreme Executive of its premier political organisation—perhaps the most fateful ever made.

As soon as the perennial European crisis appeared to be nearing a new acuteness, it was suggested that an emergency meeting of the Congress Working Committee should immediately take place. The President actually issued the notice of the meeting. But a few days later, when the international situation did not show any sign of easing, the meeting was postponed. That was an intriguing step which kept the politically alert guessing about the possible result of the secret diplomacy carried on by the Congress leaders, at least by a few of them. Two events preceded the postponement of the emergency meeting of of the Working Committee.

Even before it was called, the Congress Premiers from all the provinces met, according to a plan made previously, in a conference at Poona under the presidentship of the Chairman of the Parliamentary Sub-Committee. The Premier's Conference was to discuss what the Congress Ministries should do in case of a war in Europe. It is reported that the question was discussed for four days. But the Conference ended without announcing any decision. The only decision, known to the public, was to temporise,—the last thing to do in a critical moment. Nevertheless, that strange decision, not to decide anything, naturally stood on the way to any emergency meeting of the Working Committee. It would be ridiculous to hold an emergency session which would make no decision. The argument for temporising just when decisive action was needed was that the next move must come from the side of the Government. Unless there had been any secret move from the side of the Congress, the expected move of the Government was to be made in reply to the oft-repeated resolution of the Congress, reaffirmed by the Working Committee in its last meeting. Since the Poona Conference, the Government has made two moves, in quick succession. The later move—declaration of war by the British Government—is a check which threatens a mate, unless the opposing party has up its sleeves a sure plan to back through the attack. As far as we know, there is no such plan. So, the danger of our leadership giving up the game is imminent.

The earlier move of the Government, however, has been the more decisive. It seems that the policy to temporise was adopted in anticipation thereof. Expecting that move to be conciliatory, those who really determine and guide the Congress policy to-day did not want to prejudice the chances by any hasty declaration. That earlier, more decisive, move of the Government was to invite Gandhi together with his most trusted lieutenants to meet the Viceroy for discussing the Congress attitude in case of a war. The emergency meeting of the Working Committee was formally postponed on the arrival of the Viceregal invitation for Gandhi, although that decision had actually been made even earlier, in pursuance of the temporising policy adopted at the Poona Conference. Imperialism is anxious to come to some understanding with the Congress. But it naturally wishes to bargain from a position of vantage. The declaration of war has upset all the opportunistic calculation of the Congress leaders, and on the other hand, has placed the Viceroy in a position wherein he must dictate terms. There will be no negotiations at Simla. The Viceroy in the situation created by the declaration of war, can tell Gandhi only one thing; Take it or leave it; the war is there; either join hands or cross swords. Gandhi, being a man of peace, who wants peace at any price, will have no hesitation as regards the choice. The Congress stands on the eve of a capitulation!

This disturbing and shameful perspective is not altogether new. It was opened up by the behaviour of our leaders ever since the meeting of the AICC at Delhi in September last year. At that time also, Europe was trembling on the brink of a war on the Czechoslovakian issue. In that psychological moment, for the first time, the hint came from the Congress that it might accept office also in the Centre if Imperialism would shelve the ill-conceived Federal Scheme. It was expected that if the imminent war broke out, Imperialism would be compelled to pay a good price for Congress co-operation without which its position in India was sure to be very precarious. With that expectation, the AICC was persuaded to arm the Working Committee with plenary powers which would enable it to close a bargain with Imperialism in distress, and later on have it endorsed by the Congress. Emergency places disorganised democracy at a discount.

The AICC having passed the very significant resolution, and given it the power to make or mar the future of India, the Working Committee for a number of days remained in permanent session, holding up the olive branch and expecting the next move from the other side. That times the expected move was not made. The war was avoided in Europe. For the time being, it was not necessary for Imperialism to sue for the co-operation of the Congress.

Since then, there has been persistent rumour about back-door diplomacy and underhand dealings. Meanwhile, the Congress repeated its resolution to oppose the imposition of war on India. But, on the other hand, the logical consequences of the ministerialist policy came to be evident at least for those who cared to see. The object of the policy was to extend the 'parallel Government' beyond the limits of the provinces to the Centre. As the President of the Congress, Subhas Chandra Bose himself announced that the Congress was running a race towards Delhi and that it was sure of beating others in the game The Chairman of the Parliamentary Sub-Committee having busied himself with electoral arithmetics, came to the conclusion that the Congress could capture a majority even in the Federal Legislature. But the subsequent failure in coming to some understanding either with the Muslim League or with the Princes, compelled the Congress leaders to look for a different way to the establishment of the 'Parallel Government' in the Centre. The Congress would stand a better chance of capturing a majority in the Central Legislature, if the Federal Scheme was shelved for the time being, and it is re-elected according to the old Constitution. Consequently, all efforts were bent for the introduction of interim responsibility in the Centre. Imperialism, on its side, appeared to favour the idea which would offer it a graceful exit out of the impasse over the introduction of the Federal Scheme. There being agreement on principle, what was needed was an opportunity to put it into practice. The war would afford the opportunity.

One would ask, how could this policy be reconciled with the oft-repeated resolution of the Congress to oppose the imposition of a war on India. It is not a very difficult question. The answer is contained in the famous phrase itself. The Congress is committed to oppose war if it is imposed on India. Otherwise, if Imperialism acts in consultation with the representative of the Indian people, there will be co-operation. This is the clear implication of the Central idea of the oft-repeated

Congress resolution on war. But it is no longer necessary to interpret the text. Pursuing the policy, inaugurated by the Delhi AICC resolution, the Congress leaders reached a stage where the position had to be a little clarified to encourage the desired response from Imperialism. The first step in that direction was taken at Tripuri. It is contained in the famous resolution on 'National Demand' which, curiously enough, has become the political mainstay of the otherwise unstable conglomeration sailing under the false colour of Leftism. In the AICC meeting at Calcutta, still another step was taken in the direction of a possible understanding with Imperialism in the case of war. Finally, the resolution of the last meeting of Working Committee makes the attitude of the Congress abundantly clear. The text of the oft-repeated resolution is repeated once again, 'to oppose all attempts to impose a war on India.' But the same resolution ends with a rider giving the authoritative interpretation of the text:

> In the event of a war crisis leading to danger to any part of India from the air or otherwise it may be necessary for protective measures to be taken. The Committee will be prepared to encouragae such measures if they are within the control of popular Ministries.

That is clear enough. Only, the wlllingness to co-operate with Imperialism in the case of a war is justified on an imaginary pretext. In case of a conflict, either in Europe or in the Far East, no part of India could ever be really in danger of an attack from the air or otherwise. That is an imperialist scare which should not perturb any intelligent Indian. In any case, should the present conflict in Europe develop into large scale armed hostilities, any danger to India is altogether out of the question. It is simply fantastic to imagine German aeroplanes coming all the way to bombard India. No serious attack from Japan is militarily conceivable. Italy may stay out of the conflict. So, there is no necessity for taking any serious measure for the defence of India hereslf. She will participate in the war as a part of the British Empire—as a source of supply. Yet, by the resolution of Working Committee the Congress is committed to encourage measures to be taken by Imperialism with the object of scaring India under its protecting wing. Having deliberately placed themselves in this position, the Congress leaders must go ahead with eyes open to co-operation with Imperialism, on its terms.

The encouraging resolution of the Working Committee, naturally, elicited the desired invitation from Simla, as soon as it become once again urgent for Imperialism to secure Congress co-operation. Had war not been declared in the meantime, the Simla negotiation might not have been conclusive. Now the Congress leaders are confronted with an accomplished fact. War has been imposed upon India. Now it is for them to oppose it or to fall in line. At Simla, this straight question will be put to them across the table...Who do the men of peace know about the technique of massacre? They will have to simply take the experts on their words, and act according to their own commitment to encourage measures against that danger, that is to say, play the imperialist game.

Yet another thing will be done for the same purpose—to secure the answer desired by Imperialism. Popular Ministries in the provinces will be asked to shoulder the responsibility of introducing those measures. And this concession for securing Congress co-operation will most probably be extended also to the Central Government which will be reconstituted so as to be 'popular'...When all this is kept in view, there still remains the chance, just a chance, of the Congress leaders refusing to play the game of Imperialism. In that case, they may not leave Simla free men, or find themselves prisoners before long. The Congress as a whole will be declared an illegal organisation; the Ministers will follow their mentors to jail; thousands of others will also have the doubtful glory of wearing the martyr's crown of thorns; but there will be no opposition to the war imposed on India.

By its blind faith in the leaders, the Congress has allowed itself to be placed in this tight corner. The Congress resolution on war could never be enforced unless deliberate preparations were made for capturing power, and thereby break India's relation with British Imperialism in the first critical moment. The leaders of the Congress would not allow any such preparations. The idea of the Indian people capturing power did not enter into their scheme of political action. They were striving for a gradual, peaceful transfer of power, and were hopefully waiting for the opportunity when Imperialism would be compelled to transfer to them a large measure of power for securing their indispensable co-operation. The long looked for opportunity has come. They will naturally avail of it, and settle the problem of Indian freedom in their peculiar way. It would be stupid to accuse them of betrayal. They have been deliberately moving in this direction...There is a large grain of truth in the saying that a movement gets the kind of leadership it deserves.

The crucial test is for the so-called leftists who have been crying themselves hoarse against the war danger and promising all manner of heroic performance when Imperialism would be involved in a first-class war in Europe. If the present European conflict will really develop into large-scale armed hostilities, which is not yet certain by any means, the Indian crusade's against the war danger would not be able to do even what they can, namely, to shout bombastic slogans. They will also find their way to prison and will not be able to put up any greater reinstance than the Congressmen who at least never promised to do anything more spectacular than to go to prison by way of a struggle against Imperialism.

This however, is not a matter of flippancy. It is a heart-rending tragedy. Whoever had his eyes could see that events were all heading towards capitulation in the case of a war. Yet, the leftists could do no better than stump for united leadership which they wished to wield as the lever for pushing the present leadership of the Congress to a struggle against Imperialism. They could do no better. Having no confidence in their ability to assume the leadership of a revolutionary movement, they discovered an ingenious way of shirking responsibility. They talked ceaselessly about struggle. But they did not know that local and partial struggles could be developed into a general mass struggle for the capture of political power only under the leadership of a revolutionary party. But having preconceived notions, acquired from superficial book-learning about the role of different classes, they pityfully failed to see on what social basis the party to lead the present Indian revolution could be built. Consequently, in the beginning, they fought against the Congress; later on they joined the Congress, but with mental reservations about its role and future. They themselves did not try to build upon the foundation already laid. What is worse, the sole object of their activity was to prevent others from doing that. The result has been the complete absence of organisational conditions, which must have been created if imperialist war was to afford India a golden opportunity for gaining freedom.

The only hope is that a large scale war in Europe may still be avoided. In that case, the anti-imperialist forces in India will have another chance to do what has not been done untill now, so that when the next opportunity comes they may rise up to the occasion. If the almost certain disaster is avoided by chance, they should learn from bitter experience and apply themselves to the hard task of building up the instrument for the masses to capture power, instead of wasting time in shouting impractical slogans and carrying on ineffective agitation and finding fault with others who may not be tempted by these easy methods for gaining notoriety.

During the Quit India Movement, Pant was in Jail from August 1942 to March 1945. After a year, he was again elected the Chief Minister of U.P. and during his tenure, as usual, he was busy in several developmental scheme. The Zamindars abolition was the biggest achievement of his ministry. Besides, there was remarkable development in the fields of agriculture, industry, education, public health, *Harijan* uplift, panchayats, labour welfare and several other reforms.

References

1. Nehru, Jawaharlal: *An Autobiography* (New Delhi) 1962, p. 306.
2. Whitcombe, Elizabeth: *Agrarian Conditions in Northern India* (New Delhi) 1971, p. 197.
3. Siddiqi, Asiya: *Agrarian Change in a Northern India State*, 1819-1833 (Oxford) 1973, p. 44.
4. See his article on 'Landlords and Lords of the Land Estate Management and Social Control in Uttar Pradesh, 1860-1920' in *Modern Asian Studies*, 1972, pp. 257ff.
5. Home Pol. File 33/XVI, K.W., 1931.
6. Neale, Walter C: *Economic Change in Rural India: Land Tenure and Reform in Uttar Pradesh*, 1800-1955, (Yale University Press) 1962, pp. 114-15.
7. Gopal, S: *Jawaharlal Nehru, A Biography, Vol. I.* 1889-1947, (Delhi) 1976, p. 154.
8. *The Tribune*, 12 March 1929.
9. *Agrarian Distress in the United Provinces*, pp. 88-112.
10. *Ibid.*
11. *Ibid.*
12. See Gopal, S: *Selected Works of Jawaharlal Nehru*, Vol. IV (New Delhi) 1973, pp. 391-92.
13. *Ibid.*
14. Brown, Judith M: *Gandhi and Civil Disobedience, The Mahatma in Indian Politics*, 1928-34 (London) 1977, pp. 215-16.
15. Home Poll. File 33/XI, 1931.
16. Home Poll. File 33/IX, 1931.
17. *The Leader*, 12 October 1931.
18. *Agrarian Distress in the United Provinces*, pp. 238-41.
19. *Ibid.*
20. Home Poll. File 33/XVI, K.W., 1931.
21. *A.I.C.C., Papers.* File 54, Part III, 1931.
22. *The Tribune*, 25 October 1931.
23. Home Poll. File 33/37, 1931.
24. *A.I.C.C. Papers*: File G-140, pt. III, 1931.
25. Home Poll. File 33/36, 1931.
26. *The Leader*, 18 November 1931.
27. Gopal, *op. cit.*, pp. 167-68.
28. *The Leader*, 27 November 1931.
29. *The Pioneer*, 27 November 1931.
30. *Templewood Papers*; Willingdon to Samuel Hoare, 13 December 1931.
31. *The Bombay Chronicle*, 7 Dec. 1931.
32. Home Poll. File 18/12, 1931.
33. Home Poll. File 33/XI, 1931.

34. *Halifax Papers*: Viceroy to Secretary of State, 26 December 1931.
35 Home Poll. File 31/97, 1932.
36. Nehru, *op. cit.*, pp. 304-5.
37. *Ibid* , p. 299.
38. *Ibid.*, p. 236.
39. *New Age*, September 1939.
40. *Independent India*, 10 September 1939.

5

The Assessment

Govind Ballah Pant indeed was a giant among the most prominent Congress leaders of his time. Born in a remote hilly village in the Himalayas, he rose to the position of the Premier of his own state and later on, the Home Minister, Government of India. By profession, he was an exceptionally brilliant lawyer, who gave up his legal practice at the call of Mahatma Gandhi. His sacrifices for the cause of India's independence are unique in every respect. He was imbued with simple habits and always identified himself with the problems of the masses not only of his own province but of the whole of India. He gained popularily in his own region at a fairly young age. Indeed his energy of any kind of public work was amazing.

He was a true Gandhian and lived a simple life. At the call of Mahatma Gandhi, he not only joined the satyagraha but also gave up his legal practice. He was arrested and convicted during the freedom struggle and suffered in the jails along with other Congress satyagrahis. When the members of the Simon Commission visited India, he felt much agitated and gave vent to his feelings in the U.P. Council as well as in public. When the Commission reached Lucknow, he, along with Jawaharlal Nehru and other leaders of the province, organised a non-violent rally against it. As a result thereof he received several injuries from the police lathi charge which greatly affected his physique for the whole life.

He was a very fine and impressive speaker. In fact his fluency of speech in simple and meaningful words greatly influenced the audience. In the U.P. Council his colleagues listened to his arguments with respect and much attention. When he was a leader of the Swaraj Party in the U.P. Council, he contributed much in the solution of the socio-economic condition of the people in his province. 'His presentation of facts and marshalling of figures, his persuasiveness and method of speaking, coupled with a peculiar indecisiveness and directness in speech, when necessary, made him quite a towering personality—a towering personality as he actually is in his figure in the Council.'

In the Central Assembly from 1935-37 his performance had an effective bearing on various problems for which he sought a solution within the framework of the constitution. He argued well and this always placed the treasury benches in an uncomfortable posture. He was well-conversant with the parliamentary procedure. His oratory was superb and very often he could convince the bureaucrats with his comprehensive arguments. Above all, he never acted in a way which was against the discipline and established norms of the Assembly.

When the Congress took charge of the ministries in a few provinces in 1937, Govind Ballabh Pant was elected as the Premier of the U.P. With his superb administrative zeal, he not only controlled the administrative machinary but geared it up towards several socio-economic measures. He showed much keenness for the development of education, roads, electricity, irrigation projects, panchayat system and several other works for the welfare of the people of U.P. His capability and sincerity in the administrative work as the Premier of a big State, with several problems, were greatly praised by the then Governor of U.P., Harry Haig. 'He was a model Prime Minister with a high reputation as the ablest administrator in India'.

Pandit Pant was a loyal party worker and throughout his long career, he functioned as a disciplined soldier of the Congress Party. He did not like any kind of rift among the leaders and whenever he found such a situation, he used his good offices for its resolution. He was a fine negotiator and a peace-maker. Thus he was always on the alert to fight for liberty and justice with balanced and reasonable views which could suit both the sides.

He was a very popular leader among the poor and weaker sections of our society. He moved freely among them and listened to their problems and tried to solve them. Pandit Madan Mohan Malaviya opined, 'His personal life is based on simplicity, truthfulness, purity and tolerance—and patriotism and selflessness have added lustre to it.' In fact he never pretended any kind of sophistication. He was modest and unassuming. Hard work never tired him as his physical energy was amazing. He always felt happy to meet as many people as he could, particularly the rural folk and solved their numerous problems. He indeed was a far-sighted politician who alway had his hand on the pulse of the nation. By temperament, he was courteous, polite and affable. He spoke the language of a common Indian and respected his sentiments.

As Chief Minister of U.P. and Home Minister, Government of India his contribution to several socio-economic measures is unique. His arguments, as usual, were fairly comprehensive during the debates in U.P. Assembly as well as in the Lok Sabha. He listened to the point of view of the opposition with respect and replied to their quaries with politeness. He died on 7 March 1961 after a long career in the service of our country. Undoubtedly his dedication was unique and this fact brought him in the forefront of our freedom struggle. The country's highest honour 'Bharat Ratna' was conferred on him on 26 January 1957.

In Lok Sabha, Shri Satya Narayan Sinha, the Minister of Parliamentary Affairs, read out the following message from the Prime Minister, Jawaharlal Nehru on the passing away of

Pantji:

"What we have been expecting fearfully, during the last two weeks, has come to pass and the last glimmer of hope that Pantji might recover has been snuffed out and we are left desolate and forlorn. Dear friend and comrade, great captain of our people during the days of our struggle for freedom, great in leadership after freedom came, the wisest of counsellors, gentle and yet firm of purpose, with malice to none, child of our beloved Himalayan mountains, carrying with him something of their calm and imperturbability, rock of stability and lighthouse to guide people's minds and paths, how shall we replace him or find his like again. He shone in Parliament but, even more, he shone in life itself and loved with passion our motherland and the well-being of all her children. We pay our homage to him and give our pledge to devote ourselves to the cause to which he gave his brilliant mind and all his strength and energy, in spite of physical ailments and disabilities. To the last moment of his days, so long as consciousness lasted, he gave his unremitting labour to the service of India. Even so, may it be given to us to labour with joyful heart in this dear service till the last breath of life."

Morarji Desai, Minister of Finance opined, 'His services of the country will never be forgotten and they will be equalled by few. He had been in public life for about forty-five years, as far as 1916 I find he was a Member of the AICC, as it was even then called...He was a tower of strength to the party and the Government here by his wise counsel his debating skill and the great amount of thought that he gave to every problem that he dealt with. I was always wondering how he could remember every point without making any notes. People who might make written speeches might forget something but he never forgot a single point and dealt with everything in proper sequence.

He will be missed always in this House in the Government and in the Congress where he was a tower of strength. The country has lost one of the greatest patriots produced by it, who gave his whole life to the struggle for freedom and after freedom had been obtained, to the work of consolidation and bringing prosperity to the country. I never saw him ruffled even once. I was connected with him from 1937 from which time I had the privilege of getting his affection and I can never forget the wise counsel that he always gave me and others. I shall always miss him; we shall all miss him, I have no doubt. We can only remember what he has done for all of us and for the country. He lived a rich life and has left us traditions in the matter of wisdom which if we follow I have no doubt that we will all enrich ourselves.

S.A. Dange, observed, 'In paying tribute to the memory of Pantji we pay tribute to one of the stalwarts of the old independence movement led by the Congress and the people in this country against British rule. And throughout his life he carried the sign of the struggle not only in the memory of the people, but on his own personal body. He embodied in fact, the spirit of independence.

After independence, and in particular lately, he had to discharge heavy duties. Everybody knows, Sir, that it is very difficult to be popular when you wield the Home Ministry particularly. But then he had that particular quality that even when he did an unpleasant job, he did not leave bitterness behind. He had the peculiar quality, as I saw him in many surroundings, to bind people together, to synthesize and not to dissipate, even where differences existed. Even when we differed, when ever we differed and parted, we did so not as permanent opponents, and without bitterness. That was the greatest quality which endeared him to all circles. He did not mind even keeping contacts with smaller subjects...The nation will remember his services not only during the period of struggle for Independence but also during the later period when it was his ambition to develop the country and strengthen its Independence, and a tribute to his memory will ever be given.

Asoka Mehta stated, 'It is not easy to express in words the sense of loss and grief that we feel. I am reminded of the words that Gandhiji used at the time of the demise of Pandit Motilal Nehru. He said, "The rock of ages has cleft for me". In that way, as our own Prime Minister pointed out the other day, Pandit Pant was the great anchor. In this storm-tossed sea, when our journey is so full of difficulties and dangers, here was someone to whom all of us instinctively turned. We turned to him for security, for guidance. Even those of us who belong to another party would always go to him; his commanding and yet affectionate personality was there before us. I know, as many of my colleagues know, that we used to go to him with our doubts and difficulties, and sometimes with our woes, and we were always assured not only of warm welcome, of wise counsel; somehow or other, we came back after meeting him, with a feeling as if we had left our worries to him. He was willing to carry the Cross for all of us and it is very rare that one can have a person of that kind, massive in body, massive in mind and massive in spirit.

On a number of occasions I had the privilege to see him, I saw in his eyes and in his heart the great agony that he felt about many things that are going wrong in the country, many things for which perhaps many of us are responsible. But I also saw that there was always in him an unshakable faith in the future of our country and in the wisdom of our people. It is that faith and it is that anguish that I hope we shall try to remember.

He was one of the great torchbearers of the freedom-fighters and one of those who have been privileged to consolidate that freedom. He has been removed, but I hope the torch which has been made brighter by his great personality, by his remarkable services, will be kept aloft by those who will always remember him and cherish him in their thoughts.

N.G. Ranga opined, 'On the death of Shri G.B. Pant, many people like me and I see so many here feel a terrible loss. We have been together for the last 35 years as colleagues, as comrades as friends, as almost members of the same family. It was a privilege to be embraced by him. He was a great man, a good man and a wise counsellor. It could be seen from the debates that he did recognise political differences but he never recognised personal differences. He had a tremendous capacity for love, to love everybody. More than anything else, he set an example as a great follower of our great leaders, Mahatma Gandhi, Sardar Patel and Bhulabhai Desai.

Frank Anthony said, 'I have had the opportunity and the privilege of working closely on many occasions with Pantji for about 20 years. We had our differences, but in that not negligible period, inevitably perhaps; I came to regard him not only with the highest esteem, but with deep affection.

One finds it impossible to describe and pay a tribute even inadequately to his many and multifaceted gifts, but I would like to refer to two outstanding examples of his work with which I was closely associated. The House will remember the vitally important States Reorganisation Bill. The more I saw him work the more amazed was I. Some of us were conversant with some of the provisions, but not one of us except Pantji was conversant with every provision. I think he was flanked by four Secretaries in our deliberations lasting about a fortnight. I do not think he referred to them once. He was seized not only of every provision, whether it was legal, administrative, financial or constitutional, but he was seized of the nuance, and meaning of every word.

Again, he presided over the parliamentary committee on official language. Never in my fairly long public life have I been in a committee which was bedevilled by such fierce conflicts. I say this that perhaps none but Pantji with his skill, his patience and his unruffled nature could have brought its deliberations to any conclusion. It is not for us to attempt to assign a place to Pantji. I have no doubt history will do that. I also feel that it will assign to Shri Govind Ballabh Pant a place in Indian history perhaps greater than what we have assigned to him today.

Acharya Kripalani stated, 'I associate myself with all that has been said here about our beloved leader. I have been associated with him personally ever since, the national movement started under Gandhiji. There are innumerable occasions which come to my mind. It is, therefore, not only a national loss, but a personal loss to me and at such time, words are not adequate to do justice to the great qualities of head and heart that he had.

In him we have lost a great patriot, a great guide and a great parliamentarian, a man who was never ruffled and who always had a sweet word for everybody. Therefore, our loss is very great and I pay my humble tribute of reverence to his memory.

Atal Behari Vajpayee said, 'He was as firm as the Himalayas and as deep as the ocean. He devoted every moment of his life to the service of the country. For the coming generations his life would always be a beacon of light and a source of inspiration.

Ananthasayanam Ayyangar opined, I fully associate myself with all the sentiments that have been expressed on the life and services of Shri Govind Ballabh Pantji. In him we have lost one of the main architects of India's freedom. My association with Pantji started as early as 1935 when, for the first time, the Congress resolved to contest seats in the Central Legislature and both of us were returned Members of the then Legislative Assembly. He became the Deputy Leader of the party and the Government of the day always paid the greatest regard for his words. He proved very easily to be one of the greatest parliamentarians. Without offence, rancour or bitterness and with an easy-flowing style he would meet all the arguments of his opponents. He was invincible in his argument and even his opponents developed great regard and respect for him. After coming here to our Parliament he became an asset to us and on all crucial matters Parliament looked up to him for an answer. In spite of his poor health he never hesitated to undergo any amount of sacrifice and service for the country's freedom. As the Home Minister sometimes he had very unpleasant duties to do but he was strong and, at the same time, good.

Dr. M.N. Kunzru opined, 'Mr. Chairman, having had the privilege of knowing Pandit Govind Ballabh Pant for more than forty-five years, it is difficult for me to give expression to my feeilings on this occasion. Sir, the very first day that I came to know him, I realised that he was far above all of us. Having followed his career, I can say without fear of contradiction that in his judgement of a situation, his grasp of facts, his administrative ability he had few equals in the country. I should add that he had qualities which made him not merely an administrator but also a statesman. And, it is the combination of these qualities that made him occupy so large a position in the eyes of our countrymen. We know, Sir, the ability and skill with which he took part in the debates in this House. I feel that his parliamentary skill was superb. I have not known it equalled, Sir, during the few years that I have been in Parliament. The skill that he showed was not a matter of artificial management of facts or of men. It showed that he had the rare quality of being able to put his point of view in such a way as to excite the least opposition. Sir, this is not the time to review the work that he did, but I should like to say that in spite of all that he suffered in the days when he was fighting bravely for the freedom of his country, he never allowed himself to be embittered by his sufferings. Whether it was the influence of Mahatma Gandhi or his own nature that made him rise above his sufferings, I cannot say, but I think it will be acknowledged by all those who came in contact with him that when one talked to him about the past, one did not notice the slightest trace of bitterness in what he said about it.

Dr. S. Radhakrishnan, Chairman stated, 'Friends, I wish to associate myself with the sentiments so feelingly expressed by the representatives of the different groups here. We have lost a great leader, a great parliamentarian and a great national leader also. His place in the struggle for freedom and also in the post-independence years is significant and secure. I heard of his activities as the Chief Whip of the Swaraj Party in the old Central Assembly when there were many stalwarts like Motilal Nehru, Malaviya Jayakar, Srinivasa Iyengar etc. I came to know him a little more intimately when I took charge of the Banaras University affairs from 1939 to 1948 and when he became the Leader of this House, our connections became closer and more intimate. It is a matter of great pride for me that in the last months when both of us happened to be here we used to meet at least twice a week to discuss not parliamentary affairs but the results of our reflections on the affairs of this country etc. His last intervention in Parliament was in this House and when he took ill he was preparing the reply to the Debate on the President's address which he hoped to deliver on the 21st morning. Till the last moment his devotion of duty at the risk of his health stood out...Reference was made to his great parliamentary skill. I have noticed it here; all of you have noticed it. Very soothing, very conciliatory, very civilised in his appeal, he made few errors, tuffled few rempers and disarmed every kind of opposition. You had in him a combination of commonsense, clarity, balance of judgement and patriotism. It will be difficult for us to get another of the same calibre. Reference was made to his physical sufferings which he sustained during the struggle for freedom, but as was said these physical ailments did not produce in him any embitterment of spirit. He was human, humane and always anxious to find any fault with himself more than with others. Of course, as a parliamentarian when the opponents played into his hand he was devastating with a great sense of humour and yet he left no bitterness benind. His life is an example of service for the country. Till the end that was his one ambition and he has left behind an inspiring example for us all to follow. There is no doubt that we will feel his loss for many many years to come.'

life for independence years is significant and secure. I heard [illegible] his activities as the Chief Whip of the Swaraj Party in the [illegible] Central Assembly when there were many stalwart [illegible] Motilal Nehru, Madan Mohan Malaviya, Jayakar, Srinivasa Iyengar etc. I [illegible] came to know him a little more intimately when I took charge [illegible] the Banaras University affairs from 1939 to 1948 and when he became the Leader of the House, our connection became closer and more intimate. It is a matter of great pride for me that in the last months when both of us happened to be nearly [illegible] used to meet at least once a week to discuss not [illegible] [illegible] affairs but the results of our reflections on the future of this country etc. His last intervention in Parliament was on this House and when he [illegible] the [illegible] on the Debate on the President's Address which he hoped [illegible] [illegible] on the 21st morning. [illegible] the last moment his [illegible] [illegible] [illegible] Whatever was [illegible] [illegible] [illegible] I have noticed [illegible] [illegible] have [illegible] very [illegible] conciliatory [illegible] [illegible] [illegible] [illegible] [illegible] [illegible] [illegible] [illegible] [illegible] [illegible] [illegible] [illegible] [illegible]

[illegible]

Glossary

Ahimsa	non-violence
Bapu	Father; name often used in respect for Mahatma Gandhi
Bharat	India
Charkha	spinning-wheel
Desh	Country
Dharma	religion
Ghat	bank of a river
Guru	Teacher
Harijan	a name which Mahatma Gandhi used for an untouchable
Hartal	stoppage of work and business
Himsa	violence
Inquilab	revolution; a slogan raised against the *Raj*
Istri	woman
Jai	victory
Khadi	hand-spun and hand-woven cloth
Kisan	a peasant
Lakh	100,000
Lathi	stick
Mahila	a woman
Mahatma	high-souled person, often used for Gandhi
Nari	woman
Purna	full, complete
Raj	kingdom; commonly used for British rule in India
Sabha	an association

Sainik	sepoy
Samaj	association
Satya	truth
Satyagraha	non-violent resistance
Swaraj	self-government
Swadeshi	principle of using only articles of indigenous make
Thana	police station
Vidyapith	an institution of higher learning
Zalim	cruel
Zamindar	landlord
Zindabad	a word used for victory
Zulum	oppression

Bibliography

Primary Sources

A.I.C.C. Papers
Speeches and Writings of Govind Ballabh Pant
Nehru Papers
Halifax Papers
Reports of the annual sessions of the Indian National Congress
Debates, U.P. Council and Legislative Assembly.

Newspapers and Journals

The Hindustan Times
The Leader
The New Age
The Independent
The Pioneer
Times of India

Secondary Works

Beasant, Annie, *How India Wrought for freedom*, Madras, 1915
Bhagwan Singh, M.C. Shah (edt.); *Pandit Govind Ballabh Pant: The Collosus Speaks*, New Delhi, 1987
Banerjee, S.N., A *Nation in Making*, Calcutta, 1964
Bose, N.S., *Indian National Movement*, Calcutta, 1982

Chalapathi Rau, *Govind Ballabh Pant*, Delhi, 1981
Chirol, V., *Indian Unrest*, London, 1910
Jugal Kishore, *Congress Government in U.P.*, Allahabad, 1940
Nehru, Jawaharlal, *An Autobiography*, Delhi, 1962
Newinson, H.W., *The New Spirit in India*, London, 1908
Rastogi, M.K., *Govind Ballabh Pant*, Nainital, 1987
Srivastava, Gopi Nath, *When Congress Ruled*, Lucknow, 1940
Tewari, B.K., *Govind Ballabh Pant*, Allahabad, 1947

Index